America: Where Great Things Happen

Donald L. Gilleland

BLACK ROSE writing™

ISBN: 978-1-61296-447-8

PUBLISHED BY BLACK ROSE WRITING

www.blackrosewriting.com

Printed in the United States of America

Suggested retail price $16.95

America: Where Great Things Happen is printed in Traditional Arabic

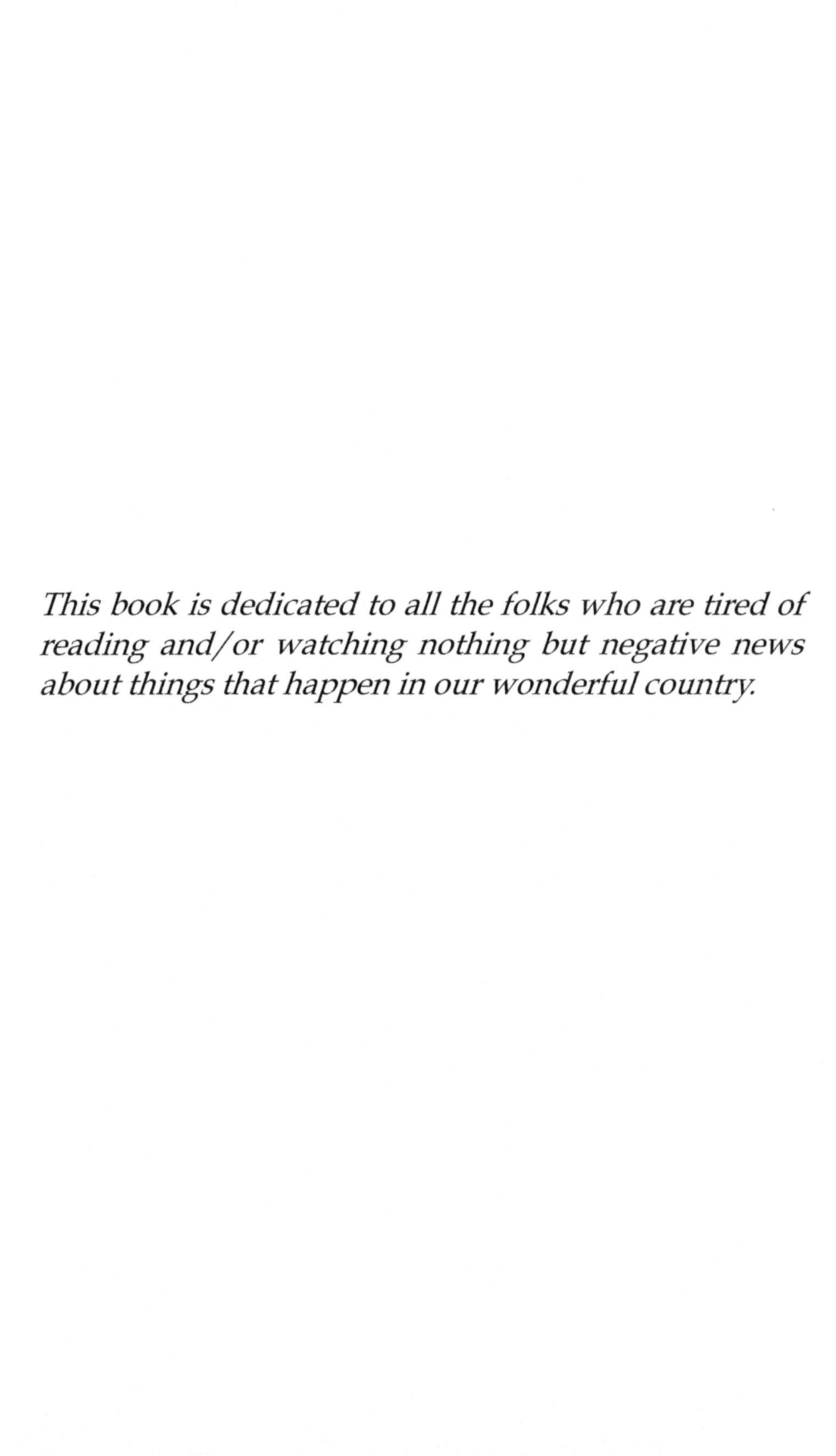

This book is dedicated to all the folks who are tired of reading and/or watching nothing but negative news about things that happen in our wonderful country.

America:

Where Great Things Happen

Observations of a Proud American Citizen

Table of Contents

Preface

Every day wonderful things happen throughout the United States, but you would never know it reading newspapers or watching network television news coverage.

There is a simple philosophy that seems to drive the headlines in many, if not most newspapers and evening news programs: "if it bleeds, it leads."

That is not to say there is never any positive news, but as often as not the positive stories are unique or unusual, not ordinary nice stories that just make us feel good. They tend to be like the story of a dedicated father who pushes or pulls his disabled son in a wheel chair through a marathon run, not a second grade student who sells cookies or candy and gives all the money to a worthy charity.

Shootings, muggings, robberies, car crashes, rapes, scatological public behavior, scandalous celebrity conduct, corrupt politicians, teenagers who mug old people for money and an assortment of similar stories will almost always drive the cookie story off the front page and send it to page 14.

For instance, here are a few samples of recent front-page negative headlines:

Female Serial Killer Hunted Men for Fun (Huffington Post).

Drunk 13-Year-Old Kills 6-Year-Old Girl (The Stir, a cafemom blog).

Expungement of Criminal Records OK'd (The Anniston Star).

Mass Killer Winked at Victim's Families (The Huntsville Times).

Arrest Made in 'Goodfellas' Heist (Anchorage Daily News).

7th Bighorn Death Logged in Catalinas (Arizona Daily Star).

Defense Chief Orders Review of Nuclear Force After Gaffes (The Denver Post).

A CIA Prison's Secret History in Poland (The Washington Post).

Kerchner makes deal, gets prison (Florida Today).

Justin Bieber's DUI Arrest and More: A Timeline of the Singer's Bad Behavior (E News).

Judge Orders Hospital to Remove Pregnant Woman From Life Support (New York Times)

These are all legitimate front-page stories, but they all cover something negative, and none of them were accompanied by positive human-interest stories on the same page.

Every day we are blasted out of our chairs by television commentators announcing "breaking news," which is almost always negative, almost always covering something wrong with our society. I wonder how many times a positive story is bumped off the front page of a newspaper by a late breaking gang rape story or a bank heist or a grisly murder or a politician caught with his hand in the till.

You won't find any of those kinds of headlines in *America: Where Great Things Happen*. Instead, you will find uplifting stories about wonderful things that occur every day in our great country, things you rarely read about, things that make you smile and feel proud to be an

American. These too are legitimate headline stories, some of which may appear on the front page of a local newspaper, but rarely make the national news.

Think about how many times you have turned to your neighbor or friend or co-worker and said: "I wonder why they never run any positive stories on the front page?" Or, "why doesn't the evening news ever lead with something that will make us feel good!"

Well, whether or not you've ever said something like that, if you've ever thought about it, this is the book for you. It is full of incredible things that happen every day in America--things about regular citizens who excel someway or who do something wonderful for a perfect stranger, yet go unnoticed.

It's about senior citizens who accomplish amazing things that you would never expect. It's about corporations that have a strong sense of responsibility for their communities. It's about organizations that make you feel good because of the wonderful things they do for their communities. It's about people who start out in life dirt poor, but become wealthy because of their hard work, steady focus, and perseverance. It's about men and women who care enough about their fellow citizens to donate organs to help extend their lives. It's about things that are not adequately covered by the mainstream news media. And, it's about inspirational, humorous, and encouraging things that just make you feel good.

There is no coverage of stabbings, shootings, burglaries, rapes, highway disasters, political shenanigans or scandals of any kind.

This is a book about great things that happen in America. You can get your negative news from the mainstream news media!

Donald L. Gilleland

Chapter 1

DEDICATED AND TALENTED YOUNG PEOPLE

If you had nothing but news reports to rely on, you might think wayward teenagers are all you can find in the United States. Almost every time you see a young person in the newspaper it's because he or she did something wrong.

Teenagers are often depicted as lazy, listless, unmotivated and uninformed. In November 2009, Outsidethebeltway.com reported that an Oklahoma survey of public high school students revealed that 77% of them couldn't name our 1st President.

The overwhelming majority couldn't answer even simple questions about the U.S. government and our history. Forty-three percent could not name the two major U.S. political parties; 26% didn't know what we call the first ten amendments to the U.S. Constitution, and 27% didn't know the names of the two parts of the U.S. Congress.

Ten percent didn't know how many Justices are on the U.S. Supreme Court; 61% could not name the ocean on the West Coast of the U.S.; and another 61% didn't know the difference between east and west.

This is the kind of stuff that tends to make us think the future of our country is in great jeopardy because today's young people will become tomorrow's leaders, and too many of them seem to be terribly uninformed at best and woefully ignorant at worse.

If that makes you feel uneasy about our future, let me assure you the findings in Oklahoma probably are an anomaly, not an accurate reflection of our nation's youth.

Since the beginning of time, young people have been doing wonderful things that just don't make the headlines the way juvenile delinquents do. Even in biblical times young people did exceptional things. The most obvious example was young David vs. Goliath. Jesus himself was still young and living with his parents when he began to teach the elders in the temple (Luke 2:42-49).

Current examples are not difficult to find, but you have to search for them. While some of the outstanding young contributors to our country may have received recognition when they were young or during their lives, few have been included in our history books, and many, if not most, have been swallowed up by time. Some don't even receive the recognition they deserve while they are making their contributions.

Fortunately, some of our earliest contributors have been documented in books, magazines, and newspapers that are preserved in our nation's libraries. As technology evolved, the Internet began to play a role too.

A Frenchman may have said it best:

To accomplish great things, we must not only act, but also dream; not only plan, but also believe.
~Anatole France (1844 – 1924) , French poet, journalist, and novelist.

Read on and be pleasantly surprised at some of the wonderful things talented young people do or did. They dream, believe and accomplish incredible things, often overcoming huge obstacles, frequently with little or no public recognition.

We must never forget that young people are our future leaders. They will set the tone for our country for generations.

Jack Andraka (1997 –)

Seventeen-year-old Jack Andraka was born in 1997 in Crownsville, Maryland. His father is a civil engineer and his mother is an anesthetist. In 2012, he won the Intel Science Competition, the world's largest high school science research competition, for his groundbreaking research on pancreatic cancer.

The Maryland high school student developed a test for pancreatic cancer that is 28 times cheaper and faster, and also 100 times more sensitive, than current tests. When his name was announced in June as winner of the Gordon E. Moore Award, named in honor of the co-founder of Intel Corporation, for the Grand Prize of $75,000, the expression of pure elation on his face was priceless. A video showing his stunned reaction went viral almost immediately. "I did not think I was going to win a single award," he said to Intel.. "It's unbelievable, I can't believe this is happening to me. This means so much to me."[1]

Andraka told the Wall Street Journal Live about his future plans to patent his test and take it nation-wide: "I'm incredibly excited about that aspect of this endeavor."

Andraka also won other prizes in smaller individual categories for a total of $100,500 in prize money.

During his research on pancreatic cancer, he found that one reason for the poor survival rate from pancreatic cancer was the lack of early detection and a rapid, sensitive, inexpensive screening method. According to his account, he was not deterred by his teenage optimism, and he went on to consult "a teenager's two best friends: Google and Wikipedia", and also drawing on content from YouTube. He began to think of ways in which cancer growth could be detected, prevented and terminated before the cancer cells become invasive.[2]

---

[1]

18 Under 18: HuffPost Teen's List of The Most Amazing Young People of the Year, December 31, 2012.

[2]

Jack Andraka, Wikipedia, The Free Encyclopedia, March 29,

and frequently played a violin Virginia had made."[7]

According to Chaz Allen, who wrote *The Violin Maker*, Virginia was a perfectionist and construction of the instruments had to be perfect, right down to the kind of wood she used to make them.

With one viola, she was happy with the wood she used on the front part of the frame, but wasn't satisfied with the wood for the back. So, she searched and searched for just the right wood, which she found in a telephone booth. In those days phone booths had a wooden shelf, which she thought was perfect.

The telephone company wouldn't let her have the shelf, so she took it anyway and replaced it with a different piece of wood. Evidently, the phone company never knew what happened, but the piece of wood she took from the telephone booth was perfect.

By all accounts, the viola she made from the telephone booth shelf was one of the finest instruments she ever made. She became known as the violinmaker, but that isn't what she is remembered for today, even though she was a great musician and instrument maker.

No, the wonderful musician and violin maker is better known because her name can sometimes be heard in a hospital delivery room, because of her system for evaluating the health of babies, and for becoming one of the first American women to specialize in anesthesia.

She was one of the few women to complete her graduation during the 1930s from Columbia's College of Physicians and Surgeons, completed a residency in surgery at Columbia, finished her training in anesthesia and in 1938 became director of the newly formed division of anesthesia.

In 1959, she obtained a master's degree in public health from Johns Hopkins and also held an executive position with the March of Dimes, and worked hard to improve the health care of infants and children.

She published sixty scientific papers, and her book *Is My Baby All Right?* (1972), co-written with Joan Beck, became a popular parenting

---

[7]

The Violin Maker, from American Goddesses? Extraordinary Women by Chaz Allen.

hardback. It is available on Amazon.com in either Hardcover or Paperback.

But, despite all her medical credentials and accomplishments, many musicians still remember her as a young masterful maker of violas and violins. Anyone interested in learning more about Dr. Apgar's early avocation, should read *The Violin Maker* from *Extraordinary Women – The Things They Have Done That You Never Knew*, by Chaz Allen, available on Amazon.com in Paperback or Kindle.

Ever heard of Dr. Virginia Apgar? I didn't think so. Except for politicians and Hollywood celebrities, it doesn't take long for some of the most wonderful contributors in our society to fade into history.

Unfortunately, they rarely even show up in our history books; so, unless you've spent some time in a hospital delivery room, there is little reason you should have ever heard about Dr. Apgar. Unless, of course, you happen to own one of the cellos or violas she built.

John M. Browning (1855 – 1926)

According to the Utah Division of State History, everyone who has ever fought with the U.S. military has benefited from John M. Browning. For over 50 years, U.S. infantry units have used the hard hitting, mobile Browning Automatic Rifle, better known as the BAR, a light automatic weapon, to provide quick bursts of concentrated fire.

Designed by John M. Browning, the BAR could be fired from the shoulder or the hip, while on the move. According to Robert R. Hodges, Jr., in *The Browning Automatic Rifle*, the BAR was first used in 1918 during World War I. It was then used in every major theater of World War II and went on to be used in Korea and in the opening stages of the Vietnam War.

It saw service with the U.S and other armed forces across the world for much of the 20th century. This author first fired the BAR in the Air Force 1962 and can vouch for the fact that it is heavy and somewhat clumsy, but it is also powerful and deadly effective.

Hodges says that Brig. Gen. S.L.A. Marshall's pioneering study of men in combat revealed the tremendous psychological boost the BAR gave to a squad in the field; Marshall discovered that riflemen were so glad to have a BAR in their midst that they readily volunteered to carry extra ammunition for their gunner.

What is not well known is how young Browning was when he first started making guns. According to Utah history, Browning started to make guns with his father when he was only six. His father was a gunsmith in Nauvoo, Illinois, and went west with the Mormons in 1852.

"John Browning made his own first gun at age 10. It didn't have a trigger, and you had to pour gunpowder into the barrel for every shot. He made the gun out of scraps from the shop's garbage pile, and he didn't tell his father until after he had finished. He and his brother, Matt, tested it out by firing at prairie chickens–and brought the chickens home to the family for dinner that night."[8]

Browning's inventions dominated the field of firearms during his lifetime and are the basis for many weapons still in use today. Winchester, Colt, Remington, Stevens, and Fabrique National (FN) of Belgium, as well as the Browning Company manufactured his designs.

Highlights from The Browning Legacy, posted in the John M. Browning Museum, point out that four generations of Browning inventors are represented at the Museum with original models and production examples from Jonathan, John's father, Val, John's son, and Bruce, his grandson.

"John M. Browning was granted over 128 patents, his designs include the "Model 1911" Colt 45 pistol, the "BAR" Browning Automatic Rifle, the "Model 94" Winchester lever action rifle and many other famous machine guns, cannons, shotguns, rifles and pistols."

According to *The Guns of John M. Browning* by Richard L. Baird, "John M. Browning was the greatest firearms designer who ever lived or ever will live."

Unfortunately, while he spent much of his life designing guns to help protect American soldiers, some of his guns also made it into the hands of criminals. Gangsters and others used his guns to commit crimes

---

[8] *I Love History*, Utah Division of State History, Utah Department of Heritage & Arts.

all across America.

With all this marvelous background, if you asked the average man on the street who John M. Browning was, I doubt more than a very few could tell you, even those whose lives were dramatically affected by his inventions. But, if you ask an active duty or retired military man who has served in a combat environment with a BAR, he may not know much about Browning's background, but he will likely be able to tell you who built the BAR.

Bessie Coleman (1893 – 1926

Born in 1893, one of 13 children born to a part Cherokee father and a Black African/American mother, Bessie Coleman, at age 29, became the first black woman in the world to earn a pilots license.

Coleman was raised in Texas and faced the kinds of difficulties many Black Americans faced at that time, including segregation and disenfranchisement.

She worked hard in her childhood, picking cotton and helping her mother with laundry. But, she didn't let her environment keep her down. She graduated from high school and moved to Chicago, where she became interested in flying.

After seeing newsreels on aviation, listening to and reading stories about World War I pilots, she decided she wanted to become a pilot, but no U.S. flight school would accept her because she was Black and a female.[9]

So, "she took it upon herself to learn French and move to France to achieve her goal. After only seven months, Coleman earned her license from France's well known Caudron Brother's School of Aviation."[10]

In 1922, a time of both gender and racial discrimination, Coleman

---

[9]

Little Known Black Americans, by Carol Bainbridge., About.com, Parenting Gifted Children.

[10]

Bessie Coleman biography, www.biography.com/people/bessie-coleman-36928.

broke societal barriers and became the world's first black woman to earn a pilot's license.

When she returned to America, she wanted to start a flying school for Black African/Americans; but, instead, she "...specialized in stunt flying and parachuting, and earned a living barnstorming and performing aerial tricks. In 1922, hers was the first public flight by a Black African/American woman in America.

Unfortunately, Coleman had a tragic ending. She left Orlando, Florida by train to give a benefit exhibition for the Jacksonville Negro Welfare League, scheduled for May 1, 1926. "Her pilot, William D. Wills, flew her plane into Orlando, but had to make three forced landings because the plane was so worn and poorly maintained.

On April 30, 1926, Wills piloted the plane on a trial flight, while Coleman sat in the other cockpit to survey the area over which she was to fly and parachute jump the next day. Her seat belt was not attached because she had to lean out over the edge of the plane while picking the best sites for her program. At an altitude of 1,000 feet, the plane dived, then flipped over, throwing Coleman out. Moments later Wills crashed. Both were killed.

Although the wreckage of the plane was badly burned, it was later discovered that a wrench used to service the engine had slid into the gearbox and jammed it.[11]

"Coleman had three memorial services, in Jacksonville, Florida, Orlando, Florida and Chicago, Illinois, the last attended by thousands. She was buried at Chicago's Lincoln Cemetery and gradually, over the years following her death, achieved recognition at last as a hero of early aviation."[12]

Coleman is still considered to have been a female pioneer of women in the field of aviation, but is rarely mentioned today except in accounts of outstanding Black accomplishments, reported during Black History

---

[11]

Wikipedia, The Free Encyclopedia, February 16, 2014.

[12]

Bessie Coleman, Encyclopedia of World Biography.

Month. Shouldn't America's authentic heroes receive more attention? Bessie Coleman should be mentioned in every American history textbook used to teach our students. She was a critically important female aviation pioneer who deserved more attention in our history books than she gets today.

Taryn Davis (1985 –)

Taryn Davis, founder of the *American Widow Project*, is a little known hero of giant proportions. According to the Huffington Post, she was just 21 when she received the devastating news that her husband, Corporal Michael Davis, had been killed in Iraq.

It was June 22, 1972 when two Naval Casualty Assistance representatives showed up at her front door to tell her that her husband's helicopter had crashed at sea and he had been lost.

CNN reported that Ms. Davis felt lost and isolated after her husband's death. "While she struggled with her grief, it seemed that those around her found it easier to move on with their lives. Other military wives avoided her as though she represented their deepest fears. Family and friends insisted that her youth should provide solace.

"After the funeral I felt ostracized," Davis said. "Everybody liked to write off my grief due to my young age. They liked to say: 'Well, at least you're young. You'll get remarried.'"[13]

Davis attended some grief groups, but met mostly widows over age 65; few were anywhere near her age. She traveled the country to find other young military widows in her age group and eventually founded the *American Widow Project*, which provides a network of support for military widows all over the country.

Since 2001, over 6,600 U.S. service members have lost their lives in Iraq and Afghanistan. That number does not include the thousands more that have lost their lives due to sudden illness, accident, homicide

---

[13]

Connecting a new generation of military widows, by Danielle Berger, CNN, May 26, 2011.

or those who have taken their own lives due to Post Traumatic Stress Disorder.

The American Widow Project recognizes the sacrifices made by the families of our fallen military and believes that no military widow should feel alone in her grief.[14]

The American Widow Project is a 501(c)3 non-profit organization that provides support to a new generation of military widows grieving the loss of a spouse in the armed forces. Its mission "…is to provide vital support to military widows with peer based support programs designed to educate, empower, inspire and assist in rebuilding their lives in the face of tragedy."[15]

The American Widow Project believes "Each military widow deserves the opportunity and tangible tools available to help rebuild her life." Because of that, this wonderful organization provides the emotional and educational support necessary to maximize success, healing and hope for a widow's brighter future.

The American Widow Project offers many tangible opportunities for military widows to learn about project benefits:

On Site: Built to house ideas, stories, and advice, they have compiled a list of resources to help with the lifetime of struggles that come along with being a military widow.

A DVD film: A 75-minute documentary gives a candid look into the stories, struggles and perseverance of six military widows. Everything is covered from meeting the love of their life, to the knock on the door, life as a single parent, and decorating a headstone. The film is distributed free of charge to all military widows and widowers as key to the healing process.

The film, *In Their Boots*, is a web based documentary series about the impact the wars in Iraq and Aghanistan are having on people at

---

[14]

2014 American Widow Project.org.

[15]

Ibid,.

home in the United States. A preview can be viewed on YouTube.com and the series can be seen on PBS-TV.

Newsletter: Compiled and created by widows, the newsletters range in content and keep the widows up to date on all happenings of the American Widow Project.

Hotline: No counselors answer the calls, just widows who are going through the same trials and tribulations. 1-877-AWP WIDOW.

Widow U: A series of scholarship-based courses and related resources provides military widows with the tools, empowerment and education for the next steps on their journey.

All of these services are available because one young woman, Taryn Davis, decided to devote her life to a cause bigger than herself. As a result, more than 3,600 young military widows and 46 widowers face a brighter future.

If you are not a military widow or the family of a military widow, you probably have not heard of this exceptional effort by a caring young woman, despite the limited media coverage of her cause and that of other dedicated young volunteers.

Ms. Davis remarried several years later, had a son, got her college degrees and taught school, but has never forgotten her first husband. "I could still practically build in my mind all the time we spent together. His life, and death, has shaped my entire adult life."[16]

She became a widow again in 2008, when her second husband died from a heart attack. But, she says she is rebuilding her life and is happy again. Nevertheless, she says she will never forget the day those Casualty Assistance representatives showed up at her front door. We should never forget either, because it was the beginning of her effort to form a marvelous organization to help other military widows rebuild their lives.

It's too bad every American doesn't know about this remarkable organization, because it could certainly use wide financial support to help out the military widows. It's also too bad more people don't know about Taryn Davis. She is certainly a splendid example of a talented

---

[16]

Ibid.

young woman who exemplifies the wonderful things that are happening in America.

Robert James "Bobby" Fischer (1943 – 2008)

Robert James "Bobby" Fisher was born on March 9, 1943 in Chicago, Illinois. He was an American chess prodigy, grandmaster, and the eleventh World Chess Champion, considered by many to be the greatest chess player of all time.

Nicknamed "the bad boy of chess," his career and legacy were marred by eccentricities that developed into what some believe was full-blown mental illness that made him an exile from the United States, which he represented in the greatest proxy battle of the Cold War, and from the game he loved.

"The young Bobby grew up without a father with his mother and older sister. It was his sister who introduced him to chess when she bought a chess set when Bobby was six years old. Reportedly possessed of a super genius I.Q. of 180, Bobby had a remarkably retentive memory. A monomaniac when it came to chess, his memory combined with an uncanny knack for the game and a determination to win transformed him into the greatest chess player in the world."[17]

Bobby Fischer's lifetime tournament and match results were: 415 wins, 248 draws and 85 losses out of 748 games played from 1955 through 1992 for a performance average of .721 or 72.1%. But that doesn't tell the whole story of his genius.

Fischer became a National Master at the age of 12 and won America's Junior Chess Championship at the age of 13. As a 14-year-old, he won the U.S. Chess Championship in 1958. He became the youngest World Chess Federation Grand Master in history.

He quit high school at the age of 16 to make a living as a chess player. By 1962, at the age of 19 he was considered by the chess world to be the best non-Soviet chess player in the world.

Fischer hated Soviet chess players because he thought they drew matches between themselves so they cold concentrate on beating non-

---

[17]

Bobby Fischer Biography, www.IMDb, 2014.

Soviet players like him. But, he liked and respected Boris Spassky, the reining world champion. Spassky is believed to have returned the affection and esteem.

By 1972, Fischer was in a position to make good on his boast of being the greatest chess player in the world. He accepted Spassky's suggestion that they play a championship match in Iceland. However, negotiations were so prickly, Henry Kissinger intervened to personally persuade Fischer to not drop out of the match, which was seen as a proxy battle in the ongoing Cold War between the United States and the Soviet Union.

Fischer embraced the Cold War rhetoric, declaring the match was "the free world against the lying, cheating hypocritical Russians."

"Fischer won the third game of the match, the first time he had beaten Boris Spassky in 12 years. For the rest of their play in 1972 and their 1992 rematch, Fischer never fell behind Spassky in terms of play or points. Spassky was baffled by Fischer's innovative moves, as he played new lines and combinations that Boris had never encountered before. Fischer won the match and became World Chess Champion by a score of 12.5 points to 8.5 on seven wins, one loss and 11 draws in 19 games."[18]

After the 1972 World Chess Championship, Fischer did not play a competitive game in public for nearly 20 years. However, in 1977, he played three games in Cambridge, Massachusetts against the MIT Greenblatty computer program, winning all of them

Fischer did not play competitively again until 1992, when he met Boris Spassky for a rematch on the resort island of Sveti Stefan in Montenegro, which was part of all that remained of Yugoslavia. Fischer beat Spassky, winning $3.35 million in prize money (approximately $5.65 million in 2012 dollars).

After beating Spassky, Fischer withdrew into seclusion, in part because he had violated U.S. restrictions on participating in events in Yugoslavia. On July 13, 2004, he was detained at the Narita Airport in

---

[18]

Bobby Fischer Biography, www.IMDb.com, 2014.

Tokyo where authorities discovered that his U.S. passport had been revoked.

Fischer fought deportation to the United States, where he faced criminal charges for violating sanctions against the former Yugoslavia. He was granted Icelandic citizenship and within days was flown to Reykjavik, the site of his world-famous encounter with Spassky.

After the 9/11 attacks on the World Trade Center and the Pentagon, Fischer, became an American pariah, a citizen of Iceland, and a recluse. He became openly and vociferously anti-semitic and anti-American, but was rarely heard from again, especially in chess circles.

Although he is still considered to be the greatest chess player in the history of the game, during his lifetime Fischer went from the heights of international stardom to virtual obscurity.

Fischer died on January 17, 2008 in Reykjavik after having been gravely ill with degenerative renal failure. At his death he was 64-years-old, which was a bit symbolic, since a chessboard has 64 squares.

As popular as Fischer was as a child prodigy and later as a world-class champion chess player, since his death he has virtually drifted into obscurity, with few young people outside of the chess environment even knowing who he was.

Robert G. Heft (1941 – 2009)

I doubt one out of a thousand people could identify Robert G. Helf, yet at a very early age he came up with an idea that affects us all. At the tender age of 17 Helf designed the current American 50-star flag, while he was still a high school student.

Heft spent his childhood in Lancaster, Ohio, where he created the American flag as a school project. In 1958, a history teacher assigned Heft and his classmates at Lancaster High School to each redesign the national banner to recognize Alaska and Hawaii, both nearing statehood.

Heft un-stitched the blue field from a family 48-star flag, sewed in a new field, and used iron-on white fabric to add 100 hand-cut stars, 50 on each side of the blue canton (upper left quarter).[19]

Unfamiliar with a needle and thread and unable to get help from his mother who feared her son's projects would be desecrating the flag, Heft spent 12 ½ hours one weekend arranging and sewing a new combination of stars. He arranged the 50 stars in five rows of six stars alternating with four rows of five stars.

"Heft originally received a B– for the project. After discussing the grade with his teacher, Stanley Pratt, it was agreed that if the United States Congress accepted the flag, the grade would be reconsidered. Heft's flag design was chosen and adopted by presidential proclamation after Alaska and before Hawaii were admitted into the union in 1959. According to Heft, his teacher honored their agreement and changed his grade to an A for the project."[20]

When Alaska and Hawaii were being considered for statehood, American citizens submitted more than 1,500 designs to President Dwight D. Eisenhower. Archived in the Eisenhower Presidential Center in Abilene, Kansas, only a small fraction of the proposed designs have ever been published.

Heft became a high school teacher and later a college professor, and also served as Mayor of Napoleon, Ohio, for 28 years. After retiring from teaching, he became a motivational speaker.

He travelled over 100,000 miles annually from his home in Napoleon, spreading the gospel of patriotism and the story of how he had designed the flag. He was very popular as a speaker and averaged about 150 speaking engagements a year.

"The flag that made Heft famous is soiled and faded from frequent

---

[19]

Wikipedia The Free Encyclopedia, Robert G. Heft, February 18, 2014.

[20]

A half-century ago, new 50-star American flag debuted in Baltimore, by Frederick N. Rasmussen, *The Baltimore Sun*, Saturday, July 3, 2010.

display. It has flown over every state capital building and over 88 U.S. embassies. An uneven patch at a lower corner is evidence of an attack on the embassy in Saigon in 1967. Heft claimed it is the only flag in America's history to have flown over the White House under five administrations.

His place in history is already secure as the designer of our nation's 50-star flag 55 years ago, but he dreamed of having a second and succeeding versions adopted too. He claimed he had copyrighted designs for American flags with 51 to 60 stars. "There's a very good chance that I'd be the very first person in America's history to design two of the nation's flags, if it comes to pass," Heft said.[21]

Unfortunately, he died before another star was added to the flag. On December 12, 2009, Heft died from a heart attack at Covenant Medical Center at age 67.

William D. Swenson (1978 –)

William Swenson appeared to be an ordinary young soldier, who during a critical period in his life did something extraordinary, for which he was awarded our nation's highest military honor: the Medal of Honor.

He was the first living United States Army officer to receive the Medal of Honor since the Vietnam War, as well as the sixth living recipient in the War on Terror.[22]

A resident of Seattle, Washington, Swenson graduated from Seattle University with a Bachelor of Science degree in political science. He

---

[21]

Designer of America's Current National Flag, by Jim Sielicki, United Press International, *The Exchange*, July–August 1988, www.usflag.org.

[22]

After long wait, Seattle man gets highest military honor, The Seattle Times, Sept. 16, 2013.

was commissioned from Officer Candidate School as a U.S. Army Infantry Officer in 2002.

His military education included Infantry Officer Courses, Ranger School, and Airborne School. He deployed overseas three times, once to Iraq and twice to Afghanistan. Before being awarded the Medal of Honor, he had already been awarded the Bronze Star Medal (with two oak leaf clusters), the Purple Heart, and the Combat Infantryman Badge.[23]

At the time of his Medal of Honor award he held the rank of Captain. He was assigned to Task Force Phoenix, Combined Security Transition Command Afghanistan, in support of the 1st Battalion, , 32nd Infantry Regiment, 3rd Brigade combat Team, 10th Mountain Division (Light Infantry). He was an embedded trainer for the Afghan Border Police.

While serving as one of two Army advisors and mentors to the Afghan National Border Police, Swenson and a contingent of 12 Marine Corps advisers to the Afghan National Army and one Navy corpsman were making their way to the village of Ganjgal, about 10 miles from the Pakistan border. They were to meet with the village elders over tea and discuss improvements to a mosque and how Afghan National Security Forces could help them.

Swenson was working with Afghan security forces in the volatile Kunar province near Pakistan's border when he and his troops were suddenly ambushed, flanked on three sides. An immediate withdrawal was called for. Swenson radioed for white phosphorous smoke to shield the retreat as well as artillery placement, but both were denied several times on the basis that the civilian population was too close. The battle raged for more than six hours and when all was said and done --three Marines and a Sailor were killed and Swenson's partner and friend, Sgt. 1st Class Kenneth Westbrook, was mortally wounded. Eight Afghan soldiers died too.

Meet William Swenson

A fifth soldier, Sgt. First Class Kenneth Westbrook -- the man

---

23

Profile: William D. Swenson, U.S. Army.

Swenson helped load onto a helicopter -- later died from his wounds too.

According to CNN, President Obama recounted to an audience of fellow soldiers and families of the fallen how Swenson braved enemy fire again and again to recover the bodies of the dead Americans and Afghans.[24]

"In moments like this, Americans like Will remind us of what our country can be at its best, a nation of citizens who look out for one another, who meet our obligations to one another not just when it's easy, but also when it's hard," Obama said. "Maybe, especially when it's hard."

Part of Swenson's rescue efforts was recorded by a rescue pilot's helmet camera. In the heat of battle, with bullets flying and dust blocking any clear vision of the surrounding situation, Swenson is seen helping Westbrook, who had been shot in the throat, back to a helicopter.

After placing him in the helicopter, Swenson bent down to kiss his forehead before running back to the battle to retrieve other fallen Americans and Afghan fighters.

"I was just trying to keep his spirits up. I wanted him to know it was going to be OK. And I wanted him to know that he had done his job, but it was time for him to go," Swenson told CNN.

In the aftermath of the battle, Swenson was critical of several senior Army officers who failed to provide the coverage and artillery requested of them at Forward Operating Base Joyce. Swenson and Marine Cpl. Dakota L. Meyer were both nominated for Medals of Honor by Marine Gen. John R. Allen, commander of the International Security Assistance Force at the time. It was only the second time in half a century that two men from the same battle have been awarded the medal. But, only Meyer's Medal of Honor packet made it to the president.

24

Medal of Honor recipient braved gunfire to retrieve bodies of the fallen, by Chelsea J. Carter and Barbara Starr, CNN, November 4, 2013.

Meyer was awarded the medal at a White House ceremony, Sept. 15, 2011. Because of a processing error, the recommendation for Swenson's award was lost and didn't surface until 2013. He had resigned his commission in February 2011.

In the presentation ceremony for Swenson in November 2013, Secretary of the Army John McHugh acknowledged the errors in the submissions process of Medal of Honor packets and offered his apology and changes to the process.

"Will Swenson is truly a hero amongst heroes," he said. "Today he'll have his name enshrined along with those who have gone before, forever part of our nation and our Army's history and his name will be displayed alongside such others as Alvin York and Audie Murphy…"

During the ceremony honoring Captain Swenson, McHugh acknowledged the Army had lost Swenson's Medal of Honor packet, and said he was implementing changes to ensure such an occurrence would not happen again.

A new directive now requires Medal of Honor nominations be sent immediately to Army Human Resources Command, known as HRC. "As soon as an honors packet is created at battalion level, we will have immediate visibility at Army headquarters," the secretary said.Each subsequent review of the package must also be forwarded to HRC. The command will also follow up with the original command every 30 days until that award packet reaches its final review.

"This will be a parallel process that will provide greater oversight," McHugh said. The change will improve how the Army takes care of its Soldiers."Our heroes have always taught us many things, and that's true here today," McHugh said. "But sometimes our heroes teach us how to make ourselves better, and Will, for that as well, I want to 'thank you.'"

Secretary of Defense Chuck Hagel also apologized for excessive delay in the award of Swenson's Medal of Honor: "We're sorry that you and your family had to endure through that, but you did and you handled it right, and I think (that) deserves a tremendous amount of attention and credit."

Following the presentation of his framed citation and the personal Medal of Honor flag, Swenson spoke briefly. "I look at this crowd and I see the strength of a nation and I see the strength of a fighting force, one that I fought proudly with," he said. "I look at my fellow Marines, Army, Navy and Air Force, a team that I fought side-by-side with as brothers. It's the proudest moment of my life and I'm honored and privileged to know these men."

I'm sure I speak for many American citizens when I say that we are incredibly fortunate to have such men represent us in our armed forces. They voluntarily go into harms way to serve on our behalf to ensure that the freedoms and exhaustive benefits guaranteed to us by the U.S. Constitution and Bill of Rights are preserved for future generations of our citizens. We will forever owe such men our eternal debt of gratitude.

Child Prodigies

While we can document many wonderful teenagers and young adults who have done exceptional things, there is a special category that almost always mystifies us—child prodigies.

A child prodigy is someone who at an early age masters one or more skills at an adult level. They are typically younger than 15 years old and perform at the level of a highly trained adult in very demanding field of endeavor.[25]

Examples of child prodigies would include Wolfgang Amadeus Mozart in music, Carl Friedrich Gauss in mathematics, and Pablo Picasso in art. The term Wunderkind, from German, meaning "miracle child" or "wonder child" is sometimes used as a synonym for prodigy, although the term is discouraged in scientific literature.

"From a seven-year-old-surgeon to a 16-year-old who speaks 23 languages, the seemingly superhuman intelligence of child prodigies has long been a subject of public fascination. And it's no wonder—while most of their peers are still learning to read, these wunderkinds have accomplished feats unimaginable even to many adult experts in their fields."[26]

---

[25]

Child prodigy, FactualWorld, 2014.

[26]

Child prodigies have been around for centuries and exist in virtually every country in the world. America is no exception, and this section provides a glimpse into the lives of some of the American child prodigies.

Jacob Barnett (1998 –)

Jacob L. Barnett was born in Indianapolis, Indiana on May 26, 1998. He is a mathematician and astrophysicist. "When he was two years old, he was diagnosed with moderate to severe autism, a form of Asperger's Syndrome. Doctors said that he might not be able to talk, read, or become independent in basic daily activities." They said he may not even be able to tie his shoe laces.

But they were extraordinarily mistaken. He proved the doctors wrong when he was able to recite the alphabet forwards and backwards —at three-years-old.[27]

His parents taught him privately and his mother eventually wrote a book about his educational journey.

While visiting a planetarium as a three-year-old, Barnett was able to answer the presenter's question of why the Martian moons are oddly shaped. Later, he enrolled at Indiana University-Purdue University in Indianapolis at age 10.

While working on his degrees, he asserted that he might one day disprove Einstein's Theory of Relativity. He is currently working on his PhD in Quantum Physics.

At the age of 15 he became a PSI-student at the Perimeter Institute for Theoretical Physics in Waterloo, Ontario, Canada and is expected to receive a Masters degree in late 2014.

Barnett has been working on Albert Einstein's theory of relativity and thinks he will one day be able to amend it or even to prove it

---

Child Prodigies: 20 Astounding Young Wunderkinds From Around The Globe, Huffington Post, March 7, 2014.

[27]

Jacob Barnett, 10 Modern Child Prodigies, www.listverse.com, July 9, 2013.

wrong. He also expressed doubts about the Big Bang Theory and thinks he will be able to amend it too.

So far nothing written or postulated by him on those topics has been peer reviewed. Professor Scott Tremaine of the Institute of Advanced Study wrote, "The theory that he's working on involves several of the toughest problems in astrophysics and theoretical physics. Anyone who solves these will be in line for a Nobel Prize."[28]

With an IQ of 170, which is believed to be higher than that of Albert Einstein, Barnett has flourished at the university, astounding his professors, peers and family with his spectacular intelligence. He even tutors other college students in subjects like calculus and is a published scientific researcher.

His mother says that, while he makes it all look so easy, he has to work hard on a daily basis to handle his autism. "He overcomes it every day. There are things he knows about himself that he regulates everyday," his mother told the Indianapolis Star.[29]

In April 2013, Kristine Barnett's memoir about her family's experience with autism, "The Spark: A Mother's Story of Nurturing Genius," was released and a movie deal is said to be in the works. Barnett hopes his mother's book will inspire other children to be doing something they like.

His heroes are the physicist Richard Feynman and Donald Trump. He says simply, "I respect people who are good at their fields."

Michael Kevin Kearney (1984 –)

Michael Kevin Kearney was born on January 18, 1984 in Honolulu, Hawaii. He became known as the world's youngest college graduate at

---

[28]

Jacob Barnett, Wikipedia, The Free Encyclopedia, April 10, 2014.

[29]

Jacob Barnett, 14-Year-Old With Asperger's Syndrome, May Be Smarter Than Einstein, Huffpost Good News, May 11, 2013.

the age of 10, when he graduated from the University of South Alabama with a Bachelor's Degree in anthropology. He also received a Master's Degree in biochemistry from Middle Tennessee State University at age 14, and a Master's Degree in computer science from Vanderbilt College at age 17.

Kearney was homeschooled by his parents, especially his Japanese/American mother. He was diagnosed with ADHD at an early age and his parents refused to use the prescription drug Ritalin. His younger sister, Maeghan, is also a child prodigy.[30]

Kearney spoke his first words at four months. At the age of six months, he said to his pediatrician "I have a left ear infection" and learned to read at the age of ten months. When Kearney was four, he was given diagnostic tests for the Johns Hopkins precocious math program and achieved a perfect score.

He finished high school at age 6, enrolled at Santa Rosa Junior College graduating at 10 with an Associate of Science in Geology. He is listed in the Guinness Book of World Records as the world's youngest university graduate at the age of 10, receiving a Bachelor's Degree in anthropology. For a while, he also held the record for the world's youngest postgraduate student.

In October 2006, he became a finalist on the Mark Burnett/AOL quiz/puzzle game *Gold Rush*, winning $100,000. In November 2006, in front of a national audience on Entertainment Tonight, he went on to win the grand prize of an additional $1,000,000. Kearney was also a contestant on Who Wants to be a Millionaire which aired on April 25 & 28, 2008. He left with $25,000.

Kearney was also a contestant on Million Dollar Password, which aired on June 14, 2009, but did not pass the elimination round after losing in the tiebreaker.

He is a cultural hero in Japan, partially because his mother is Japanese/American, but also because they view brilliant youngsters as

---

30

Michael Kearney, Wikipedia, The Free Encyclopedia, March 12, 2014.

national assets, not upstart smart-alecks. But his parents discovered what many people already know, Americans don't have much time for smart kids, and Kearney has a measured IQ of nearly 200. To put that into perspective, the IQ of the average American citizen is about 100.

Kearney's dad, Kevin, a former U.S. Navy officer, says the U.S. society is simply not prepared to deal with super-bright young people. Kearney's parents discovered that rearing a child with a mind like their son was a full-time job.

Kearney's dad gives full credit to his wife, Cassidy, for teaching him though high school and guiding his college studies. "She was the juku here," Kearney explains, in a dual reference to the intense after-school academic programs common in Japan and to his wife's Japanese-American heritage. "Instead of giving Michael Ritalin, like the two million other kids who have been diagnosed hyperactive, she gave him school. Cassidy had to be a Power Ranger of motherhood."[31]

Trained as a teacher, she previewed material in a home-study program to stay ahead of him. She attended college classes with him, and the two of them would cover the text material two weeks ahead of any test so the class session itself functioned essentially as review.

Kearney's family now lives in Alaska, but little else is known about him now. When he was last heard from for an ABC News story in 2005, he said all he wanted was what he called a "normal" life. He had someone new in his life, Megan Clancy, who said, "He's told me before that I'm something that keeps him kind of grounded." The boy who was too young to go to his high school prom finally had someone to take to a college ball.

With his rare intellectual ability Kearney is sure to turn up somewhere in the United States for a future follow-up article.

31

The Smart Money Is on This Young Genius: Michael Kearney, 10, is the world's youngest college graduate and a cultural hero in Japan but finds a less enthusiastic response ion the U.S., by Richard Kahlenberg, Los Angeles Times, January 15, 1995.

Saul Aaron Kripke (1940 –)

A rabbi's son, Saul Aaron Kripke was born on November 13, 1940 in Bay Shore, New York, but grew up in Omaha, Nebraska. By all accounts he was a true prodigy. He is a logician and philosopher who is considered to be one of the most powerful thinkers in Anglo-American philosophy.

In the fourth grade he discovered algebra, and by the end of grammar school he had mastered geometry and calculus and taken up philosophy. While still a teenager he wrote a series of papers that eventually transformed the study of modal logic.

One of them earned a letter from the math department at Harvard, which hoped he would apply for a job until he wrote back and declined, explaining, "My mother said that I should finish high school and go to college first." After finishing high school, the college he eventually chose was Harvard.[32]

Kripke is the oldest of three children born to Dorothy K. Kripke and Rabbi Myer S. Kripke. His father was the leader of Beth El Synagogue, the only Conservative congregation in Omaha, Nebraska, while his mother wrote educational Jewish books for children.

Kripke was labeled a prodigy, having taught himself Ancient Hebrew by the age of six, read the complete works of Shakespeare by nine, and mastered the works of Descartes and complex mathematical problems before finishing elementary school.[33]

In 1962 he graduated from Harvard with the only degree he ever received that wasn't honorary, a B.S. in mathematics. He remained at Harvard until 1968, first as a member of the Harvard Society of Fellows

---

[32]

Saul Aaron Kripke: Invited to apply for a teaching post at Harvard while still in high school, 10 Extraordinary Child Prodigies, www.oddee.com, April 6, 2009.

[33]

Saul Kripke, Wikipedia, The Free Encyclopedia, March 5, 2014.

and then as a lecturer. Kripke taught logic and philosophy at Rockefeller University from 1968 to 1976 and at Princeton University, as McCosh Professor of Philosophy, from 1976 until his retirement in 1998.[34]

He delivered the prestigious John Locke Lectures at the University of Oxford, in Oxford, England, one of the leading universities in the world, in 1973 and received the Rolf Schock Prize in logic and philosophy, an equivalent of the Nobel Prize, awarded by the Royal Swedish Academy of Sciences, in 2001. In 2003 he was appointed distinguished professor at the City University of New York.

Although a prolific thinker and problem solver, Kripke did not publish many of his works. Nevertheless, some of his unpublished papers have been influential through lectures, seminars, and informal circulation among colleagues and students.

Many philosophers consider Kripke to be among the most important 20th century contributors to the subject of philosophy. He made important contributions to the theory of truth and the solution of the semantic paradoxes.[35]

The Saul Kripke Center at the Graduate Center of the City University of New York is dedicated to preserving and promoting Kripke's work. The Saul Kripke Center holds events related to Kripke's work and is currently working to create a digital archive of Kripke's previously unpublished recordings of lectures, lecture notes, and correspondence dating back to the 1950s.

Mabou Loiseau (2006 –)

Mabou Loiseau, a 5-year-old Queens, NY prodigy, scored in the 99th percentile on the city's test for gifted and talented children. She can speak seven languages and play six instruments.

---

[34]

Saul Kipke, Encycloopedia Britannica, October 23, 2013.

[35]

Overview: Saul Aaron Kripke, Oxford Index, Oxford University Press, 2014.

Loiseau speaks Creole, English and French, and is learning Spanish, Mandarin, Arabic and Russian. She can sing her ABCs in Spanish, count in Mandarin, read fairytales in Russian, and already has an ambitious list of career goals.[36]

She says she wants to be a firefighter, a doctor and a dancer, but she also wants to be a princess. "And I want to be an actor, and I want to be a musician, and I want to be a singer, and I want to be a veterinarian, and I want to be a mom."

Her favorite language is Russian. "I just hear something and, if I don't understand I say, 'What does that mean?' and they'll tell me," said Mabou, whose house is plastered with flashcards in different languages.

"Mabou has her own dance studio with a mirrored wall where she learns tap and ballet. Her mom recently got rid of the kitchen table to make room for a full-size drum set. She's also learning to play the harp, clarinet, violin, guitar and piano. When she's not taking ice-skating or swimming lessons."

Her parents spend $1,500 a week on tutors and lessons, and she spends seven hours a day in some type of instruction, with Sunday's off. Friends and neighbors were initially shocked that her parents started Mabou on such a tough regimen so early in her life, instead of letting her just be a kid.

Esther Loiseau, Mabou's mom, who taught piano and French at an American school before leaving Haiti for Queens in 1996, said: "All the sacrifices in the world for her. Furniture is not important. Education is. But I make sure I leave enough time for her to play. All she knows is learning. What becomes fun for someone is what he or she knows. Honestly, I just want to open doors for my daughter. She is really my princess."

Loiseau tells the tutors to play with Mabou, speaking in their native language for half of the lesson. They spend the other half reading,

---

36

It's Supergirl. 5-year-old Queens prodigy can speak seven languages, play six instruments, by Erica Pearson, New York Daily News, May 18, 2011.

writing and practicing vocabulary.

"It's a great experience for me, honestly. A lot of even adult people can't understand what she does," said Rogneda Elagiona, 24, Mabou's Russian tutor. "We like to read together. We started with the alphabet and connecting letters, and now she can read folklore."

Mabou's dad works 16 hours a day as a parking attendant in Manhattan to pay for everything, and the Loiseaus have also started hosting other students for classes at their house.

No one can predict what Mabou will actually do when she becomes an adult, but for sure, even at age 7 today, she is a child prodigy.

Yo–Yo Ma (1955 –)

Born in Paris, France on October 7, 1955, by Chinese parents, Yo-Yo Ma started playing the cello under the guidance of his father when he was four years old. He is now one of the most prolific cellists of our time.

His mother, Marina Lu, was a singer, and his father, Hiao-Tsiun Ma, was a violinist and professor of music at Nanjing National Central University. The family moved to New York City when Ma was five years old.

Initially, Ma began studying violin, and later viola, before settling on the cello in 1960, at age four. He performed for Presidents Dwight D. Eisenhower and John F. Kennedy when he was seven. At age eight, he appeared on American television with his sister, Yeou-Cheng Ma, in a concert conducted by Leonard Bernstein.

Ma had his first public recital when he was five and performed at Carnegie Hall at age 9. He attended Juilliard School under the tutelage of Janos Scholz (1904 – 1993) and Leonard Rose (1918 – 1984), both celebrated Cellists and renowned teachers.

Ma graduated from Harvard University in 1976, at age 21, with a humanities degree. He wanted a traditional liberal arts education to expand on his conservatory training. In 1991, at age 36, he received an honorary doctorate degree from Harvard University.

Ma plays two instruments, a 1733 Montagnana cello from Venice and the 1712 Davidoff Stradivarius cello. According to www.bookofjoe.com, Ma's 1733 Montagnana cello, which was crafted by Domenico Montagnana, is valued at more than $2 million. The 1712 Davidoff Stradivarius cello, named after Karl Davidoff, a prominent Russian cellist, referred to by Tchaikovsky as the "Tsar of Cellists," is valued at between $2.5 – $3 million.[37]

Ma founded the Silk Road Ensemble, a 31-member ensemble, whose members represent 20 counties, to express his spirit of exploration and sharing. "What we tried to do in music and in culture is look at what do we have in common," he said.

He has carefully built trust among ensemble members, each of whom is a virtuoso within his or her own tradition. Yet they easily collaborate and improvise with each other.

What Ma calls "passion-driven" education is at the heart of the ensemble's mission. After tours, Silk Road members often stay behind to conduct music classes in locales like China, Azerbaijan, Turkey, and Brazil. In the United States, Silk Road Ensemble members offer workshops in conservatories and public schools.[38]

Ma plays as a soloist and with many major orchestras. His 75 albums have received 15 Grammy Awards. In addition to recordings of the standard Classical repertoire, he has recorded America bluegrass music; traditional Chinese melodies; the tangos of Argentinian composer Astor Piazzolla; Brazilian music; and collaboration with Bobby McFerin.[39]

He was awarded the National Medal of Arts in 2001, Presidential

---

[37]

www.yo-yo-ma.com/yo-yo-ma-biography, The Official Yo-Yo-Ma Site.

[38]

Silk Road Ensemble Celebrates Cultural Harmony, by Adam Phillips, Voice of America, News/Arts & Entertainment, January 11, 2014.

[39]

Yo-Yo Ma, Wikipedia, The Free Encyclopedia, March 7, 2014.

Medal of Freedom in 2011, and the Polar Music Prize in 2012.

On November 3, 2009, President Barrack Obama appointed Ma to serve on the President's Committee on the Arts and Humanities.

Yo-Yo Ma is arguably the premier contemporary American cellist. Some authorities believe Ma ranks among the all time best cellists of the last century, which include Pablo Casals and Mistislav Rostropovich.

William Joseph Mosconi (1913 – 1993)

Nicknamed "Mr. Pocket Billiards" "Willie" Mosconi, as he was known, was an American professional pocket billiards (pool) player from Philadelphia, Pennsylvania. He played professional billiards at age six.

Willie's father owned a pool hall where he wasn't allowed to play, but Willie improvised by practicing with small potatoes from his mother's kitchen and an old broomstick. His father soon realized that his son was a child prodigy and began advertising challenge matches, and though Willie had to stand on a box in order to reach the table, he beat experienced players many years his senior.[40]

In 1919, an exhibition match was arranged between six-year old Willie and the reigning World Champion, Ralph Greenleaf. The hall was packed, and though Greenleaf won that match, Willie played very well launching his career in professional billiards. In 1924, at the tender age of eleven, Willie was the juvenile straight pool champion and was regularly holding trick shot exhibitions.

Between the years of 1941 and 1957, he won the BCA World Championship of pool an unmatched fifteen times. Mosconi pioneered and employed numerous trick shots, set many records, and helped to popularize the game of billiards. He still holds the officially recognized straight pool high run record of 526 consecutive balls.

Shooting Straight Pool on Depression Era tables in poor upkeep

---

[40]

10 Extraordinary Child Prodigies, by Grace Murano, Oddee, 2014.

taught Mosconi to compensate for any conceivable playing condition. His record might stand forever since manufacturers have made scoring tougher on their tables in recent years.

"Whoever his adversary, the poor soul would squirm in their seat waiting for Willie's inning at the table to end. Having the bad luck to play Willie, their custom cue might as well have been a broomstick."[41]

In 1961, Mosconi was the technical advisor on the film The Hustler, starring Paul Newman and Jackie Gleason. Mosconi's job was to teach Newman how to walk, talk, and shoot like a real pool hustler. Newman had never even picked up a pool cue prior to filming, but his relative inexperience was undetectable due to Mosconi's expert instruction.

Mosconi said Gleason already knew his way around a billiard table, so he recommended him for the role of the original "Minnesota Fats."

Mosconi also had a cameo role as himself, acting as a stakes holder during the first match-up between the film's characters "Fast Eddie" Felson and "Minnesota Fats". Gleason can be heard saying "Willie, hang on to that" (the stakes money) when the match commences. At various points in the extended scene, a keen eye can spot Mosconi in the audience watching the match.

The documentary short "The Hustler: The Inside Story", featured on *The Hustler* Special Edition DVD revealed that whenever the camera cut to Fast Eddie's hands it was really Mosconi taking the shot.

Willi Mosconi was among the first Billiard Congress of America Hall of Fame inductees. He was to pocket billiards what Tiger Woods, Jack Nicklaus and Arnold Palmer are to the world of golf.

Part of his greatness at the game probably stemmed from the fact that he was a child prodigy, but more than likely it was because he was alleged to have practiced pool six hours a day, seven days a week, for over 30 years!

Ruggiero Ricci (1918 – 2012)
Born on July 24, 1918, Ruggiero Ricci debuted in San Francisco in

---

41

Willie Mosconi, aka "The Mosc," by Matthew Sherman, About.com,.

1928 at the age of 10-years-old, playing a formidable program of violin works by Vieuxtemps, Saint-Saens, Mendelssohn, and Wieniawski. He astounded the audience and his performance started him on the road to stardom.

According to the New York Times, Ricci grew up in San Francisco, the son of an Italian immigrant and amateur trombonist who insisted that all seven of his children learn to play instruments. Ruggiero Ricci preferred the piano, but his parents had other plans. "They bribed me with fiddles," he told the New York Times in 1976. "I'd wake up in the morning and there would be another one. Once I had five fiddles under my bed."

His parents initially named him Woodrow Wilson Rich, but later gave him his Italian-sounding name because it seemed a better fit for a musical prodigy. Throughout his life he was called Roger.

At 13 he performed at the Hollywood Bowl and held the audience spellbound. He was said to be a "wunderkind" of classical music with marvelous showmanship and beautiful tone.[42] According to the Los Angeles Times Ruggiero Ricci made the rare leap from child prodigy to serious artist, and was regarded as one of the greatest violin virtuosos of his generation.

According to his official biography, Ricci made his first tour of Europe in 1932 at the age of fourteen, a highly sensationalized series of concerts with the world's greatest orchestras; he continued to play extensively until, ironically, the Army Air Force put a stop eleven years later to his world travels.

He enlisted at the beginning of World War II in 1942 and served as "Entertainment Specialist Ricci" until 1945. During those three years he played and broadcast hundreds of concerts under a variety of unusual conditions, often without an accompanist, exploring and presenting the largely unexploited solo violin repertoire.

He remained an enthusiastic exponent of the solo recital, basing a majority of his programs on the solo works of Bach, Paganini,

---

[42] *Ruggiero Ricci dies at 94; violin virtuoso began as child prodigy*, by Valerie J. Nelson, *Los Angeles Times*, August 22, 2012.

Wieniawski, Kreisler, Ernst, and Bartok.

His was the first recording of the unadulterated Paganini Caprices, and he performed the U.S. premieres of both the Fourth and Sixth Concerti. He recorded the complete 24 Caprices, Op.1, in their original form.

Not surprisingly, Ricci is recognized as having greatly contributed to the world's renewed appreciation and affection for the great Nineteenth Century composers, though he maintained a broad repertoire of over 50 concerti. He performed over 6,000 concerts in 65 countries during his 70-year solo career. He also made over 500 recordings, on every major label.[43]

Ricci taught at Indiana University, the Juilliard School, University of Michigan and the Mozarteum in Salzburg, Austria. His book, "*Left Hand Violin Technique*" is published by G. Schirmer. Ricci was particularly well know for his recordings of the works of Paganni.

His last performance in the United States was October 12, 2003 at the Smithsonian Institution in Washington, DC. He retired to Palm Springs, California and taught Master Classes in the greater Los Angeles area, under the auspices of the Jascha Heifetz Society.

On August 6, 2012, Ruggiero Ricci died of a heart attack at his home in Palm Springs, California. He was 94.

Gregory R. Smith (1989 –)

Gregory Robert Smith is an American child prodigy who graduated "cum laude" from high school at 9 by completing 10 grades of school in just 3 years by skipping some of them and completing some within a matter of months. He received his Bachelor degree in mathematics at the age of 13 years from Randolph-Macon College, USA. At age 16 he went for his Ph.D. in Mathematics at the University of Virgina.[44]

---

[43] *Ruggiero Ricci*, Wikipedia, The Free Encclopedia, September 13, 2013.

[44] *Six Child Prodigies Doing Ph.D at 15*, by Valli in Education,

Born in West Reading, Pennsylvania, Smith has been recognized as a prodigy since early childhood. His IQ reportedly tests "off the bell curve," Smith was memorizing and reciting books at 14 months, adding numbers at 18 months and taking in the information presented to him by his parents and earliest teachers like a super computer.

It only took him one year, for example, to advance from second to eighth grade, and he began college on June 9, 2003 on his 14th birthday, focusing on graduate work in mathematics.

He said he especially likes "the thinking and logic that comes with the study of math," and sees how the ability to think logically through complex problems can directly benefit future political, business and social activities in which he might become involved.[45]

Smith graduated college with a master's degree at age 16 and pursued a Ph.D in mathematics, the first of several doctoral degrees he planned to obtain. He studied for four doctorates–in math, aerospace engineering, international relations and biomedical research.

But, when Smith was not studying and learning, he traveled the world as a peace and children's rights activist. He founded International Youth Advocates, an organization that promoted principles of peace and understanding among young people throughout the world.

He has served as youth ambassador for the Christian Children's Fund and youth spokesperson for World Centers of Compassion for Children. His travels have taken him to nine countries on four continents and he also travels extensively throughout the United States to promote peace.

"That optimistic spirit has led Smith to organize humanitarian aid projects for East Timor orphans and youth in Sao Paulo, Brazil; to help Rwanda build its first public library; and, while youth ambassador for

October 17, 2007.

45

Another notch on the educational belt of prodigy and peace activist Greg Smith, by Kathleen D. Valenzi, Inside UVA Online, May 19, 2006.

the Christian Children's Fund, to launch a $350,000 campaign to build a "peace school" in Kenya for the children of three warring nomadic tribes — the idea being that, with joint formal education, these tribal children would have the knowledge necessary to come up with innovative ideas for how to live and coexist peacefully.

"Over the years, Smith has met with former U.S. President Bill Clinton and former Soviet Union President Mikhail Gorbachev, plus Nobel Peace Laureates, including Betty Williams, Archbishop Desmond Tutu and Jose Ramos-Horta, to talk about his educational and peace plans and to learn from them about "how they've dealt with difficult situations" so that he can follow their example, he said."

In 2002 and 2003 he was nominated for the Nobel Peace Prize at ages 12 and 13, and was among 43 students in the United States to receive scholarships up to $50,000 a year for six years from the Jack Kent Cooke Foundation for his graduate studies.

By almost any definition Gregory R. Smith was an American child prodigy.

Stephen R. Stafford II (1997 –)

We generally think of young blacks excelling in sports, and sometimes music, but there are many talented young blacks who are achieving extraordinary success at high levels in science, math, classical music, chess and other knowledge based areas. One such individual is Stephen R. Stafford II, who was born in Lithonia, Georgia in 1997.

Nothing says "I'm smarter than you" better than going to college at a time when most 16-year-old's are just worried about getting a license to drive or getting out of sophomore year of high school. But that's exactly what Stephen R. Stafford II has going on. In fact, the young man started studying at Morehouse College in Atlanta, Georgia when he was 11, and wasn't just studying one major, but three: pre-med, mathematics and computer science.

Stafford's genius has garnered him much media attention. Now 17, Stafford continues to do a slew of public speaking, and the young man and his mother like to do outreach programs and provide support for other young and gifted teens. He did drop one of his majors (pre-med), and is currently sticking with computer science and mathematics. He hopes to be done at Morehouse when he turns 17

Stafford started at Morehouse College at age 11 because his mother, Michelle Brown-Stafford, who was homeschooling him, could not keep up with his potential. She saw how much potential he had while she was teaching him and she just could not keep up with his academic skills. So, she took the unusual step of enrolling him at Morehouse College.

Stafford became the youngest student in the 150-year history of Morehouse College. Few people can bend their minds around the idea that a young black African/American could be halfway through college by the time he was 14. Of course, it's also difficult to comprehend that a young boy could learn advanced mathematics at age 6, geometry at age 7 and Algebra II at age 9.

"Stafford's mother and father detoured him and his older sister, Martinique, from an underachieving educational career when they home-schooled him and protected his growing mind like it was a priceless exhibit at the Smithsonian Institute."[46]

The college student is also a talented classical pianist; he began to play the piano at the age of two, and started his multiplication tables in kindergarten. When asked about his exceptional abilities, the teen replies: "I'm just like any other kid. I just learn very, very quickly."[47]

Stafford is an inspiration to everyone around him. He shows them that you can do almost anything with focused effort, hard work and perseverance. He is also a great example of what can be achieved through home schooling.

"What floors you as much as Stephen's keen intellect…is how blasé he is about his uninterrupted upward trajectory into the infinite horizons.

"I wouldn't call school 'exciting.' I mean, it's school. Who calls

---

[46]

Mr. Stephen R. Stafford II Profile, Zoominfo, 2014.

[47]

Stephen R. Stafford II, YES!, Hicktown Press, March 15, 2014.

school 'exciting?'" he says incredulously…The thing is, [going to Morehouse] is like a normal school except the kids are older, and the coursework is a little more advanced.

"There's nothing you can say to that, except to pay homage to Stephen's father, Stephen Sr., who carved out a career sufficient enough to enable his wife, Michelle, to stay home. And you must praise Michelle, who tended to her children's education as if her own life depended on it. Her tireless research and how she applied it helped her son to catapult beyond what didn't seem remotely possible."[48]

One must be extremely proud of a child as gifted as Stephen R. Stafford II. But what is somewhat scary is to realize there must be other gifted kids like Stafford and his sister in our educational system, who are growing up in quiet desperation, searching for ways to free their creative minds from the traditional constraints of an ordinary education.

---

[48] Ibid.

Chapter 2

SENIOR CITIZENS WHO MAKE A DIFFERENCE

To often we think only of young people as major contributors to the welfare of our communities. The truth is that senior citizens are frequently responsible for major happenings around our country. Their contributions often don't seem to count for much in a nation where mass media, technology and advertising generally speaks to young people. But, there are thousands of gray haired people making significant contributions to our society.

Depending on who you ask, a senior citizen can be as young as 50-years-old; although I suspect most folks think the term "senior citizen" applies more to those who are eligible for Social Security, which has traditionally been closer to age 65.

The day when your image of a senior citizen was that of a retiree sitting tied to a rocking chair in an assisted living facility, waiting for someone to take him to the bathroom, is probably long gone. Today, many senior citizens don't even retire when they hit the Social Security age.

In 1900 life expectancy was around 40. In 1935, when President Franklin Roosevelt established Social Security, with an entitlement age of 65, life expectancy was age 60 and very few people lived to collect it.

Today, with life expectancy at age 79 for men and 82 for women, and lengthening more every year, almost everyone lives long enough to collect Social Security (a problem we'll save for another discussion), you are more likely to find senior citizens taking orders behind the counter at McDonalds or ushering at the local movie theater, if not still employed by a major corporation.

There was a time when senior citizens didn't show much interest in advanced education because they thought going to school was for young people. As you will see a bit later in this chapter, more and more of them are returning to college, and recently the oldest college graduate was 95 when her college president handed her the college degree. Later she received her Masters Degree at age 98.

Today, senior citizens who are truly retired are likely spending their days serving their communities in a variety of volunteer positions, or fulfilling long held dreams of a second career or avocation.

I'm a prime example. While I've had over 500 articles published over the last 30 years, I had my first book published at age 78. It is titled, *America: A Cultural Enigma,* published by Black Rose Writing, in which I explore major changes to our society that occurred over the past 50 years. For those who might be interested, the book is available online at Amazon.com, Barnes&Noble.com and BooksaMillion.com. When not writing I volunteer at my church.

My wife, Peggy, is even more active than me. At age 75, she volunteers at the Brevard Association for the Advancement of the Blind, covered in Chapter 3. She reads books, magazines and articles for a Library of Congress program. Her readings are recorded and sent to the Library of Congress, after which they are made available to American libraries for visually impaired citizens to check out and listen to. She has a gift for dialects and by disguising her voice can read all the parts.

Peggy is also a very busy volunteer at our church at which she runs the Information Center where people check with her and other volunteers for information about the church and its programs. She literally runs the Information Center at services on Wednesday evening, Saturday evening and two services on Sunday morning. She also attends Bible study classes on Thursdays.

So much is available for senior citizens to do in virtually every American city it boggles the mind. Parks and Recreation Departments usually have listings for seniors that might include tours around the city, classes in everything from computers and photography to martial arts classes for seniors. Senior centers often have programs that focus on exercise or ballroom dancing or card games or any one of a number of other ways for seniors to feel connected and/or relate to their local community.

Local community colleges and four-year degree colleges generally offer a variety of credit and non-credit courses tailored for senior citizens to take as a hobby or to use in a new career. It is not unusual to hear working senior citizens declare that retirement isn't in their future. This chapter is devoted to just such senior citizens.

In 1988, while serving as President of the United States, Ronald Reagan declared August 21st to be National Senior Citizens Day. It is not a national public holiday, but a day to raise awareness of older people and for recognizing their achievements. It is an observance that was established to honor senior citizens in the United States who make positive contributions to the communities in which they live. It is also a day to bring awareness of social, health, and economic issues that affect senior citizens.[49]

America is full of senior citizens who have done or are doing incredible things that call into question the stereotypical image of the elderly in a ratty bathrobe and worn out slippers shuffling down a hallway. Some of these people are well past the age for a bucket list.

Baby Boomers have been called the first self-indulgent generation. They are accused of not wanting to grow old. Well, perhaps today's Baby Boomers are the first generation of citizens who aren't going to allow that to happen. Some of them are even older than the parents of yesterday's Baby Boomers.

Makes one wonder at what age in the 21st Century you should start your "bucket list?" Jack Nicholson and Morgan Freeman might just have to make an update to their 2007 movie " *The Bucket List.*"

Anyway, here are some truly impressive and extraordinary senior citizens.

CHARLES ATLAS (1893 – 1972) Physical Fitness Advocate

Born Angelo Siciliano in Acri, Calabria, Italy, on October 30, 1892, Charles Atlas turned to bodybuilding after moving to the United States.

---

[49]

Senior Citizens Day in the United States, timeanddate.com, 2014.

He partnered with pitchman Charles Roman to market his weight-free "Dynamic-Tension" program in the 1920s, creating a lucrative mail-order business that made Atlas a household name. The strongman died on December 24, 1972, in Long Beach, New York, though his business remains active.

Atlas' family arrived on Ellis Island in 1903 and settled in Brooklyn, New York, where neighborhood bullies often harassed him. At that time he was a shy, scrawny little boy.

"Two events changed Siciliano's life: one was a trip to the Brooklyn Museum, where he was awed by the physiques depicted in statues of Hercules, Apollo and Zeus, and was inspired to begin bodybuilding. The second was a visit to the Bronx Zoo. Watching a lion stretch, he realized that the enormous animal was undergoing a natural workout by "pitting one muscle against another." He abandoned weight training to focus on isometric and isotonic exercises, which helped him quickly build an impressive physique."[50]

He trained himself to develop his body from a "scrawny weakling" to become the most popular muscleman of his day. Deciding to make a career out of bodybuilding, Siciliano legally changed his name to "Charles Atlas," after a friend told him he resembled the statue of Atlas on top of a hotel in Coney Island. [51]

In 1928 Atlas teamed with Charles Roman, who was a marketing genius who created popular "Hey Skinny" and "97-Pound Weakling" advertisements designed to appeal to young boys. TogetherAtlas and Roman created Charles Atlas Ltd.

Atlas was the popular bodybuilder and Roman was the marketing genius. Atlas served as an inspiration for Americans to improve their

---

[50]

Charles Atlas. Biography, bio.true story, A+E Networks, 2014.

[51]

Charles Atlas, Wikipedia, The Free Encyclopedia, March 14, 2014.

health and well being through physical fitness. He marketed his program for the "97-pound weakling."

One famous ad featured a young man on a beach accosted by a sand-kicking bully while his date watches. Humiliated, he goes home and, after kicking a chair and gambling a three-cent stamp, subscribes to Atlas's "Dynamic-Tension" program. Later the now muscular protagonist goes back to the beach and beats up the bully, becoming the hero of the beach. His girl returns while other women marvel at how big his muscles are.

Different versions of this ad ran for many years. By the 1950s the Dynamic-Tension regimen had been translated into seven languages and sold to nearly one million customers worldwide. The Atlas program became popular for years; however, when his wife died of cancer in 1965, Atlas sold his half of the company to Roman, but remained involved in the company as a consultant.

In addition to his bodybuilding course, Atlas also started a string of successful gyms. He practiced what he preached, and even into his 60s and 70s was working out in a gym every day, his body sculpted and toned to a degree that put to shame many men half his age.

Distraught after his wife died, he continued to sculpt his own body. He took long runs on the beach near his home in Palm Beach, Florida, and kept up a morning routine of 50 knee bends, 100 sit-ups and 300 push-ups.

When Atlas died on December 23, 1972 at the age of 79, he was still excelling at what he knew best, how to keep his body in terrific shape. He was able to do things with his body that men half his age were not able to do. His program was literally the beginning of the modern day fitness boom.

His program of Dynamic-Tension continues even today. It is available on the Internet, only a click away in banner ads on youth-oriented sites. The company says it now does 80 percent of its business online.

In addition to his Dynamic-Tension course, courses in boxing, wrestling, self-defense, hand balancing and weight training, are still being sold over the Internet by his company, Charles Atlas, Ltd., of New York City.

Charles Atlas had a pure image. Throughout his life he neither drank alcohol nor smoked, and his personal life was free of scandal. One of his famous phrases was, "Nobody picks on a strong man."

"He sprang from the back pages of comic books and promised every bullied, insecure young man the means to take control of his life. If he hadn't been real, no one would have believed him."[52]

In 2005, Atlas was posthumously enshrined in the initial class of inductees to the National Fitness Hall of Fame.

ELLIOTT COOK CARTER, JR. (1908 – 2012) Centenarian Composer

Elliott Carter was born in New York, New York on December 11, 1908. He was encouraged towards a career in classical music by his friend and mentor Charles Ives. While attending Harvard University he studied under composers Walter Piston and Gustav Holst and later studied with the legendary teacher Nadia Boulanger in Paris, France.[53] He was considered by many to be one of the most enduring voices in contemporary American music.

In a field that sets a high value on youth, Carter celebrated his 100th birthday at Carnegie Hall on December 11, 2008, where the Boston Symphony Orchestra and pianist Daniel Barenboim played his *Interventions for Piano and Orchestra*, which he had written at age 98. In fact, between the ages of 90 and 100, Carter wrote more than 40 published works, which represented an extraordinary burst of creativity at an age when most people would be making peace with their mortality. His first opera premiered in 1999. He produced 10 works in 2007 and six more in 2008.[54] After his 100th birthday he published at least 20 more, with his final work, *Epigrams* written for piano trio in

---

[52]

Charles Atlas: Muscle Man, by Jonathan Black, Smithsonian Magazine, August 2009.

[53]

Elliott Carter, Elliottcarter.com, The Amphion Foundation, Inc., 2014.

2012.

"He received numerous honors and accolades, including the Pulitzer Prize on two occasions: in 1960 for his String Quartet No. 2 and in 1973 for his String Quartet No. 3. Other awards include Germany's Ernst Von Siemens Music Prize and the Prince Pierre Foundation Music Award.

Carter was the first composer to receive the United States National Medal of Arts, and is one of a handful of composers inducted into the American Classical Music Hall of Fame. He was recognized twice by the Government of France: being named Commander of the "Ordre des Arts et des Lettres," and receiving the insignia of Commander of the Legion of Honor in September 2012."[55]

On February 7, 2009, he was given the Trustees Award (a lifetime achievement award given to non-performers) by the Grammy Awards. He was on the faculty of the Tangewood Music Center, in Lenox, Massachusetts, where he gave annual composition master classes. In June 2012, the French government named him a Commandeur de la Legion d'honneur.

While Carter wrote complex musical compositions throughout his life, it was as a senior citizen that he created much of his work, at an age most world-renowned composers never attained. And, while audiences did not always appreciate his work, performers who cherished the way he wrote for their instruments loved it.

Also, while Carter's compositions were respected throughout the music world, it is highly probable that lots of people from heartland America who read this book will never have heard of him. It is unlikely his music would have appealed to folks who frequent pop music icons such as Guns N Roses, Led Zeppelin, The Rolling Stones or Bruce

---

54

Elliott Carter, 1908-2012, The New York Times, March 26, 2014.

55

Elliott Carter, Elliottcarter.com, The Amphion Foundation, Inc., 2014.

Springsteen, although Franz Joseph Haydn, Wolfgang Amadeus Mozart, and Franz Schubert were pop music icons of their day.

SISTER CECILA GAUDETTE (1902–) Oldest Absentee Voter

A 106-year-old American nun living in a convent in Rome could well be the oldest voter to cast an absentee vote in the 2008 U.S. Presidential election.

Sister Cecila Gaudette, who last voted for President Dwight D. Eisenhower in 1952, registered to vote on an absentee ballot in the 2008 election. Before the election she said she would vote for Senator Barrack Obama. "I've never met him, but he seems to be a good man with a good private life. That's the first thing. Then he must be able to govern," she said.[56]

At the time, the diminutive nun had lived in Rome for over 50 years and had no plans to return to the United States. "I am too old to go back to the U.S. Life has changed too much."

When asked about what she hopes for the United States under a President Obama, she said: "Peace abroad. I don't worry about the Iraq war because I can't do anything about it. Lord knows how it will end."

According to BBC News Sister Gaudette seemed uninterested in the row inside the American Catholic church over Senator Obama's support for pro-choice policies on abortion.

Although hearing impaired, she keeps herself informed by reading newspapers and watching TV at the convent. She watches "very important events" on TV and says the election comes under that category.

According to Reuters, Sister Gaudette became a minor celebrity after she appeared on television saying she would vote for Barack Obama, and was startled by all the attention she got for saying so. She wanted to return to the comfortable obscurity that characterized her life

---

[56]

106-year-old voter chooses Obama, BBC News, 2008

before the media discovered that she was one of the oldest Americans to vote. She would rather be left alone.

She was born in Manchester, New Hampshire and, despite living in Rome for over 50 years, she was very proud to be an American. She keeps an American flag in her office.

In Rome she taught music and art; before that she taught French in the United States. She has lived through 11 pontificates, starting with Pope Leo XIII and concluding with Pope Francis.

In 2012, when asked why she thinks God has allowed her to live so long, she replied: "I am wondering why. I often say that it is time for me to go." She's looking forward to meeting God. When asked what she will say to Jesus upon meeting him, she smiled and said: "I'm pleased to see you, I'd think."[57]

In 2013, at age 111, she was interviewed for a movie on the World's Oldest People, and is still going strong.

DOROTHY P. COLLEEN GEEBEN (1908 – 2010) Oldest U.S. Mayor

Dorothy P. Geeben was born on March 31, 1908 in Mondovi, Buffalo County, Wisconsin. She and her husband, Cornelius "Neal" Bunting, an electrician, founded Bunting Electric, with her working as their bookkeeper.

In 1952, she and her husband retired to Ocean Breeze Park, Florida and bought a mobile home. After her husband's death, she married Albert Geeben in 1963, but he died less than two years later.

She began serving on the Ocean Breeze Town Council in 1960 and in 1976 she began serving as the council president for 31 years. In 2001, after the death of Mayor Ruth Hoke, Geeben was selected to be the next mayor. For the next two elections no one ran against her.

"When she was ninety-four years old, Geeben saved Jansen Beach

---

[57] *At 110-years-old, Nun Advises Young to Draw Close to God,* Kaldaya.net, April 5, 2012.

Christian Church from closing down. At the time, the church lacked a minister and had four parishioners remaining. Geeben's efforts revived the church, enabling it to retain a pastor and increase church membership to 100 people."[58]

In January 2012, America's oldest, active mayor died after complaining of a cold. She was 102 years old and would have turned 103 in March.

"We had a council meeting on Monday," said David Myers, president of the Ocean Breeze Town Council. "She was supposed to be there, but called in to say she wasn't feeling well. She thought it was a cold. About 1:30 p.m., the paramedics went to her home and took her to Martin Memorial Medical Center where she passed away."[59]

Myers said Geeben had devoted much of her life to Ocean Breeze Park and its residents. "She was a kind, sweet woman who always had a smile," he said.

Gregory Minchak of the National League of Cities in Washington, DC said Geeben was definitely the oldest, active mayor in the country before her death.

The U.S. House of Representatives recognized Geeben as the nation's oldest mayor in April 2008. The Meals on Wheels Association of America survey also recognized her status. National Conference of Mayors officials said that while they don't keep a record of mayors' ages, they knew of no one who was older and still actively running a government.

She had always claimed the secret to her long life was keeping busy. "I have a good time. I'm on the go a lot. I guess that's half the battle."

---

[58]

Dorothy Geeben, Wikipedia, The Free Encyclopedia, December 22, 2013.

[59]

America's oldest active mayor dies at 102, by Joe Crankshaw, TC Palm, January 12, 2010.

On her 100th birthday, Geeben received letters from First Lady Laura Bush and Florida Governor Charlie Crist in tribute of the special occasion.

At the time of her death, she was survived by her son, John Bunting, two grandchildren, seven great-grandchildren, and four great-great grandchildren.

RUTH HAMILTON (1898 – 2008) Oldest Blogger at 109-years-old!

At age 109, Ruth Hamilton was a vibrant and engaging person who died three months before turning 110. She was the World's Oldest Blogger.

Born in Alta, Iowa in 1898, Ruth married Carter Hamilton, who set a single game strikeout record playing baseball for the University of Iowa. He later became a prominent radiologist, had a successful career and died in 1949. Ruth remained a widow the rest of her life.

After graduating from college, Ruth developed a passion for teaching. She first became a teacher in 1916 in a country schoolhouse in Iowa. As technology evolved, so did Ruth. When radio became popular, she began to use it to help her teach and became the first women to have her very own radio show in New York City. On the radio program she taught speech, elocution and English. Later, she moved to Los Angeles and taught diction to Hollywood starlets.[60]

She also taught through the newspaper, writing articles, travelogues and letters to the editor. Later, with the invention of the Internet she taught as a blogger. Using a computer as a blogger, she discovered the entire world could be her audience. She was, in fact, an Internet pioneer. As a world traveler well into her 90s, she lectured all across the country.

In her final years, she lived in an assisted living center in Orlando, Florida and, as Ruth1898, was a member of Growing Bolder, a social

---

[60] *Web's oldest bloggers: Olive riley and Ruth Hamilton,* Stories.OneWebDay. Org, September 22, 2012.

networking web site. Ruth was thus touted in the media as the "world's oldest blogger", inheriting the title at age 109, after a younger woman, 108-year-old Olive Riley of Australia, died. She had been previously touted as the oldest living blogger.

In 2007, Ruth sat for an interview on Growing Bolder, a radio and television program that features stories about ordinary people pursuing extraordinary lives. It is a weekly program that has appeared on over 600 public broadcast stations in more than 177 markets, including commercial television. The television version of Growing Bolder's Surviving & Thriving appears in prime time on the CBS affiliate in Orlando, Florida.

During her interview on the Growing Bolder radio program Marc Middleton told his listeners about this remarkable lady. "She started as a teacher, married a professional baseball player, became one of the first women to host her own radio show, came face to face with Hitler in 1937, taught diction to Hollywood starlets and became the first woman elected to the legislature in New Hampshire."[61]

Middleton described Ruth as a national treasure. As a blogger, she had so much to offer, so much guidance, inspiration, knowledge and experience to share. Because of her blogs, her wit, wisdom and curiosity will live on even longer than her 109 years on earth.[62]

Ruth Hamilton was one of a kind. Everyone should celebrate the fact that a 109-year-old woman could be so thoroughly dedicated to teaching the rest of us how to live.

MARY ALLEN HARDISON (1910 –) Oldest Paraglider

---

[61]

Radio interview with Ruth Hamilton on the Growing Bolder radio community, Marc Middleton & Bill Shafer, posted on June 3, 2007.

[62]

Web's oldest bloggers: Olive Riley and Ruth Hamilton, Stories.OneWebDay.org, September 22, 2012.

Mary Allen Hardison celebrated her 101st birthday by going paragliding over the skies of her hometown of Ogden, Utah, and now owns the Guinness World Record for the "Oldest Female to Paraglide Tandem."

"Hardison, who set the record in front of a group of spectators that included her children, grandchildren, great grandchildren and great-great grandchildren, admitted that part of the reason she took to the skies was out of competition with her 75-year-old son.

"I don't want my son to do anything I can't do, so I decided to go have fun like he did," Hardison told the local television station, right after the record-breaking flight, which was done with the help of her instructor, Kevin Hintze.[63]

"She wanted me to go upside down – do whatever I wanted," Hintze said. "She was hardcore."

It was the very first paragliding trip for the centenarian. With her family cheering hundreds of feet below, she soaked in the view. "I felt very serene. I looked all around, looked at the buildings, and looked at the mountains," she said.

Hardison didn't even know she had set the record. For her, the whole thing was a bit of a lark, but it wasn't the first time she did something different for her age. On her 90th birthday, she went to Disneyland and went on all the adult rides that were open. She said she doesn't just sit at home and groan about being old.

Paragliding is a long way off from her hobbies of knitting garments for the less fortunate: hats for children's hospitals, crocheted bandages for leopards (yes, leopards) in India and knit caps for premature babies. But, she didn't let it go to her head.

"I feel very humble in setting a new Guinness World Record," she said. "My desire is for the elderly to keep on going, do things as long as you are physically able. Be positive. Friends don't like a grumpy

---

63

Mary Allen Hardison, 101, Sets Guinness Record For Oldest Paraglider, by David Moye, Huffington Post Weird News, March 19, 2012.

person."[64]

Hardison also urges other senior citizens to keep moving and to continue to challenge themselves, even if it means they may break her record.

Obviously, Hardison's family, including all her grandkids, is very proud of her accomplishment.

BERT KILBRIDE 1914 – 2008 Scuba Diving at 93!

In 2004, for his 90th birthday, Gunness Book of World Records proclaimed Bert Kilbride to be the "oldest scuba diver" in the world. Kilbride had been a diver for almost a century when he died in 2008.

In an article for Squidoo, titled: *In Memory of the Last Pirate of the Caribbean,* Kilbride said his mom taught him how to swim before he could walk. He could not remember a time that he couldn't swim. He "…was bringing up treasures, in the form of rings and watches, from the depths of Lake Loraine in the 1920s. His mother made a dive mask for him when he was only eight years old.

"I have been an inventor, a builder, a contractor, and an entrepreneur. I have bought and developed two barren islands, one as a Scuba Destination hotel. I owned a SCUBA Diving tour business for 30 years. I am a husband, a father, and I'm aiming to live to be 100. I have a date with Jean–Michel Cousteau to go diving in the British Virgin Islands (BVI) for my 100th birthday."

According to his own web page, Kilbride had been a treasure seeker around the British Virgin Islands for over five decades, where he resided from the 1950s through 2005. He charted 138 shipwrecks, including famous shipwrecks such as the RMS Rhone, the Astrea, and what he called the Crown Site. The Crown Site is the location of an unknown wreck on Anegada Reef in the British Virgin Islands, where he found lots of musket balls, cannon balls and flints.[65]

64

Ibid.

65

The Last Pirate of the Caribbean, by A.J. Bernstein, Sport Diver Magazine, 2014 Sport Diver.

Kilbride created what he called the "Resort Course" for beginners interested in Scuba Diving. It is now taught worldwide under the name "Introductory SCUBA course." In 1967 he was made "Receiver of the Wrecks" by Queen Elizabeth and called a "pirate" by others in the BVI Government, when he wouldn't produce a map of the wrecks he had found on Anegada Reef.

Kilbride was instrumental in the 1977 movie The Deep being made around the RMS Rhone. He introduced the producer to the RMS Rhone. His third wife, Jackie, became Jacqueline Bisset's underwater stunt double, and Bisset's white T-shirt was Kilbride's idea.

A.J. Bernstein, author of *The Last Pirate of the Caribbean*, describes Kilbride as a New England Yankee by birth, who was drawn to Virgin Gorda for the warm, clear water and the treasures left behind centuries ago by Blackbeard, Henry Morgan and Sir Francis Drake.[66]

In 1989, after Hurricane Hugo blew through the BVI and temporarily killed off the dive business, Kilbride opened a "Pirates Pub,"which attracted a diverse crowd, including such celebrities as Robert DeNiro, Walter Cronkite and Geraldo Rivera.

At age 85 he was still busy. For ten years he worked with the Drake Exploration Society to locate Sir Francis Drake's lead coffin from the waters off Panama and sail it home to England. Of course he never did find it, but he continued to dive into his 90s.

He attributed his long life to his love of young women. His fifth wife, Gayla Kilbride, who was 34 years younger than Kilbride, maintains his web page.

Kilbride passed away in Etna, California on January 8 2008. His oldest son, Gary, arranged with Neptune Memorial Reef to have Bert's ashes placed in one of the gate columns with a brass plaque reading:

Bert

Kilbride

"Last Pirate of the Caribbean"

1914 – 2008

Mar 8 Jan 8

---

[66] Ibid.

The Neptune Memorial Reef is an artificial reef 3.25 miles east of Key Biscayne, not far from Miami, Florida. Built as an artistic interpretation of the Lost City of Atlantis, the Neptune Memorial reef is a memorial site. Those who choose cremation for final needs may opt for their remains to be deployed to the Reef.

FRANCOIS HENRI "JACK" LALANNE (1914 – 2011)
Physical Fitness

Jack LaLanne was born in San Francisco, California on September 26, 1914. Even though he was only 5'5" tall, he was an American fitness, exercise, and nutritional expert, as well as a motivational speaker, who is sometimes called "the godfather of fitness."

LaLanne was a Chiropractor, bodybuilder, and personal trainer who gained worldwide recognition for his success on his television show that ran nationwide for 34 years.

Throughout his career, LaLanne won many awards including the Horatio Alger Award, President's Council of Physical Fitness Silver Anniversary Award, and he has a star on the Hollywood Walk of Fame.

As a young man LaLanne was a sugar addict who ate a lot of "junk" food. He was influenced to change his habits when he heard Paul C. Bragg, a nutritionist who spoke on health and nutrition. Bragg motivated Lalanne to focus on his diet and exercise habits.

"He studied Gray's Anatomy of the Human Body, concentrated on bodybuilding, Chiropractic and weightlifting, something virtually unheard of in the 1930s. In 1936 he opened the very first modern health club and developed some of the modern equipment whose principles are still used today."[67]

Lalanne believed in daily, vigorous, systematic exercise and proper diet. These are all things that doctors today recommend to their patients as the principle keys to a longer and healthier life. Every health club in America owes a debt of gratitude to Jack Lalanne for advancing the concept of daily exercise and healthy food for a long and vigorous life.

---

[67]

Jack LaLanne, www.jacklalanne.com, 2014.

He was a superb salesman, and used stunts and other marketing tactics to draw attention to the importance of fitness and to lure more viewers to his show. His was one of the most popular daytime television shows for decades.

In addition to his television program, over the years Lalanne performed amazing feats of strength. At age 41, proving it was possible to escape from Alcatraz, he swam from Alcatraz to Fisherman's Wharf in San Francisco while wearing handcuffs. At age 45, he completed 1,000 push-up and 1,000 chin-ups in an hour and 22 minutes, with blisters under his calluses. At 60, he swam from Alcatraz to Fisherman's Wharf handcuffed, shackled and towing a 1,000-pound boat. At 70, while battling currents and handcuffed and shackled, he towed 70 boats holding 72 people for a mile and a half across Long Beach Harbor.[68]

His book, *Live Young Forever*, was critically acclaimed. It contains an overview of his life and how he lived it. There are never before seen photos of every aspect of his career and even tips on juicing.

"In 2002, Jack LaLanne scored a big success by endorsing a juicer. More than a million Jack LaLanne Power Juicers were sold between 2002 and 2004, according to *BusinessWeek* magazine. In addition to the juicer, he lent his support to a line of swimming pools and sold an assortment of books, videos, and other products through his own website."[69]

For decades he got up early every day and exercised for two hours: one hour of strength training and another hour of swimming. He then had a protein shake for breakfast. He was adamant about never drinking milk or eating dairy products. "Am I a suckling calf," he once told *Sports Illustrated.* "No other creature uses milk after they wean."

He remained in superb physical condition throughout his life. Even at the age of 95, Lalanne continued to have a great physique and to

---

[68]

Jack Lalanne Biography, All Men Must Die, www.IMDb.com, 2014.

[69]

Ibid.

encourage his fans with health and fitness tips through videos and writing. He died in his home in Morro Bay, California, of respiratory failure and pneumonia on January 23, 2011. To the day he died, he lived by what he preached to others. His message was simple: "Get out of your seat and onto your feet." One of the last things he said was: "I can't die, it would ruin my image."

His wife released a statement on his passing, saying "I have not only lost my husband and a great American icon, but the best friend and most loving partner anyone could ever hope for." The couple had been married for 51 years. In addition to his wife, his three children survive LaLanne.

NOLA OCHS (1911 –) Oldest College Graduate Ever!

At age 95, this 5' 2" great-grandmother, who is the matriarch of a family that includes three sons (a fourth died in 1995), 13 grandchildren and 15 great-grandchildren, is the oldest American member of a university graduating class.

When Vernon, her husband of 39 years died in 1972, she decided to start taking community college classes. She started college when she was 65. Ms. Ochs did some of her work on line, although not all of it. That wasn't even possible when she began more than 30 years ago. She finished up graduating from Fort Hayes State University, in west-central Kansas, with her granddaughter, living in an apartment on campus.[70]

Not only did she receive her degree in General Studies, but she also entered the Guinness World Records (known until 2000 in the U.S. as The Guinness Book of World Records) as the oldest person to be awarded an earned college degree.

She never ever doubted she would finish. According to an interview she had while still a student, she said she had great support from her family and other students. "You'd be surprised how well I have been

---

[70]

The Oldest People Who Have Done Things You Wouldn't Expect Them To Do!, www.squidoo.com, Copyright 2014, Squidoo, LLC.

accepted. That is one of the biggest reasons that I enjoy myself so much. I am just another student.

"I give thanks every day for each new day that the Lord allows me to live and enjoy life to the fullest."[71]

One of Nola's greatest thrills was the fact that Alexandra Ochs, her 21-year-old granddaughter, wore the cap and gown alongside her for the Class of 2007 graduation at Fort Hays State University. She received a Bachelor of Arts degree in History.

Nola Ochs set another record by earning her Masters Degree at age 98, and wrote a book at age 100. According to a report by LJ World in 1911, she has a good start on the book, which is about her life experiences. "I'll call it 'Nola Remembers"…and I depend on the name Nola to sell it," she said, laughing. (She is widely known and honored around campus simply as 'Nola.'"[72]

Among her other accomplishments, she was named the 2007 Kansas Woman Leader of the Year, and was given her undergraduate diploma by Kansas Governor Kathleen Sebelius. She earned a spot on *The Tonight Show* one week after she graduated, sharing a laugh with Jay Leno. After graduation, Princess Cruises hired her as a guest lecturer on a nine-day Caribbean cruise. [73]

Features on Ochs aired on The Early Show, MSNBC, and CBS News, among others. Ochs once said: "I don't keep track of my age, but I can tell you I was born in November of 1911." She also

---

[71]

Ibid.

[72]

Nola Ochs, World's Oldest Masters Degree at 98, Now Writing a Book at 100 Years Old!, Senior Editor, Helping You Care, Care-Help LLC, 2012.

[73]

Nola Ochs, Wikipedia, the Free Encyclopedia, February 24, 2013.

commented, "I've led a long, interesting life. We went through the dust storms. We had some difficult times in our marriage, financially. But, it's been the Lord's will that I've lived this long life, and I thank Him kindly for it."

Nola Ochs should be an inspiration to every senior citizen who lives alone, or who every thought of going back to school.

DR. PAUL E. SPANGLER (1899 – 1994) Long Distance Runner

Dr. Paul E. Spangler was born on March 18, 1899 in Oregon. He graduated from the University of Oregon and the Harvard Medical School, after which he joined the U.S. Navy and participated in World War I. He was Chief of Surgery at the naval hospital near Pearl Harbor, when the Japanese bombed Pearl Harbor on December 7, 1941.

Spangler retired from the Navy in 1959, then joined the charitable hospital ship SS Hope as its chief medical officer. He later moved to San Luis Obispo, California and took the job as Chief Surgeon at the nearby California Men's Colony prison.[74]

He later became chairman of his chapter of the American Heart Association and in 1966 at age 67 he took up long distance running. He once said, "My only mission in life now is to convince people this is possible. With proper living, they can eliminate coronary heart disease."

He enjoyed being a weekend athlete, but decided playing tennis, climbing mountains and digging clams, was not enough to stave off heart disease.

He was a bit of a Renaissance man. In addition to running long distances, he took up flying and became the first doctor, according to his family, to obtain a pilot's license. He also formed barbershop quartets all over the world, and had already given long service to his country.

However, running became his career. "Running has meant everything to me," he said before competing in the 1989 New York

---

[74]

Paul Spangler, Wikipedia, The Free Encyclopedia, December 25, 2013.

City Marathon at the age of 90. While he had completed 10 marathons, he had to drop out after 19 miles, having tired himself out before the race. He said he had given too many interviews. He completed the 1991 New York City Marathon at the age of 92.[75]

Before dying at age 95, Spangler claimed 85 national age group records at various distances. He still holds the American record for 90-year-olds in every metric distance race between 800 meters and 10,000 meters, including the 5,000-meter race-walk, with all records set in 1989 at age 90.

He also holds the 85-year-old record for 3,000 meters and also completed the New York Marathon in 1989. He continued to train for the marathon, with the goal of competing at age 100.

He was a pioneer into the limits of senior athletics by frequently being the oldest competitor, paving the way for successors into the upper age brackets.

He died shortly after turning 95 while doing one of his regular seven mile training runs, which he did three times each week. The Lifelong Fitness Alliance, a senior health organization, sponsors an annual eight-kilometer run for seniors at Stanford University named in honor of Spangler.

The USA Track & Field (USATF) named its annual award for the outstanding Masters Long Distance Running athlete after Spangler. Spangler was also elected into the USATF Masters Hall of Fame in its second year, 1997.

Paul Spangler was truly a senior citizen who believed in setting a sterling example in physical fitness for others his age. He life was living evidence that his theory on longevity was correct.

BESS TANCRELLE (1907 – 2010) Oldest Biker Chick

Bess Tancrelle died on March 17, 2010, at the Hanover Regional

---

[75]

Dr. Paul E. Spangler, 95, Dies; Took Up Fitness Running at 67, by Robert McG. Thomas, Jr., The New York Times, April 14, 1994.

Medical Center, in Wilmington, North Carolina, less than two months short of her 103rd birthday. As a member of the Westminster Presbyterian Church in Wilmington, she was a faithful Christ follower. She was also a loving wife for 53 years and an adventurous spirit.

Wearing her motorcycle helmet with "I'm About To Develop An Attitude" stenciled on it, she celebrated her 102nd birthday with a ride on a Harley Davidson motorcycle. Accompanying her on the ride in a sidecar was her 98-year-old sister, Clara Sternberger.

Tancrelle was born on May 12, 1907 in Franeker, The Netherlands, to Sytze and Tetje van der Wal and, together with her two sisters, they sailed to America in 1912.

She graduated from New Hanover High School, got an office job at the Atlantic Coast Line Railroad, and in 1931 married Louis Tancrelle. They had a son, Louis Tancrelle, Jr., who died in 2009.

After her husband died in 1984, Tancrelle lived with her widowed sister, Clara Sternberger and, together, they traveled the world and drove all over the United States.

Tancrelle had an adventurous spirit and had been a tomboy most of her life. Over the years she had often ridden horses, but for her 102nd birthday she wanted to ride a Harley-Davidson motorcycle; so, she hitched a ride, with her sister keeping an eye on her from a sidecar.[76]

It all started with a conversation about wishes between girlfriends at Lake Shore Commons Retirement Community. "I said I would like to ride a Harley someday," said Tancrelle, "and another lady said "I'd like to drive an 18-wheeler.""[77]

Kelley D. Hamilton, Chief Executive Officer and co-owner of the Bonaventure Senior Living facility, said some senior adults are content to sit in a comfortable chair and catch up on Law and Order reruns, but

---

[76]

Bess Tancrelle Obituary, Wilmington Star-News, March 20, 2010.

[77]

[w] *Wilmington woman was born to be wild 102 years ago*, by Amanda Greene, StarNewsOnline.com, May 12, 2009.

there are many who go above and beyond as an advocate for their age.

Mrs. Bess Tancrelle was an example of a senior citizen setting the bar for physical prowess. In 2009, at age 102, she received a gift from the coastal Carolina Harley Owners Group: a brand–new Harley Davidson motorcycle. She and her sister were both thrilled about getting to ride the "Harley" at their age.

Tancrelle and her sister took a cruise around Greenfield Lake before returning to a standing ovation from her friends at the Lakeshore Commons retirement home. Miss Bessie, as she was known, said she had ridden on a horse, a camel and even on an elephant, but it was nothing compared to riding a "hog." She continued, "It was a great thing; it's the greatest thing I've experienced in life."

Jeff Granato, a family friend, had the honor of driving the pair around town. He said the ladies were overjoyed to finally be able to ride a motorcycle, and it was a great experience for everyone involved.

Chapter 3

CORPORATIONS WITH A CONSCIENCE

Corporations are mostly known for maximizing their profits. In fact, some folks feel like most corporations are greedy, don't pay enough taxes and have no heart for the "little people." But, as you will see in this chapter, many corporations feel a social responsibility for the communities in which they have business operations. Many are placing nearly as much emphasis on how they treat people and our planet as they put on generating profits.

While it's true they must fulfill a responsibility to their shareholders or owners, corporations often play a vital role in the welfare of the communities in which they operate.

Unfortunately, except for the local community that benefits from the corporate largess, most of us never get a chance to read or hear about the length to which some corporations go to fulfill what they consider to be their social conscience.

In this chapter you will read about extraordinary things some corporations do to benefit the physical and spiritual health and welfare of their communities. These are corporations that earn a profit, but also feel a special obligation to support the communities in which they operate.

In return, very often, community support for these corporations is awesome. For instance, when Chick-fil-A was embroiled in a public controversy over the position it's chief executive officer, Dan Cathy, took against same-sex marriage, there was a movement by LGBT (lesbians, gays, bi-sexuals and transgender) activists to boycott Chick-fil-A.

However, despite huge protests by activists groups, the public largely supported Chick-fil-A. "In response to the controversy, former Arkansas Governor Mike Huckabee initiated a Chick-fil-A Appreciation Day movement to counter a boycott of Chick-fil-A, launched by same-sex marriage activists. More than 600,000 people RSVPed on Facebook for Huckabee's appreciation event.

"On August 1, Chick-fil-A restaurants experienced a large show of public support across the nation with the company reporting record-breaking sales. A consulting firm projected that the average Chick-fil-A restaurant increased sales by 29.9 percent and had 367 more customers than a typical Wednesday."[78]

The public recognized that, despite the controversy over same-sex marriage, by almost any other standard Chick-fil-A is a prime example of a corporation with a conscience and a great neighbor.

CHICK–FIL–A

Every now and then an individual, group or corporation does something so extraordinary for their community, that it defies logic. Even a great imagination would not predict such behavior. In 2014, Chick-fil-A did such a thing.

For those who might not know, Chick-fil-A is an American fast food restaurant chain headquartered in the Atlanta suburb of College Park, Georgia, specializing in high quality chicken sandwiches. It may be best known for its humorous billboards, which show cows holding signs that say "Eat mor chikin." It's cows are an instantly recognizable corporate logo.

Founded in 1946, it is privately held and family owned. Chick-fil-A was mostly associated with the southern United States until it began to grow in 1967. According to its company fact sheet, Chick-fil-A "has steadily grown to become the second largest quick-service chicken restaurant in the United States, with over 1,700 locations in 39 states and Washington, DC. In 2012, their annual sales were over $4.6 billion," which means it just barely missed being listed as a Fortune 500 company.

---

[78]

Wikipedia, The Free Encyclopedia, February 3, 2014.

Founded by S. Truett Cathy, who is Chairman Emeritus, and lead by Dan T. Cathy, Chairman, President and Chief Executive Officer, the company's culture is strongly influenced by its founder's Southern Baptist beliefs. All Chickl-fil-A restaurants are closed for business on Sunday, and the corporation has a strong social conscience, which many people across the nation may not know about.

Their social conscience was never more evident than in January 2014, when much of the United States was covered in a sheet of ice and a blanket of snow. We all read about the snow and cold temperatures, but many of us didn't read about the magnificent generosity of some companies. This was particularly true in the South, where many, if not most, cities rarely see snow and are not equipped to deal with it. Some don't have plows or salt or sand or other ice melting chemicals.

Such was the case for cities around Birmingham, AL. What some weather forecasters were calling a "polar vortex," caused a problem not often seen in the South.

What many people thought would become a light dusting of snow, became much more. Soon interstates and highways became clogged with cars and trucks, and quicker than many folks thought possible, people began to become stranded in their cars.

As Todd Starnes said in Todd's American Dispatch, published on January 29, 2014,[79] "…a good number of those stranded motorists were able to find shelter in the storm thanks to the kindness and generosity of Chick-fil-A restaurant employees and the restaurant's owner, Mark Meadows."

Meadows closed the restaurant and sent his staff home, but many of them returned because they couldn't get to their homes. The highways had become a huge parking lot, with some people stranded for as much as seven hours without any food or water. So the Chick-fil-A staff decided to help them.

Starnes continued, "The staffers braved the falling snow and ice,

---

79

Chick-fil-A Gives Free Food to Motorists Stranded in Southern Snowstorm, Todd's American Dispatch, January 29, 2014.

slipping and sliding, as they offered hot juicy chicken breast tucked between two buttered buns. And Chick-fil-A refused to take a single penny for their sandwiches.

"The meal was a gift – no strings attached. For the frozen drivers, it was manna from heaven. Chick-fil-A then opened their dining room to anyone who wanted to sleep on a bench or in a booth. The next morning Chick-fil-A served chicken biscuits to the stranded drivers and their passengers, once more at no cost to the visitors.

The Chick-fil-A web page says "…giving has always been a part of our company culture." Their theme may well be a quote from the Gospel of Matthew: "I was thirsty and you gave me something to drink, I was a stranger and you invited me in."

Chick-fil-A's web page says they are dedicated to serving the communities in which they operate. "From the day Truett Cathy started the company he began applying biblically-based principles to managing his business."

Wouldn't it be great if all companies did that? And wouldn't it be great if you could occasionally read on the front page of your local newspapers stories about such generosity as that displayed by Chick-fil-A during the 2014 snowstorm in and around Birmingham, AL?

Our mainstream news media doesn't do a very good job of keeping us informed about the great things happening around our country. They focus almost exclusively on stories that are really ugly, with little regard for morally uplifting stories that validate the fact that we are truly a great nation!

Other corporations like Chick-fil-A are all over our nation; we just don't her about them nearly often enough.

OTHER ORGANIZATIONS WITH A CONSCIENCE

AMERICAN APPAREL

While many U.S. apparel companies move their manufacturing operations abroad to third world vendors, American Apparel has kept its operation local. With its headquarters and manufacturing facilities in downtown Los Angeles, and 2012 sales revenue of $617 million and gross income of $327 million, American Apparel operates the largest apparel manufacturing facility in North America.[80]

American Apparel believes "…that having manufacturing under the same roof as design, marketing, accounting, retail and distribution gives us the ability to quickly mobilize all departments, to respond directly to changes in the market, and to have complete visibility over our produce – start to finish. An added bonus – this business model is inherently sustainable."[81]

The company pays its average factory worker $12 to $14 per hour, which the company says is the highest pay worldwide for the manufacturing of apparel basics, and significantly more than the California minimum wage. They think of their 5,000 employees as part of their corporate family.

American Apparel is politically active, and regularly uses its billboards, advertisements, press contacts and even printed t-shirts to speak out about important issues, such as the need for immigration reform and support for gay rights.

After printing a few hundred Legalize Gay t-shirts for a rally they attended, the company received thousands of requests from people all over the world who asked for us to expand it. "We've since given away over 50,000 of these shirts and run protest advertisements." [82]

The company is proud of the ways in which it fulfills its corporate responsibility to give back to its customers and the American public. Making over one million garments each week means they are poised to lend a hand to small groups working to make a difference in their community and elsewhere.

"As proud as we are of this ability, we also try to use our resources in big ways too. When disasters hit, we pick, box, and ship these garments where they are desperately needed within hours."

80

Market Watch, The Wall Street Journal, February 18, 2014.

81

www americanapparel.net.

82

Ibid.

Examples of American Apparel's sense of corporate responsibility.

2005: Packaged and delivered over 80,000 shirts to the victims of Hurricane Katrina in the Gulf Coast.

2007: Sent a truck across the U.S. to deliver 250,000 garments to people in need.

2008: Since the passing of Proposition 8 in California, the Company has given away more than 50,000 "Legalize Gay" t-shirts to everyone from LGBT clubs on college campuses to the Harvey Milk School in San Francisco.

2009: Sold over 15,000 overstock pieces at a sale in their parking lot and donated 100 of the proceeds to immigrant rights groups.

2010: Donated over 80,000 garments to support Haiti Relief.

2010: Donated roughly 15,000 pieces to Soles4Souls for the victims of the Nashville floods that caused over $1 billion in damages. American Apparel was the first relief group on the scene.

2011: Donated t-shirts and other garments to LGBT Youth Organizations.

2012: Supported those affected by Hurricane Isaac via Operation USA and the wildfires in Colorado via Family Center.[83]

---

[83] Ibid.

Whether or not you agree with their community outreach efforts, one must acknowledge that American Apparel epitomizes what is meant by the term "corporations with a conscience." They are consistently and deeply involved in corporate outreach programs that support their sense of responsibility to their community.

AMERICAN TELEPHONE & TELEGRAPH (AT&T)

The senior leadership at AT&T believes that investing in a well-educated workforce may be the single most important thing they can do to help America remain the leader in a digital, global economy.

AT&T has a program it calls *Aspire*, which is its signature philanthropic initiative to raise high school graduation rates. To that end, it committed to investing $350 million in education, to help prepare students for college and for careers. Their goal is to help students succeed in school, in the workforce and in life.[84]

Since the program launched in 2008, over one million students have benefited in all 50 states. AT&T accomplished this extraordinary achievement by providing support to more than 1,000 national and community organizations, including school districts, higher education institutions and education–serving non–profits organizations.

In 2012, AT&T launched their Aspire Local High School Impact Initiative, which focused on high school success and college–and–career–readiness programs, by funding local programs that have strong, evidence–based practices grounded in data–driven outcomes demonstrated to improve high school graduation rates.

In 2014, the AT&T Aspire program "…will provide up to $10 million to eligible organizations implementing verifiable, evidenced–based interventions to improve the retention, promotion and graduation rates of students at risk of dropping out of high school."[85]

AT&T reports that more than 60 percent of America's black

---

[84]

about.att.com/content/csr/home/people/aspire.html, 2014

[85]

Ibid.

African-American and Hispanic school children are living in poor or low-income families, and more than one in five children overall are in poverty, putting many of these students at risk for educational failure. But there is a promising new strategy for providing at-risk students with the academic and non-academic supports they need for educational success.

Integrated Student Support (ISS) promotes academic success by securing and coordinating specific supports tailored to the specific needs of at-risk students. These supports include tutoring and mentoring, linking students to physical and mental health care, and connecting their families to parent education, family counseling, and food banks. A key ingredient is the use of assessments to identify what is needed and to monitor progress over time.

AT&T and Bloomberg Philanthropies provided funding for Child Trends, a nonprofit, nonpartisan research center that provides valuable information and insights on the well being of children, based in Bethesda, Md., to conduct a study to determine how they can help at-risk students.

Child Trends drew on research in child and youth development, examined the empirical research on the factors that affect school success, conducted additional quantitative analyses, examined existing program evaluations, and interviewed leading practitioners in the Integrated Student Support field.

They found a positive return on investment in ISS, that ISS as a student-centered approach is firmly grounded in child and youth development research, that ISS is also aligned well with empirical research on the varied factors that promote educational success, and high-quality implementation is important to achieve positive outcomes.

However, they concluded that the evidence is mixed and inconclusive and warrants further study.

Meanwhile, AT&T established a Mentoring Academy and works with many education and dropout prevention non-profit organizations to provide mentoring opportunities. In addition to AT&T employees, who are invited to share life skills, personal stories about their career path and advice to help students succeed in school, AT&T works with such organizations as: Big Brothers Big Sisters, Boys & Girl Clubs of

America, Communities in Schools, Jobs for America's Graduates, Junior Achievement and We Teach Science.

AT&T is also focusing on "game-changing" approaches to education: development of interactive electronic games that foster learning, creation of educational programs that enable students to do things such as clean up simulated oil spills or extract DNA from bananas, sponsorship of "hackathons" to encourage U.S. technologists to develop new educational tools, sponsorship of mobile app contests, and promotion of e-mentoring.

General Colin L. Powell, (USA) Ret., puts AT&T's Aspire program in a more concrete perspective:

"America's Promise Alliance was founded on the belief that young people must be our nation's greatest priority. Helping youth achieve their full potential is not just good for our country, it's good for business. AT&T understands this and is demonstrating that through its Aspire program."

General Powell is the Founding Chairman of America's Promise Alliance.

BEN AND JERRY'S

Ben and Jerry's illustrates a dramatic American success story. In 1978, two obscure high school buddies, with a vision and a dream created what has become one of the most successful franchise companies in the United States. With a $5 correspondence course in ice cream-making from Penn State University, and a $12,000 investment ($4,000 of it borrowed), Ben and Jerry open their first ice cream scoop shop in a renovated gas station in Burlington, Vermont."[86]

Ben & Jerry's ice cream shops have since become the quintessential American company that grew from an obscure little shop in Vermont to perhaps the most famous ice cream shop in America. Ben & Jerry's has become the iconic American ice cream shop. The history of this

---

[86]

www.benjerry.com

legendary company is fairly well known, as is the quality of their ice cream.

Bennett "Ben" Cohen and Jerry Greenfield, dared to enter a market fairly well dominated by Baskin-Robbins in many parts of the country. But, despite being known for its 32 flavors, Baskin-Robbins still had to compete with lots of successful ice cream parlors, and Ben & Jerry's had a vision and a dream that wouldn't be stopped.

In 1987 they introduced Cherry Garcia ice cream, named after the Grateful Dead guitarist Jerry Garcia. It was the first ice cream named for a rock legend. In 1988, President Reagan named Ben and Jerry "U.S. Small Business Persons of the Year."

In 1992 Ben & Jerry joined in a cooperative campaign with the national non-profit, Children's Defense Fund, sending over 70,000 postcards to Congress concerning kids issues.

In 2000, Ben & Jerry's became a wholly owned subsidiary of Unilever. "Through a unique acquisition agreement, an independent Board of Directors is created to provide leadership focused on preserving and expanding Ben & Jerry's social mission, brand integrity, and product quality."[87]

While Ben & Jerry's ice cream is the prime reason for its success, its philanthropy has made it a pillar of strength in communities across America.

Ben & Jerry Foundation

In 1985, the Ben & Jerry's Foundation was created with an initial gift from Ben of 50,000 shares in the company, and an unprecedented decision of the company's Board of Directors to commit 7.5% of the company's annual pretax profits to philanthropy. Even so, it is independent of the ice cream company, and has nothing to do with ordering or providing ice cream. Its interests are purely philanthropic.

---

[87]

Ibid.

However, the Foundation's web page says it limits its investment dollars to Community Development Financial Institutions (CDFI). CDFIs are private sector financial intermediaries that have community development as their primary mission and develop a range of programs and methods to meet the needs of low-income communities.

In 1994 the Foundation decided to include employees directly in grant making decisions. Through the creation of Community Action Teams at each site and the Employee Grantmaking Committee, decision-making was placed in employees' hands.

In 2000, after being acquired by Unilever, a global company with over 400 brands, the new owner committed to continuing to support the Foundation through an annual allocation that takes into account Ben & Jerry's ice cream sales. For 2013, that amounted to $2.5 million.

The Foundation's prime interest is in furthering social justice, protecting the environment and supporting sustainable food systems. They are committed to supporting non-violent, thoughtful and strategic approaches that use grassroots organizing strategies to work for social change. It is their way of giving back to their Vermont communities.

The company says the Foundation strives to fund small groups that are not on the radar screen of mainstream funders. Ben Cohen, Co-Founder of Ben & Jerry's says their goal is to change systems in our society that cause poverty. What is unique is that employee groups make all the Foundation's decisions.

The Foundation awards about $1.8 million annually to eligible organizations across the country and in Vermont. It administers four applicable grant programs, all of which use an on-line application process. For information the Foundation may be reached either by telephone: 802-846-1500 (Rebecca Golden, Director of Programs, Extension 2646), at the website: www.benandjerrysfoundation.org or by email:

info@benandjerrysfoundation.org.

In 2005, Ben & Jerry's Foundation celebrated its 20th Anniversary. If you don't live in Vermont, you probably have never heard of any of the work this exciting ice cream company and its foundation does for its communities. Nevertheless, whether or not you agree with its strategic community goals, the Ben & Jerry Ice Cream Company and its Foundation represents yet another example of a corporation with a conscience.

HOBBY LOBBY

Headquartered in Oklahoma City, Oklahoma, Hobby Lobby is one of America's best-known arts and crafts companies. David Green, who began building miniature picture frames in his garage, started the company in 1970. According to Wikipedia,[88] his first store was called Greco Products, and was the result of a $600 loan. It had only 300 sq. ft. of space.

Today, with around 16,000 employees and 589 stores, having an average of 55,000 sq. ft. of space, and offering more than 67,000 crafting and home décor products, Hobby Lobby is considered a leader in that industry.[89] It is listed as a major private corporation in *Forbes* and *Fortunes* list of America's largest private companies, and carries no long-term debt.

While Hobby Lobby was in the news much during 2013 because of its fight over Obamacare's requirement for the inclusion of contraceptive coverage for its employees, which Green considers to be a violation of his religious beliefs, it is probably better known for its cookie jars.

Each season Hobby Lobby introduces an assortment of cookie jars for sale, that many customers find hard to resist. Different cookie jars are available for seasons such as: Valentine's Day, St. Patrick's Day, Easter, Halloween and Christmas. And, while Hobby Lobby is not in the collectable business, many of their jars have become collectibles.

Green is a committed Christian who credits his success to a total dependency upon God. "In a recent interview with ChristiaNet.com,

---

[88]

Wikipedia, the free encyclopedia, December 11, 2013.

[89]

Hobby Lobby Stores, Inc., 2014, Hobby Lobby web page.

David Green shared his faith, his commitment to serving the Lord by serving his customers and employees, and his dedication to running a company that continually demonstrates the integrity of biblical principles in everything this company does and says."[90] His philosophy is simply to make sure his stores are committed to be servants of the Lord and their customers.

According to ChristiaNet.com, Green is so devoted to his employees' family time that all his retail doors close as evening approaches. Hobby Lobby Creative Centers close at 8:00 p.m. daily, and they are the only billion-dollar company, other than Chic-fil-A, that is closed on Sundays to honor the Lord.

Green's employees are so pleased with the way he runs the company that in 2000, when the United Steelworkers of America tried to organize the Hobby Lobby warehouse as a union shop, their efforts to convince employees to join failed, with 83 percent of employees voting against becoming unionized.[91]

His philosophy for running the company has paid off handsomely. According to Celebrity Networth, David Green has an estimated personal net worth of $5.4 billion. He is a Christian who believes with his whole heart that his business should be run based on Christian principles.

In keeping with that Christian philosophy, Green is very generous with his money. "He is a staunch supporter of evangelical education, and has given millions to Christian universities. He also has put almost 1.4 billion copies of gospel-related literature or books in homes in Africa and Asia," and saw that over 200 million copies of the Gospels were distributed to as many homes.[92]

While David Green is still Chief Executive Officer of Hobby

---

[90]

ChristiaNet.com, Hobby Lobby CEO, David Green, Copyright 1996–2012.

[91]

Ibid.

[92]

Lobby, his son Steve Green is President of the company, and his only daughter, Darsee Lett, is Creative Director for the Hobby Lobby stores.[93]

Hobby Lobby continues to expand its business, and now includes stores in over 40 states, as well as in China, Hong Kong and the Republic of the Philippines. It is almost certain to become iconic as one of America's leading arts and crafts empires – unless the Green family decides to dissolve its business, rather than capitulate to the government mandate to include contraceptive and abortion coverage in its employee health insurance coverage, which is anathema to the Green family's religious beliefs.

That issue is almost certain to end up in the U.S. Supreme Court, according to Bill Keller, writing in *The Conscience of a Corporation* in the New York Times. The Supreme Court makeup is interesting: six of the nine justices are Roman Catholic, and at least four members of the court are known to not think much of Obamacare.

If Hobby Lobby loses in the U.S. Supreme Court, the company could face fines of more than one million dollars per day until it complies with the Obamacare mandates. That would present David Green with a moral dilemma: pay the fine or capitulate to the governmental mandate. Of course his other option would be to close his business, in which everyone would lose. He says he might just do that!

Let's hope it doesn't come to that.

KANSAS CITY CHIEFS

If you don't live in or near Kansas City, Missouri, you might not think of a football franchise as a spirited example of a corporation with a conscience. The Kansas City Chiefs is well known for its quality football

---

Reference for business, company index, Hobby Lobby Stores Inc. – Company Profile, Information, Business Description, History, Background Information on Hobby Lobby Stores Inc.. Copyright © 2014 Advameg, Inc.

93

Wikipedia, the free encyclopedia, December 11, 2013.

team. What it is not well known for is the community work it does regularly for Kansas City and the surrounding areas.

Not well known outside the region, but recognized locally, one of the Chiefs main missions is to engage the fans and unite with the Kansas City community. The chiefs Community Relations department has created many programs to inspire young people, connect with the community, and honor outstanding folks in the region.

Chuck Castellano, Chiefs Community Relations Manager, noted that "the events that we have in place are really exciting because it's not only the players, or the Hunt family, but it's the Cheerleaders, the Red Coaters and front office staff; everybody coming together collectively as the Chiefs Community Caring Team to help uplift our neighbors and our community throughout the year."

The Hunt family refers to Clark Hunt, the Kansas City Chiefs Chairman and Chief Executive Officer. The Red Coaters, an essential part of the organization, are community and civic leaders from around Kansas City who support the team by promoting its presence in the city and getting commitments from people in the area to buy season tickets. They are a community-service organization comprised of businessmen and women who are passionate about the Chiefs and about giving back to the community.

Red Coaters participate in programs such as delivering Thanksgiving baskets to local families, collecting toys for the U.S. Marine Corps Toys for Tots program, and visiting servicemen and women in the Veterans Affairs Medical Center.

"Red Coaters participate at charitable fundraisers, community events, training camp, golf tournaments, NFL sponsored school programs, stadium events and are on the field during pre-game at Arrowhead Stadium.[94]

The Chiefs Community Caring Team, led by Clark and Tavia Hunt, along with the entire Hunt family, also includes members from the Chief's organization who participate in community outreach efforts throughout the year. They regularly participate in such events as food

---

[94]

www.KansasCityChiefs.com, January 23, 2014.

distribution around the holidays, visiting local schools, volunteering at Harvesters Community Food Network, hosting free dental work at the stadium and much more.[95]

Since 2004, in cooperation with the community, the team has raised over $4 million for local charities, such as Big Brothers and Sisters of Greater Kansas City. They support the NFL's national campaign, *Play 60,* which encourages young fans to be active for 60 minutes a day and eat healthy foods. They also have an art program which supports regional art and culture by hanging art in Arrowhead stadium.

During 2013, they had a 50/50 raffle at every home game, giving fans an opportunity to take home half of the jackpot, while the other half benefited a deserving local charity. One of the beneficiaries that year was Harvesters Community Food Network, which received $19,271 to provide meals for people in the Kansas City area.

Other beneficiaries of the 50/50 raffle included Big Brothers Big Sisters, Third and Long Foundation, Ronald McDonald House Charities, Rose Brooks Center, Camp Quality of Greater Kansas City and HyVee Homefront.

The Kansas City Chiefs organization has made corporate citizenship and charitable giving in the community a priority for the Chiefs. Is it any wonder that they are one of twelve companies included in a book titled: *Companies With A Conscience, Intimate Portraits of Twelve Firms That Make A Difference,* by Howard Rothman and Mary Scott, published by Myers Templeton, ISBN: 0-9722741-5-4?

The Kansas City Chiefs exemplify the intended meaning of corporations with a conscience. Wouldn't it be wonderful if every sporting organization in America took a page from the Kansas City Chiefs community relation's playbook? What a role model they are for the rest of the sporting world.

STONYFIELD FARM

In 2010 and 2011, Stonyfield Farms was named one of the best companies to work for and received the 2010 Business of the Decade

---

95

    Ibid.

Award. In 2014, the Boston Athletic Association named Stonyfield Farms official supplier of yogurt for the Boston Marathon. Company officials say the healthy mission came first; yogurt making came second.

According to its website, "Stonyfield Farm, Inc. is an Equal Employment Opportunity/Affirmative Action employer and provides reasonable accommodation for qualified individuals with disabilities and disabled veterans in job application procedures."[96]

The company began in 1983 as a non-profit organic farming school, on a small New Hampshire farm. Their mission was to help family farms survive, keep food and food production healthy, and help protect the environment.

So, they started making yogurt without the use of toxic persistent pesticides or chemical fertilizers. They are committed to keeping artificial ingredients out of food. They use only pure all natural and organic ingredients, premium milk from farmers who have pledged not to use the synthetic bovine growth hormone.[97]

The yogurt was a big hit, so they decided to focus on yogurt.

Today, their organic yogurts, smoothies, soy yogurts, frozen yogurts, milk and cream are sold in supermarkets, natural food stores and colleges across the country. And they make it all without the use of toxic persistent pesticides, artificial hormones, antibiotics or genetically modified organisms.

Stonyfield encouraged their employees to be civic minded and support the International Random Acts of Kindness Week during February 10–16, 2014. Employees were encouraged to "take this week to step out of your normal routine or comfort zone and attempt a new random act of kindness each day of the celebratory week" and share their stories with the company.

Here is what some of the employees reported:

---

[96]

At Stonyfield, the Healthy Mission Came First, Yogurt Making Second, by Stonyfield Amy, *Lifting the Lid,* August 24, 2013.

[97]

Stonyfield Farm, Inc., Careersinfood.com, 2002–2013.

"In my morning runs for a hot beverage, I had people pay for my order and I, in turn, paid it forward to the next person."

"I secretly picked up a tab for a group of soldiers at a restaurant to thank them for their service."

"For Christmas this year, instead of giving each other gifts, we paid off the lay-away balances for 8 families."

"I had a person in front of me at the toll booth pay for my toll. I then wanted to pay it forward and did it for someone else…"

The company also asked their Facebook fans to share some kind acts with them and were blown away by the responses – everything from helping strangers pay for groceries, to shoveling walkways and sending anonymous Valentines to nursing home residents.[98]

Stonyfield says they use trains for transportation because they believe trains are 11 times more fuel-efficient than trucks. In 2013, the company decided to map the carbon footprint of its 200 different products. To do that they tracked the entire process that each product goes through from beginning to end and calculated the resources it takes to create that product.

They track the life of the product throughout the production process, transportation and sales process, so they can determine where the company's highest emissions are and make adjustments accordingly.

"Through this process, the company has set a goal to reduce its greenhouse gas emissions to limits that are in line with the recommendations of the Intergovernmental Panel on Climate Change, or three percent annually, to 80 percent by 2050. It has also set the admirable goal of ensuring that 50 percent of its energy is sourced from renewable energy by 2017."[99]

Is it any wonder that Stonyfield Farm is one of the featured

----

[98]

At Stonyfield, the Healthy Mission Came First, Yogurt Making Second, by Stonyfield Amy, *Lifting the Lid,* August 24, 2013.

[99]

Stonyfield Farm Tracks Its Carbon Footprint, by Jan Lee, TriplePundit, February 12, 2013.

companies in *Companies With A Conscience, Intimate Portraits of Twelve Firms That Make A Difference,* by Howard Rothman and Mary Scott, published by Myers Templeton, ISBN: 0-9722741-5-4?

SUBWAY

From the very beginning SUBWAY has been a socially responsible corporation. In 1965 Fred DeLuca and Dr. Peter Buck opened their first SUBWAY in Bridgeport, Connecticut. By 1974 they owned and operated 16 submarine sandwich shops throughout Connecticut, at which time they began franchising the brand.

Today, the SUBWAY brand is the world's largest submarine sandwich chain, with more than 41,344 restaurants in 104 countries around the world, and it continues to grow.

Their web site says they are guided by a passion for delighting customers by serving fresh, delicious, made-to-order sandwiches. Their reputation for healthy food got a huge boost by an unexpected, serendipitous event. Jared Fogle lost a lot of weight eating SUBWAY sandwiches.

According to the SUBWAY web page, the Jared Foundation, created by SUBWAY restaurants' hero, Jared Fogle, is designed to raise funds and awareness in an effort to fight obesity. Jared is a former Indiana University student, whose incredible story of losing 245 pounds, on a diet that incorporated low-fat SUBWAY sandwiches and walking, has inspired many.

Today, Jared serves as an ambassador for both the SUBWAY brand and for healthy living by making more than 200 visits to schools, civic organizations and American Heart Association Heart Walks each year. Jared has worked hard to keep his weight off over the years. In fact, he finished the 2010 New York Marathon, and today, 15 years after he first started his diet, he weighs 190 pounds—down 245 from his beginning weight of 435 pounds.[100]

For many people, Jared has become the face of SUBWAY, which says its vision is to make their restaurants and operations as

---

[100]

Jared's Journey, www.SUBWAY.com, 2014.

environmentally and socially responsible as possible. They are dedicated to supporting their franchisees in the most environmentally sustainable manner possible. By streamlining their supply chains, using sustainable sourcing practices to ensuring their food quality and food safety standards are met, they help reduce energy, water usage and waste, while taking care of the environment too.[101]

In the past three years they have significantly cut their resource consumption and reduced their greenhouse gas emissions by 292,936 metric tons of CO2 (which is equivalent to 57,244 passenger cars not driven for a year) even as their corporation grew by 12%.

Other indicators of their corporate sense of community is reflected in the make up of their franchisees:

. 34 are women.

. 24% are members of minority groups.

. 10% are aged 62 or older.

. Nearly 30% employ staff members who are aged 62 or older.

. Nearly 80% employ members of minority groups.

. Members of minority groups make up 50–100% of the staffs in 25% of the SUBWAY shops.

. 98% of franchisees employ women in their restaurants.

. In 78% of the restaurants 50–100% of the employees are women.

. 66% of the SUBWAY shops are "family-operated" businesses.[102]

Giving back to their communities is a strong part of the SUBWAY brand culture. According to Michele DiNello, Director of Corporate Communications, in 2011 SUBWAY employees picked ten charitable organizations to receive corporate donations of as much as $100,000.

Each of the organizations chosen to receive the corporate donations work tirelessly to make the world a better place:

Doctors Without Borders, composed of doctors and nurses who

---

[101]

Social Responsibility, www.SUBWAY.com, 2014

[102]

Ibid.

volunteer to provide urgent medical care to people developing countries who are victims of war and disaster.

Feed the Children, a non-profit relief organization that delivers food, medicine and clothing to children and families who lack basic necessities.

Susan G. Komen for the Cure, a global leader in the fight against breast cancer.

United Nations Children's Fund (UNICEF), a global organization that works for universal equality for those who are discriminated against.

Save the Children, an organization that works to resolve the struggles children face every day – poverty, hunger illiteracy and disease.

The Jared Foundation, the popular SUBWAY spokesman Jared Fogle has become a leader in the fight to help children learn life-long healthy diet and exercise habits.

Make-A-Wish Foundation, an organization that grants the wishes of children with life-threatening medical conditions to enrich their lives with hope, strength and joy.

American Red Cross, the world's premier emergency response organization.

American Cancer Society, a nationwide, community-based voluntary health organization dedicated to eliminating cancer as a major health problem.

American Heart Association, an organization dedicated to building healthier lives, free of cardiovascular disease and stroke.

SUBWAY is particularly passionate about heart health and doing their part to fight childhood obesity by encouraging healthy eating habits and by encouraging living active lifestyles. SUBWAY franchisees support many programs that combat cardiovascular diseases and stroke.

While we take for granted that SUBWAY sandwiches are some of the best in the world, how often have you walked into a SUBWAY restaurant and given any thought to whether or not that restaurant and its employees are good neighbors in your community? When was the last time you read about any of these SUBWAY sponsored programs that benefit people around the world?

SUBWAY is yet another example of a corporation with a conscience, a corporation that genuinely cares about the welfare of communities they serve.

TOMS SHOES & EYEWEAR

Blake Mycoskie founded TOMS Shoes and Eyewear in 2006. He is the person behind the idea of One for One, which has turned into a global movement. He has given away over ten million pairs of new shoes to children in need since it began in 2006.

The TOMS web site points out that its "…humble beginnings happened unintentionally." While traveling in Argentina in 2006, Blake witnessed the hardships children faced by growing up without shoes. His solution to the problem was simple, yet revolutionary: to create a for-profit business that was sustainable and not reliant on donations, which would make possible his One for One program. His vision soon turned into the simple business idea that provided the powerful foundation for TOMS.

TOMS Shoes

His novel idea of One for One is to give away one pair of shoes to needy children for every pair he sells. According to AOL, "through a bit of trial and error, and the help of amazing editorial pickup from outlets like the LA Times and Vogue, Blake was able to sell 10,000 pairs of shoes his first summer, which translated into 10,000 pairs of shoes donated to children in need as well. After his first trip to Argentina to drop off shoes, his life was forever changed."[103]

His plan was to incorporate an active giving component into his company's overarching strategy. "He strongly believes and teaches that the more "good" companies can incorporate into their business strategies, the bigger an impact they will have on society, and in doing that, the more brand ambassadors they would have without even trying!"[104]

On April 10, 2012, TOMS instituted a new program called One Day Without Shoes, which is a challenge to participants around the world to go without shoes for one day to begin to understand how vital shoes are to overall health. According to Mycoskie, it's a program to generate awareness, because participants begin to talk about how they feel. He believes conversation leads to action, which ultimately leads to change that can affect the world of shoeless children.

The first year of the One Day Without Shoes program, more than 1,000 members of America On Line went barefoot in honor of the program. Now, the company says they are looking to increase their impact 100 times over.

TOMS shoes are made from vegan materials and include natural hemp, organic cotton, and/or recycled polyester. All of their shoe boxes are made from 80% recycled post-consumer waste and are printed with soy ink.

TOMS shoes are always given to children through humanitarian organizations who incorporate shoes into their community development programs. To date, TOMS has given away 10 million pairs of shoes to children in need around the world.

TOMS Eyeglasses

---

[103]

Blake Mycoskie, Founder and Chief Shoe Giver at TOMS, Visits AOL, by Joey Blumenfeld, March 21, 2012.

[104]

Ibid.

Interestingly enough, the One for One shoe program evolved into another exceptional example of a corporation with a conscience: the TOMS Eyewear Program. According to the TOMS web site, based on the same principle as the One for One shoe program, the One for One eyewear program has given "…sight to youngsters in over 10 countries, providing prescription glasses, medical treatment and/or sight-saving surgery with each purchase of eyewear.

Not only does a purchase help restore sight, it supports sustainable community-based eye care programs, the creation of professional jobs (often for young women), and helps provide basic eye care training to local health volunteers and teachers.

TOMS eyewear is inspired by iconic and vintage style, from wayfarer-inspired Classics to pilot frames to historic oversized lenses. Every purchase provides their customers with the opportunity to restore sight to a person in need.

To date, TOMS has helped restore sight to over 200,000 people in thirteen countries around the world.

TOMS is a member of the American Apparel and Footwear Association (AAFA) and is an active participant in the AAFA Environmental and Social Responsibility Committees. TOMS is also a member of the Textile Exchange and is working with them to support efforts to use more sustainable materials. TOMS regularly brings in outside experts to validate or improve their practices.

TOMS Shoes and Eyeglasses and the founder, Blake Mycoskie, have been featured nationally on network television shows and in such magazines as Forbes; but, still, I have not personally met anyone who has ever heard about this marvelous company or its extraordinary Founder and Chief Executive Officer.

They both deserve our full attention and support!

Chapter 4

COMMUNITY ORGANIZATIONS
THAT MAKE US PROUD

BASTROP COUNTY LONG TERM RECOVERY TEAM

It is fairly unusual for a long-term recovery team to get a community award, but the Bastrop County, Texas Long Term Recovery Team is an exception to that historical thought.

In 2011, the Bastrop County Long Term Recovery Team (BCLTRT) worked tirelessly performing miracles to rebuild their county after Labor Day wildfires killed two people, destroyed 1,691 homes and 38 businesses, and burned over 34,000 acres of property.

In 2014 the Bastrop County Long Term Recovery Team was awarded the 2013 LTRC of the Year Award from Texas Voluntary Organizations Active in Disaster. It was the first time this award had ever been given to a long-term recovery team. But the Texas Division of Emergency Management, believed it was deserved because of the long-term recovery team's "outstanding performance and lasting contributions to rebuilding in the State of Texas."[105]

Assistant Director for Emergency Management and Homeland Security, Nim Kidd added, "This award highlights the Bastrop Long Term Recovery Team's commitment to the community's recovery from the 2011 Bastrop Complex Wildfires. It's the efforts like theirs that

---

[105] Bastrop County Long Term Recovery Team receives prestigious award, Editorial by Janice Butler, statesman.com, March 3, 2014.

make me proud to be a part of the emergency management community in this state and Texas. I commend them for their dedication and congratulate them on this well-deserved honor."

In March 2014, BCLTRT completed its 100th home. The group funded over $3.9 million on 118 building projects toward the recovery efforts. Volunteers worked more than 500,000 hours on over 1,450 properties to help the thousands of fire survivors with everything from debris cleanup to the rebuilding of homes.

Other projects included the building of storage sheds, decks, handicap ramps and skirting for those who replaced their manufactured homes. They also helped ranchers rebuild fences for their livestock.

The homes were rebuilt using about 90% volunteer labor. The primary expenses were for construction materials and contractors for air conditioning systems, plumbing and electrical work.[106]

According to Butler, two years after the disaster a lot of people had given up hope of ever having their own home again, but the American Red Cross granted the county a $1.5 million grant to keep them rebuilding.

"The BCLTRT credits its success to the excellent relationships that have been established with Christian Aid Ministries, Mennonite Disaster Services, Nomads On a Mission Active in Divine Service, and World Renew for providing the volunteers for completing these homes."

An incredible outpouring of funds from a slew of other community and faith based organizations made the rebuilding possible. An otherwise devastated community is once more a vital and vibrant common core of neighborhoods, because an entire community pulled together to rebuild itself, with the help of the Bastrop County, Texas Long Term Recovery Team.

It is this kind of community spirit that needs to be promoted throughout our nation, and stories like this ought to rise to the level of media coverage that is so often reserved only for bad news.

BREVARD ASSOCIATION FOR THE ADVANCEMENT

---

[106]

Ibid.

OF THE BLIND

Located in Satellite Beach, Florida, about two miles south of Patrick Air Force Base, is an organization devoted exclusively to improving the lives of visually handicapped people. That is, the Brevard Association for the Advancement of the Blind (BAAB), helps those who are in various stages of being visually impaired as well as those who are totally blind.

A private organization staffed entirely by volunteers and supported exclusively by public donations, BAAB is a community group for which everyone in America can be extremely proud.

On Monday, Tuesday and Wednesday each week, volunteers participate in a Library of Congress program in which they record periodicals that are then preserved digitally so they can be reproduced in quantity for Talking Book Libraries throughout the country.

Each reading is closely monitored and reviewed to ensure the very best quality. It is then identified by its content and reader, electronically set to government specifications, and sent to a quality assurance screener who certifies the acceptability of the final product.

The Library of Congress has very strict program standards that must be met--without exception. Representing near perfection, the digitally mastered recordings are then distributed to libraries across the country so that visually challenged people can check them out and listen to them.

The recordings span a wide range of periodicals, offering a wonderful world of education and entertainment opportunities that would otherwise not be available to people who cannot see.

The volunteers are a group of talented readers and monitors. Some have computer skills that are used to complete the transformation from raw data to a unique tool for the benefit of sight–impaired citizens.

On Fridays, another group of volunteers make possible a *Program for Independent Living*, in which visually challenged folks attend classes to learn the skills needed to live independently.

Classes are divided into small groups of two or three people, so each student can have the personal attention of a teacher. Volunteers instruct participants on how to perform tasks that sighted people take for granted, such as brushing their teeth, sewing on buttons, or cooking meals.

Many participants are adults who may be thinking about moving to assisted living or nursing facilities because of their inability to care for themselves since losing their sight.

The classes are taught by trained and qualified volunteers who are motivated by nothing more than the desire to help these people become more independent in their own homes.

By teaching them critical skills, BAAB helps them remain safe and reasonably independent in their own homes. Volunteer teachers show them how to manage almost every aspect of their daily living, without assistance. Those with sight impairments learn how to deal with personal, social and community interests and needs.

Classes are taught in a home-like environment that replicates as much as possible the typical living room, dining room, kitchen and bedroom. The goal is to accommodate the individual student needs, so they can feel comfortable in their homes.

Many people who come to BAAB for the first time don't know what to expect. "Meeting anyone young or old – with diminished or total vision loss can be challenging because most of us take our eyesight for granted. For those with vision impairment, simple tasks can become major chores and a bewildering maze of obstacles to overcome."[107]

Instructors at BAAB teach their students an array of skills the visually handicapped need to function normally in what for them is a complex world. An example would be how to prepare meals. The simple task of cutting meat or vegetables could result in an injury, so instructors suggest they use a larger "chef" knife, rather than a small paring knife. The larger knife is easier to handle.

The volunteer director of the center's program for independent living, said students are taught how to label items. For instance, picking up a can of raid instead of a can of hair spray or a tube of ointment instead of a tube of toothpaste, could have really bad consequences, so the students are taught to label items so they can be identified by touch.

The students are also taught how to better use their sense of hearing,

---

[107]

Blind School Extends Hope to Visually Impaired, by John M. Egan II, SpaceCoastDaily.com, March 12, 2013,

smell and taste, so they can cross roads safely or smell an odor of gas. A sense of taste is critically important and could save their lives.

"Taste will tell if it is safe or is it sugar, salt or detergent, and touch will let you know is this a latch on the door or is the surface hot? Is that an open drawer I may strike, or is this a comb or something that will harm them. These are just some of the tips, our students can use to stay safe and return to independent living."[108]

Teaching blind students how to be independent and self-reliant is job one for the Brevard Association for the Advancement of the Blind. It provides the kind of community opportunities for visually handicapped people that should be available in every community across America. Unfortunately, it isn't!

Whether participating in the Library of Congress program for recording magazines, or helping to teach those with limited vision how to live independently, BAAB is a unique organization that fills a profound community need. It is truly a public treasure!

CARNEGIE HERO FUND

"The Carnegie Hero Fund is one of the less well-known of the charities created by the steel tycoon Andrew Carnegie; its investigators frequently have to tell people they're not selling Dale Carnegie courses or inviting them to play at Carnegie Hall. The fund's mission remains largely unchanged since Carnegie's time: to seek out North Americans who perform brave deeds and provide them with a medal and a $3,500 grant. In addition, widows and orphans receive Carnegie pensions, and some children of deceased Carnegie Medal winners receive college scholarships.

"In 1999, 102 Carnegie Medals were awarded: 47 for saving people from fires,20 from drowning, 11 for fending off animal attacks, 11 for assaults from criminals, five from electrocution, and one from suffocation. The youngest hero was Alana Franklin, 11, of Ocala, Florida, who helped free her six-year-old nephew from a gunman who was holding her family hostage. Two septuagenarians also received

---

[108]   Ibid.

Carnegie Medals: Burnell Gilleland of Haskell, Texas, who died saving his grandson from a well filled with propane, and Frank S. Hedingham, of Lantzville, British Columbia, who helped fight off a bear in a provincial park. "[109]

On January 25, 1904, the Allegheny Coal Company's mine in Harwick, Pennslvania, exploded, killing 181 people. After the explosion, a mining engineer and a coal miner died from inhaling poisonous gases while trying to rescue miners. Touched by their heroism, Carnegie ordered gold medals created to honor the two heroes and gave $40,000 to a fund created to help victims of the disaster.

But, wanting to do more, in March 1904 Carnegie donated "five million dollars of First Collateral Five Per Cent Bonds of the United States Steel Corporation" to create the Carnegie Hero Fund Commission. He also awarded smaller grants to create hero funds in nine other counties too.

The Hero Fund, which was established to recognize individuals who perform extraordinary acts of heroism in civilian life in the United States and Canada, was Carnegie's favorite among his charities and remains the only national Carnegie philanthropy to remain in Pittsburgh, instead of being headquartered in New York or Washington, CC.

"Administered by a 21-member board still based in Pittsburgh, the Hero Fund has awarded 9,611 medals as of June 2013 and has given $35.2 million in one-time grants, scholarship aid, death benefits, and continuing assistance. Recipients who have fully met awarding requirements have been selected from more than 85,000 nominees.

"The Commission's working definition of a hero as well as its requirements for awarding remain largely those that were approved by the founder. The candidate for an award must be a civilian who voluntarily risks his or her life to an extraordinary degree while saving or attempting to save the life of another person. The rescuer must have no

---

[109]

Ordinary People, Extraordinary Rescues, by Martin Morse Wooster, The American Enterprise, September 2000.

full measure of responsibility for the safety of the victim. There must be conclusive evidence to support the act's occurrence, and the act must be called to the attention of the Commission within two years. About 90% of the those awarded are male, and, over the life of the Fund, 20.7 percent of the awards have been given posthumously."[110]

According to Walter Rutkowski, the Carnegie Hero Fund's executive director, there has been a good deal of debate over the years about what an "extraordinary degree" of heroism means. A rescuer, Rutkowski says, "has to face a real threat…he has to fight the shark, not the possibility of a shark."

"Why do heroes act the way they do? What does it take for someone to save others from drowning, pull them out of a burning building, or pry them away from the claws of a savage bear?"

Rutkowski refers back to Andrew Carnegie's notion that "heroic action is impulsive." When medal recipients are asked this question, they usually respond, "I couldn't stand by and do nothing," or "I Learned this in Sunday school," or 'This is how I was brought up." But Rutowski says "The basic reason people get involved is one word—empathy."

CREATIVE ARTS FOUNDATION OF BREVARD, INC.

In Brevard County, midway down the Atlantic Coast of Florida, exists an organization not well known even in the vicinity of Melbourne, where it is located.

The Creative Arts Foundation of Brevard, Inc., (CAFOB) is a non-profit (501 ©(3) organization formed in 2007 to provide assistance and support to creative artists of Brevard County who are exceptionally talented in the fields of music, dance, and visual arts. Support for these programs comes from fundraisers and the generosity of concerned citizens.[111]

---

[110]

Carnegie Hero Fund, Wikipedia, The Free Encyclopedia, February 10, 2014

[111]

Opportunities are open to all artists regardless of age, gender, race, religion or socio-economic status. However, primary focus is on extraordinarily talented young students of the arts who need financial help to pursue their artistic dreams.

These are not average high school students who might try out for a senior play. They are genuine prodigies, some of whom have already performed in prestigious venues. They represent the kind of talent you might expect to see at the Kennedy Center for the Performing Arts or DAR Constitution Hall in Washington, DC, or Carnegie Hall in New York City. They are exceptionally talented young performers who don't get the attention they deserve.

The Creative Arts Foundation seeks out these artistic young people, provides them with grants to help them develop their talents, and makes available to them public venues in which they can gain experience, which will enhance their ability to take advantage of collegiate or professional opportunities.

Benefits are provided to artists through three primary methods:

•The Foundation provides venues in which performers can showcase their skills and talents, along with other young artists, in a public setting to familiarize them with how it feels to perform in public.

• The Foundation provides monetary grants to financially disadvantaged young prodigies to help them further develop their skills and/or to help them with travel expenses to audition for scholarships at universities and colleges.

• The Foundation provides venues in which young artists can compete with other talented young performers before professional judges and public audiences to win monetary awards of $1,000 for first place, $500 for second place, $250 for third place, and $125 for fourth place.

BACKGROUND
It all began with a "diamond in the rough."

---

www.cafob.com

In 2006, an amazing 13 year-old classical violinist was discovered in Brevard County, FL. Her family was of moderate means and could not afford a quality instrument, though she still hoped to compete one day on the international stage against some of the world's finest musicians. Her goal: to perform one day in Carnegie Hall.

After a fundraiser recital was held, in which she used a loaned violin, money was raised for her to compete in Ibla, Italy, where she finished in the top of her category. Among her awards was a chance to play a recital at Carnegie Hall, which she did to a standing ovation.

While most of the world knew nothing about this, the story went viral in her hometown. Afterwards, recognizing there were probably more young artists in the area, local citizens formed a foundation to search out talented young artists who might need a jump-start to pursue their artistic dreams. Thus began the "Creative Arts Foundation of Brevard, Inc."

FOUNDATION ACHIEVEMENTS

Since 2007, the foundation has issued $23,000 in grants to various music students who needed financial assistance to further their education and ambitions. Numerous competitions, shows, art exhibits and venues have been produced for artists to showcase their talents, which thus far, has resulted in monetary prizes awarded totally over $50,000. A few examples:

GRANTS

* The Foundation provided funds for a gifted 13-year-old boy, who has an extraordinary voice, to have a partial scholarship to the prestigious American Boy Choir in Princeton, NJ. It is one of only two prestigious boy choir boarding schools in the United States, which accepts boys in grades 4-8 from across the United States, as well as many international countries.

* A 16-year-old high school drummer worked one year mowing yards to buy his own drum set. He did not have enough money to buy a required special computer for school. The Foundation provided the computer.

* A 17-year-old highly accomplished concert pianist did not have

enough money to travel to major musical schools in the northern states to audition for college scholarships. The Foundation financed travel to three northern city auditions., after which she won a full four-year scholarship to the University of Michigan. She later said "it would never have been possible if not for the assistance provided by the Creative Arts Foundation of Brevard."

* A highly talented 16-year-old high school junior worked as a cleaning girl for a dance studio in exchange for free dance lessons to round out her talent. She needed funds for special training to compete in scholarship auditions for musical theater courses in college. The Foundation provided the funds.

* A 17-year-old minority student violinist could not afford fees for a scholarship opportunity at a music college. The girl comes from a needy family, with a blind father and a working mom. The Foundation provided the funds.

* The Foundation provided funds for a 16-year-old female vocalist, whose parents were on welfare, to take thirty voice lessons from an opera retiree to improve her ability to market her talent.

COMPETITIONS

Music

To date the Creative Arts Foundation has held five annual music competition programs at a prestigious local center for the performing arts, in which 12 musicians competed before professional judges in a public setting. Titled Brevard's Got Music Talent, the program is modeled after "America's Got Talent," and involved auditions of over 200 students, ages 11 to 19. As mentioned earlier, prizes include: first place: $1,000, second place $500, third place $250, and fourth place $125. . Total prizes awarded to date: $11,900.

Visual Art

"All That Art" is a competition for artists and photographers, now in its fifth year. Professional judges vet 150 to 200 art pieces each year, after which 62 pieces are hung at the Eastern Florida State College's King Center for the Performing Arts for one month. Prizes are issued to winning artists, totaling $1,500. Total to date: $6,000.

CONCERTS AND RECITALS

Music on the Hill

Music on the Hill, which began in 2010, offers venues for 3 or 4 young students of music to perform once a month before live audiences. These intimate shows are held in a local church that sits on a hill, which rents their facility to the Foundation. Music on the Hill is co-hosted by a selected youngster who performs, but also coordinates and emcees the program. The performances are open to the public for a recommended donation of $5 per person. Modest proceeds go to the performers. Total awarded to performers thus far: $5,600

Private Home Recitals

The Foundation promotes recitals in private homes where exceptional students play and sing directly to an intimate audience. Fees are collected as fundraisers, while a portion is paid to the performers.

Total Cash Layout To Date

As of February, 2014, monies provided directly to musicians, vocalists and artists through these various programs total: $55,000. This would not be possible without the love and generosity of private Brevard County donors.

LONG RANGE GOALS

The Foundation intends to increase its ability to promote and help talented young students of the arts, and expand its focus into other artistic areas such as drama and dance. It will also increase its grant program to include additional scholarships for disadvantaged youngsters.

LEADERSHIP

The Foundation has a Board of Directors, consisting of nine directors: one is a concert violinist, one is a creative artist, four are published authors and several are successful entrepreneurs. They meet monthly to figure out how best to identify local prodigies, how best to help them develop their talents, how best to provide them with public venues to gather experience performing in public and to identify donors, sponsors, and volunteers to keep the programs alive and the funds flowing to the neediest of young artists.

The foundation's ultimate goal is to find diamonds-in-the-rough, future stars of musical performance, museum artists, gifted writers and those who may otherwise never have a chance to develop and showcase their talents.

QUESTION

Wonderful things are happening in this small Florida community every day. The real question is why such a wonderful program is not better known. With a community of nearly a half-million people, it is often difficult to get more than 50 people to attend the monthly public concerts.

Do you have an organization like this foundation in your community? If not, why not? Don't truly talented young prodigies deserve at least as much public attention as the juvenile delinquents receive in America?

No doubt there are other community organizations doing much the same thing for young performers and artists, but we rarely hear about them. Imagine how spectacular it would be to have similar organizations helping bright young talented prodigies all across America.

Imagine how wonderful it would be to have these stories appear on the front page of newspapers, on magazine covers, and in the evening television news! What might that do to the image of our nation's youth? I suspect it would have a profound affect on how the average citizen views our younger generation, especially of those young performers who are completely dedicated to developing their talents and skills.

FRONT ROW FOUNDATION

According to Jon Vroman, Cofounder and Executive Director of the Front Row Foundation, the mission of the Front Row Foundation is to help individuals and families who are braving critical health challenges "experience life in the front row." They do that by providing recipients with a front row experience at their favorite concert, sporting event, theatrical performance or other form of live entertainment.

The Front Row Foundation creates unique life-changing moments that positively affect the mind, body, and spirit of each person they help. The point of the front row experience is to become a metaphor for how the people with critical health issues can live the rest of their lives.[112]

Trent Booth, Event Coordinator says, "it may not be a cure, but it can certainly brighten the quality of life for someone." Their philosophy is simply that the past is gone and nobody can do anything about that, but the foundation can give critically ill people a moment they will cherish and that their families will remember forever.

Vroman says "what brings people into the Front Row Foundation is that they value what our organization values, which is experiencing life to the fullest."

What the Front Row focuses on is that, whether or not someone is sick, they have an opportunity every day to do something great, something extremely meaningful in their life. The Foundation helps them to have a "moment in time."

The Front Row has board members and volunteers who are massively engaged in providing exceptional experiences for people who desperately need to be uplifted. Everyone involved in the Foundation firmly believes they "live life in the front row," and they want to share that sense of wonder and excitement with people who may be nearing their last moments.

Someone once asked Vroman why he puts so much effort into front row tickets. His answer is simple:

"Being in the front row feels like you're part of the event itself.
There is a tangible energy.
The music vibrating through your body.
The intensity in the faces of the athletes.
The voices of the actors.

112

Front Row Foundation web page, 2014

"Finally, it's not just sitting in the front row at any event; the goal of the organization is to have people sit in the front row to see their favorite sports team, musician or show and that is what makes Front Row Foundation so special."

Vroman's dream is to have bands, venues, and ticket agencies donating tickets for every concert, sporting event or live performance in the world. He wants every event to have someone with a health challenge sitting there, hands in the air, "living life in the front row."[113]

There are far too many examples to include them all, but here are a few of the wonderful experiences the Front Row Foundation arranged for critically ill recipients. Their names have been omitted to protect their privacy:

Stage 4 Breast Cancer

A 43-year-old single mother of two with stage 4 breast cancer is a long time fan of Jared Leto, lead singer of the band Thirty Seconds to Mars. Her friends knew she was a fan and, when it serendipitously happened that Leto and his band were coming to her hometown, friends contacted a local disc jockey who arranged for tickets to be donated and the Front Row Foundation surprised the mother with a letter explaining she was chosen as a Front Row Recipient.

The event included dinner and a meet and greet with Jared Leto and a front row seat for the band's performance. A sleek, black Cadillac Escalade showed up to take her and a guest to the hotel and casino where the performance would occur. She was escorted to a special VIP area to hang out with Jared and the band.

Jared had to conserve his voice, but he leaned over and whispered to her, "stay strong," after which she was escorted to her front row seat. Inside the Escalade, on the way home, everyone reminisced and laughed with each other about the day and how much fun they had.

Under normal circumstances she would have struggled to keep her energy up for that many hours, but the excitement kept her going.

"Thank you so much," she said. "It was perfect!"

113

Ibid.

The event was made possible by dozens of people who had one thing in common: they cared deeply for the woman with stage 4 cancer.

Stage 4 Mouth Cancer

An 84-year old matriarch of a very large, multi-generational family, known by most people as "Mamaw," was diagnosed with Stage 4 Mouth Cancer. Because of her advanced age, she was not eligible for a high-risk surgery and treatment regimen; so, she takes things day by day. Even so, she remains positive and continues to fight by getting lots of rest, eating well and laughing with her family.[114]

The one thing that "Mamaw" loves, almost as much as her extended family, is the University of Tennessee Volunteers, Women's Basketball team. She is a die-hard, passionate, raving fan who has attended dozens and dozens of games in her lifetime, but never ever got to see them from a courtside vantage point.

After receiving her application, the Front Row Foundation arranged for "Mamaw" to fulfill her dream of sitting on the court just inches away from her cherished "Lady Vols." Everyone at the Foundation scrambled and within one week they had arranged all the logistics to make her dream come true.

"The day began with some unexpected gifts in her family room: embroidery floss, a new bracelet, gift cards to her favorite restaurants, a Front Row T-shirt, and more. She was like a kid on Christmas morning–all smiles."[115]

A plush limo bus pulled up to her driveway to take "Mamaw" and some of her family to the arena. She was all smiles as she showed her front row tickets at the VIP entrance to the Thompson–Boling Arena in Knoxville.

After a complimentary lunch buffet inside The Courtside Club, she got to fulfill one of her lifelong dreams, to meet the renowned former

---

[114]

Ibid.

[115]

Ibid.

"Lady Vols" coach, Pat Summitt, who had coached the team to eight national championships.

During the game she had to stay alert in case a basketball came hurling her way, because she was just feet from the players, in the middle of all the action.

After her team crushed their opponent, she got to meet the team's mascot, Smokey. When he was told she was the "Queen for the Day" with the Front Row Foundation, "…he repeatedly bowed down to her, which cracked her up."

After the game "Mamaw" was treated to a wonderful meal at the acclaimed Cru Bistro in downtown "Old City" Knoxville. "Mamaw" said she loved being "treated like a Queen all day." Her family became emotional on the ride home, talking about how much this Front Row experience meant to them, and how special the day was.

Later, Shannon Coon, Senior Event Director, said to "Mamaw," "It was an honor to host your Front Row experience and I loved spending the day with you and your amazing family. I will remember it always. Remember to always "Live Life in the Front Row," and of course: "GO LADY VOLS!"

Duchenne's Muscular Dystrophy

A young boy, named Robert, was born with a fatal genetic disorder called Duchenne's Muscular Dystrophy, which primarily affects boys and results in progressive loss of strength. It causes serious heart and lung problems and eventually leads to death.

But, Robert was born to a family that embraces his every struggle, searches for a gift in his every challenge, and loves him exactly the way he is.

Robert's mother said one day Robert said something profound about himself. He said, "I've often thought, if I could change things would I? And I don't think I would, because then I wouldn't be Robert."

From an early age, Robert and his entire family have been Garth Brooks fans. Robert isn't sure what it is about Garth's music, but he loves it. He knows every single word to every single song and sang "Callin Baton Rouge" on You Tube, which made him a bit of a celebrity-in-the-making for a while.

His singing days are over now, however, because of a lung problem and muscle loss, but that doesn't affect his love for Garth's music. His family describes him as a warrior who continues to achieve great things. He has graduated from high school, enrolled in college, and celebrated his 21st birthday. All enormous accomplishments in the world of Duchenne's Muscular Dystrophy.

When Robert's family learned about the Front Row Foundation, they immediately nominated Robert. When Front Row saw that his number one wish was to see Garth Brooks in his hometown, they were crushed because Garth was not on tour and it looked like there would be no way to grant Robert's wish.

Then, one August evening, Front Row got wind that Garth Brooks was going to return and perform four shows at the Encore Theatre in Las Vegas. A Front Row volunteer in the Vegas area helped connect Front Row to some incredible people who also wanted to make Robert's night unforgettable.

Within a half hour of meeting with the Front Row people, Robert's mom and dad simultaneously looked at each other and asked, "Did you give him some coffee?" They told Front Row they had never heard him talk so much in his entire life. They and Front Row representatives had the pleasure of seeing Robert come absolutely alive.

After exchanging gifts, Robert and his family were escorted to the hip Asian Fusion restaurant, *Andrea's,* and were greeted by the General Manager, Roy Saunders, who showed them to their table and presented Robert with a Garth Books compact disc and personalized chopsticks.

After a delightful meal, Robert and his family made their way to the Encore Theatre, which was located in the same hotel as the restaurant.

Garth Brooks gave a 2½-hour performance, which included a few solo songs by Mrs. Trisha Yearwood and a few duos between she and Brooks, but the Brooks encore was special. It consisted of three songs: "Callin Baton Rouge," Friends in Low Places," and "The Dance," all songs the family had mentioned earlier throughout the night.

The family joked that Garth's version of "Callin' Baton Rouge" was *"okaaaaay,"* but not *quite* as good as Robert's.

After the show, Kaile Monroe, the Front Row Event Director, said to Robert: "I am blessed to call you a new friend. I want you to know that you make this world a better place. I am wishing you nothing but continued strength. Hold tight to your faith!

Support for the Front Row Foundation

These examples don't begin to describe all the wonderful experiences the Front Row Foundation arranges for recipients who suffer critical health issues, but they are a representative sample to illustrate the great work this foundation does.

The Foundation is supported by an Ambassador Team of individuals who partner with the Foundation monthly, regional fundraisers, an annual golf tournament, and special gala celebrations.

If you would like more information about the Front Row Foundation, or would like to support their programs, go to: info@frontrowfoundation.org, or write to:

For donations and billing information:
Front Row Foundation, P.O. Box 1595, Richmond, VA 23227

For all other inquiries:
Front Row Foundation, P.O. Box 531, Blackwood, NJ 08012

OPPORTUNITY VILLAGE

Opportunity Village is touted as Las Vegas' favorite charity. It is a not-for-profit organization that serves people within their community who have significant intellectual disabilities.

Their major focus is on helping citizens who are intellectually impaired. This extraordinary civic organization believes that people with intellectual disabilities and their families should have choices in where and how they are served.

Because of that, Opportunity Village provides a variety of different programs that provide men and women with all levels of disabilities the chance to lead a life that had previously been unattainable.

Many of those served by Opportunity Village want to find employment in their community. Opportunity Village provides assessment and training, as well as job placement help, job coaching and follow-on service.

During 2013, more than 475 people with disabilities received assessment, training and placement services, while another 250+ people were employed by Opportunity Village in service contracts throughout southern Nevada. There are opportunities in a variety of fields from food service and custodial duties to administrative and housekeeping functions.[116]

Opportunity Village operates three Employment Resource Centers in Las Vegas, Henderson and Clark County, Nevada. These facilities serve as learning centers for people with intellectual disabilities who are sponsored by Opportunity Village. They also provide assembly, packaging, mailing and fulfillment services for companies and local community organizations. In addition, Opportunity Village is one of the largest document imaging and document destruction companies in Nevada.

Opportunity Village operates programs that provide marketable job skills and long-term work experiences that enrich the lives of people with disabilities. Most adults usually go to work; but, according to Opportunity Village, the unemployment rate for people with disabilities constantly exceeds 60 percent. Having marketable job skills and long-term work experiences help disabled employees have much improved self-esteem.

Through the vocational training and employment programs, people with severe disabilities have a chance for individual advancement and increasingly higher levels of job responsibility. Combined, the attainment of marketable job skills and increased self-esteem makes possible an improved sense of independence.

These individuals who were previously considered to be unemployable, work in jobs throughout the community and at Opportunity Village's Employment Resource Centers, collectively earning wages amounting to more than $7.6 million in 2012. They are hard-working and diligent, proudly paying taxes and happily leading more engaged, fulfilling lives.

---

[116]

www.opportunityvillage.org, 2014

Benefits for the Community

"According to an independent Community Impact Assessment performed by Las Vegas-based Applied Analysis, Opportunity Village reduces the demand for Public Health and Human Services. The majority of programs offered by Opportunity Village to people with severe intellectual disabilities are funded by the work-related activities of those individuals and by the charitable donations of local individuals and organizations. The report states that, in the absence of Opportunity Village, state and local governments would be required to provide similar services that would increase public costs by more than $22 million annually.

"The Community Impact Assessment also states that Opportunity Village reduces the demand for other state and local services. State and local governments would have increased costs for homelessness, poverty, health care and criminal justice in the absence of Opportunity Village. While it is difficult to measure with any level of precision, the report anticipates these costs to be in tens of millions annually."[117]

Opportunity Village pays wages that permit people with severe disabilities to reduce their dependence on government benefits. Work at their three centers is often the first, and sometimes only, employment option available to people with severe disabilities. Earning wages allows them to become productive members of society and to join the ranks of Nevada taxpayers.

Ed Guthrie, Executive Director of Opportunity Village, says that, although their mission has remained constant over the years, the services they've provided have evolved as the needs of the people they serve have changed. "They've gone from being a school for people who were not allowed in the public school system to being a top employment and training organization."

His organization prides itself in its ability to adapt, whether that means constantly adding new programs to meet the changing needs of the people they serve or finding new ways to raise needed funds in a

---

[117]

Ibid.

struggling economy.

On February 24, 2014, Guthrie announced they are poised to implement major growth initiatives. Under Guthrie's direction, Opportunity Village has grown to become one of the most respected organizations of its type in the world and his team now has aggressive plans for the next five years.

They intend to double the number of people they serve, increase the number of people working in community-based competitive employment, and increase the amount of money the workers earn, to contribute towards their living expenses and improve their lives.

Community Village is a civic organization that should make every American citizen feel proud. It would be wonderful if every major community in the United States had such an organization. It would also be nice if organizations like this received national coverage by our news media regularly. Unfortunately, such coverage wouldn't meet the "if it bleeds, it leads" approach to news.

I'm sorry. I don't mean to be cynical, but stories like these just don't seem to have much appeal to the news directors who decide what is newsworthy.

Chapter 5

GOOD SAMARITANS: MODERN DAY MIRACLE WORKERS

The term "Good Samaritan" is generally used to describe a compassionate person who goes out of his or her way to unselfishly help another person. It's a term often used by newspaper reporters who like to feature such a person, because people love to read about folks who sacrifice their time, money, even their lives, to help someone in need.

Jesus Walk, Disciple Lessons from Luke's Gospel, from Joyful Heart Ministries, says that none of Jesus' parables has worked its way deeper into the American consciousness as the Parable of the Good Samaritan.

For readers who are not familiar with the parable, it's a story from the Bible. Luke 10:25–37 records this story about a man who was going down from Jerusalem to Jericho, when robbers attacked him. They stripped him of his clothes, beat him and went away, leaving him half dead.

A priest happened to be going down the same road, and when he saw the man, he passed by on the other side.

So too, when a Levite came to the place and saw him, the Levite passed by on the other side.

But when a traveling Samaritan came to where the man was, he saw him and took pity on him. The Samaritan went to him and bandaged his wounds, pouring on oil and wine. Then he put the man on his own donkey, brought him to an inn and took care of him. The next day he took out two denari and gave them to the innkeeper. "Look after him," he said, "and when I return, I will reimburse you for any extra expense you may have."

This is historically thought to be one of the best illustrations of what is meant by the term "Good Samaritan."

"Psychologists say some people have the right mix of qualities it takes for risky heroic acts: altruism, courage, knowing the right thing and being reflexive about it, as well as the ability to inhibit fear that stops many people from getting involved.

"It's not one hero gene. It's a very complex set of characteristics that converge and that person is unique, and thank God for them," said psychologist Dr. Rachel Yehuda at Mount Sinai Medical Center."[118]

This chapter highlights examples of 21st century Good Samaritans, who meet the standard set in the biblical parable, and who overcome the fear and inertia that might keep others from reacting during a critical situation in which someone's life is in jeopardy.

TAKING A BULLET FOR A STRANGER

In October 2004, 26-year-old Matt Casias, a Denver, Colorado resident and former Golden Gloves boxer, took a bullet for a perfect stranger outside his business. Looking through his office window, he saw a young man reaching for a woman's handbag. The potential robber went behind her, grabbed her, and tried to take her purse.

According to a CBS Evening News report, Brynda Turner had just visited an art gallery and was walking to her car when the mugger attacked her. "And I said, no, no, no," Turner said. "Then he showed me a gun. Then I shut my eyes; then, all of a sudden, I was on the ground."[119]

It was then that Casias came outside and got the guy off of her, held him against a car. But, that's when the mugger pulled out a gun and shot

---

[118] *Good Samaritans risk their lives to save strangers in New York City*, by Colleen Long, The Associated Press, Oneida Daily Dispatcch, December 8, 2013.

[119] *Taking A Bullet For A Stranger*, by Tatiana Morales, CBS-TV, January 19, 2005.

Casias point blank in the chest.

Casias then stumbled into his office and told co-worker Bette Phelps to call 911. An ambulance rushed to the scene while Casias lay on the floor of his new printing business thinking, "All this material stuff doesn't mean anything; all the hours I work; all this hard work; it's the relationships in your life the friends and your family and the people that are close to you – that's the only thing that matters at a time like that."[120]

Police arrested the mugger's companions, but the actual gunman got away, while Casias was taken to the emergency room of a local hospital.

After coming to the aid of a stranger Casias ended up with a bullet in his chest and thousands of dollars in medical bills. Then it was the turn of strangers to come to his aid. Art galleries held an auction to help him pay his bills. Radio stations and the Guardian Angels also raised and donated money to help him.

Casias said it was difficult for him to grasp how many people came to his aid with cards and donations for the fund that helped him pay his medical bills. When surgeon Michael Fenoglio found out how the guy he was operating on got that slug in his shoulder, "he didn't even charge me to remove it; he said the only thing he would ask is that I go talk to his son's high school," Casias says. "I'm still amazed that so many people came together to help someone they didn't even know.[121]

Knowing that he almost lost his life for a total stranger who had no money in her purse, he wondered if he had it to do over again, would he still do it. But, after seeing all the support he got from other strangers, he was sure he would have done the same thing. He thinks lots of other people would have done the same thing too.

Brynda Turner, the woman he tried to help, wasn't so sure. She said "I think Matt Casias's are rare. He is a definite hero and certainly a good Samaritan."

120

Ibid.

121

Matt Casias Takes a Bullet for a Stranger, by Pam Lambert, *People Magazine,* March 14, 2005.

In 2005, Bill Owens (R), the Colorado governor at the time, awarded the Medal of Valor to Casias, saying: "Not simply for his actions in saving Brenda, but for all he does for his family and his community. He's an example for all of us.

In addition to the bullet in his chest, Casias earned the admiration of his entire state. In 2005 the bullet was removed from his chest and he fully recovered.

The prime suspect, Michael Cordova, was eventually caught and bought to trial in 2007; however, a jury found him not guilty of the crime because they didn't feel confident in his identification as the shooter.

Casias had no such doubts. He was certain Cordova was the man who shot him. One thing is for sure, there can be no doubt that Matt Casias is a great example of a man who met the biblical standard for being a "Good Samaritan."

GOOD SAMARITAN SAVES HIT–AND–RUN VICTIM

Terry Pinkston, a 73-year-old Arlington, Texas patriarch, is alive today because a Good Samaritan reacted swiftly to save his life.

In February 2014, Pinkston was out on his daily morning walk when he was struck from behind by a driver who immediately left the scene, without any regard for the life of the person he had just hit. Pinkston was thrown several feet by the impact of the car. The driver was in a mid-1990 to early 2000, two-door, blue Chevy Cavalier, that had damage to its windshield and hood.

Pinkston is alive today, despite being critically injured, thanks to Bill Komar, a local resident who reacted quickly to call 911. Komar was watching hockey on television when he heard a noise and went out on his balcony to check it out. "He saw a car in the grass taking off," he said. "Out of the corner of my eye I saw a person lying there…and I realized someone had been hit by a car."[122] He didn't think twice about

---

[122] *Good Samaritan Credited With Saving Man in Hit-and-Run Crash,* by Ray Villeda, 5NBCDFW.com, February 17, 2014.

coming to the aid of Pinkston.

First he called 911 and then he ran to Pinkston's side. When he got to the victim, Komar saw that Pinkston was bleeding profusely from a huge head wound. "I found his wool cap he was wearing, took it off, cleaned it and applied pressure to his head and waited for paramedics and fire rescue to get here. I told him he was gonna be alright."

A local television reporter said the family feels lucky Pinkston is alive and lucky that a neighbor came to his aid at a critical time. While recovering in an intensive care hospital bed at John Peter Smith Hospital in Fort Worth, Texas, Pinkston was asked by his daughter, Shannon, what he would like to say to the driver who hit him. "I'd like to find out if it was intentional or if it was just an accident, and just come out and say so if it was accidental," Pinkston said.

Pinkston's injuries included a big gap on his head that required 20 stiches, broken ribs on both sides, broken vertebrae, busted sacrum, a pelvis that was busted in several places, and a big puncture wound on his calf.[123]

Pinkston's family cannot understand how anyone could leave a husband and father lying out on the sidewalk so seriously hurt, and just drive off. "It hurts your heart that someone is that callous," said Shannon. "If it was their daddy, would they want that to happen?"

Pinkston said, "It'd be nice if they would just step forward and own up to it, but I don't think they're going to do that."

As it turned out, several days later there was a big break in the case. Arlington police caught a suspect just as he was on a flight about to leave the country. Customs agents at the Dallas–Fort Worth International Airport caught the suspect, identified as 25-year-old Omar Mohammed, when he boarded a plane bound for Jordan. Police had received a tip that Mohammed's car had a broken windshield and other damages to the front bumper and hood. His apartment is located about

---

123

Injured Arlington senior has message for hit-and-run driver, by Teresa Woodard, WFAA.com, February 17, 2014.

one block from where the hit-and-run occurred.[124]

Since he was trying to leave the country, Mohammed is considered a flight risk and is being held without bond.

With so much damage to his body, Pinkston is in for a very long recovery, but is just glad to be alive. He and his family are thankful that Bill Komar came to his aid so quickly. By almost any standards, most people would probably agree that Bill Komar was a Good Samaritan.

FOUR GOOD SAMARITANS IN NEW YORK CITY

What makes people risk their own lives to save strangers, someone they they've never met and may never ever see again? Here are the stories of four such people.

In New York City, which often has a keep-to-yourself, don't-get-involved reputation, at least a dozen Good Samaritans were willing to risk their own safety in 2013 to save strangers.[125]

Miami ER Doctor Ben Abo

In 2013, during his summer vacation to New York City, Miami emergency room doctor Ben Abo found himself in an unusual situation as he watched a man fall headfirst onto the Subway tracks at a New Jersey commuter train stoop in Greenwich Village.

After looking to see if a train was coming, Abo jumped in, yelling for the two-dozen other people on the platform to pull a fire alarm and

---

124

Suspect Caught in Arlington Hit-&-Run Case, by Stephanie Lucero, CBSDFW.com, February 20, 2014

125

City of heroes: The New Yorkers who have risked their lives to save a stranger from the subway tracks. But what makes a person risk it all for someone they've never met?, Associated Press Reporter, MailOnline, December 13, 2013.

get help.

Meanwhile, he heaved the man up overhead, back onto the platform, as someone helped him from above, and then he tried to pull himself back up too.

He felt a gush of wind and saw headlights reflecting off the wall, as a train was approaching. At that moment, he knew he had only one chance to get himself back on the platform. Fortunately he made it, after which he set to work trying to stop the bleeding from where the victim had hurt himself when he fell to the tracks. All the while, other folks were taking pictures and videos of him with their smartphones.

"Ervin Straub, a professor emeritus of psychology at the University of Massachusetts, who has studied altruism extensively, said crowds in a big city can work against such heroism by creating a 'diffusion of responsibility.'

"When there are a bunch of people around, there is often a 'Why me? Somebody else can do it,'" he said. "But if someone else developed a strong sense of responsibility, they are not likely to wait. By seeing the others' passivity, their feeling of responsibility may kick in."[126]

Fortunately, on this particular day, Miami ER Doctor Ben Abo reacted quickly and a life was saved. He got a thank you and a pat on the back from police; then, still covered in the injured man's blood, he boarded another train and went home to Miami.

He has no idea what happened to the man whose life he saved, but he has no doubt he would do it again.

Personal Trainer Dennis Codrington

Dennis Codrington, 24, rescued a bleeding, 6'1" stranger who fell onto railroad tracks a minute before a train came. A personal trainer, Codrington jumped down onto subway tracks to save an unconscious man as a train barreled down on the Columbus Circle subway platform

---

[126] *Good Samaritans risk their lives to save strangers in New York City*, by Colleen Long, The Associated Press, Oneida Daily Dispatch, December 8, 2013.

in New York City.

"It's the way I was brought up: Always look out for each other," Codrington said. He helped pull up a bleeding, unconscious man who had fallen onto the tracks of the No. 1 train late one February night in New York City.

Codrington was headed home from a party when he saw the man at the edge of the platform and then the man disappeared. About 55 people are struck by New York subway trains and die every year, and the 24-year-old Codrington wasn't going to let this guy be one of them.

He and two others jumped down to hoist the bleeding, very heavy stranger up, as the time clock flashed that another train was due in the station in one minute. All three of these Good Samaritans could have died on the tracks if they had not worked swiftly.

Codrington said "it was really nerve-racking, but we couldn't leave him there." Codrington doesn't know what happened to the man he saved. "The last time I saw him, he was bleeding profusely and not conscious. I wish I knew whether he was alive."[127]

Plumber David Justino

Plumber David Justino used his belt as a tourniquet to stop tourist Sian Green from bleeding to death after a cab struck her and severed her leg.

During the summer of 2013, a gaggle of videotaping onlookers surrounded David Justino, a 44-year-old plumber, as he tried desperately to stop a tourist from bleeding to death after an out-of-control taxi struck her severing one leg and badly injuring the other.[128]

"I had no choice," he said. "I had to help her, someone had to.

---

[127]

Ibid.

[128]

Ibid.

Justino has since contacted Sian Green, who was a tourist from England visiting the United States, and learned that she is on the mend.

"There's good people in this world, very good people in this world that I can't thank enough," Green said on NBC's Today show in September 2013. "They saved my life. If it wasn't for them, I wouldn't be sitting here right now telling this story."

She told Matt Lauer on the Today show "…that if it weren't for the strangers who came to her aid after the collision, she would have been dead."

Justino also appeared in a picture on Facebook with celebrity doctor Mehmet Oz, who has his own afternoon television program.

Retired Salesman Alan Hall

Alan Hall, a 65-year-old Frito Lay salesman from Connecticut, who had recently moved to the Land O'Lakes area of Florida, died heroically saving a 4-year-old child who was struggling to survive in a powerful riptide.

Riptides, also known as rip currents, are extremely dangerous channels of water that can form unexpectedly and pull even fairly strong swimmers away from the beach.

Hall and his wife Eileen, and daughter Julie, had gone to Honeymoon Island, Florida to spend the day relaxing. Alan and Eileen were getting ready to celebrate their 42nd wedding anniversary, but the day quickly took a very dramatic turn.

While walking with his wife and daughter, who were collecting seashells, the couple spotted three children playing near the shoreline as a very powerful current began to build. "My dad said, 'I hope somebody's watching them. That's a pretty strong current,'" his daughter recalled.[129]

Seconds later, the children and their parents started screaming for

---

[129]

Heroic Man Dies Saving Child from Powerful Riptide, by Christina Ng, via Good Morning America, April 10, 2012.

help. The parents rushed into the water and were able to pull two of the children to safety, but the third child, a little 4-year-old girl, was still in harms way in the rough water.

Without any regard for his own life, Alan Hall rushed to the child's aid and was able to push her out of the way towards the shore, where it was safe. In the process, he had a heart attack. His heart stopped and he turned face down in the water. Nearby boaters managed to get him back to shore, where a crowd had gathered.

His wife immediately began performing CPR, but Hall was not breathing and didn't have a pulse. Emergency medics arrived and tried to revive him but were not successful. Hall was taken to a local hospital where he was pronounced dead.

A spokeswoman from the Florida Department of Environmental Protection said that no lifeguards were on that section of the beach because it is not a designated swimming area.

Four-year-old Ruby, the child Alan Hall saved, traveled to the hospital with her parents and siblings to thank the Halls. Eileen Hall spoke to the mother of the rescued child and told her not to feel guilty because even if Allan, her husband, had known the outcome, he would have done it anyway. That's how he lived his life. "He would have done it regardless. He was one of those people that actually lived what he preached," said his daughter.

Julie Hall said: "My mom said one of the things she remembers so strongly is the circle of people around him that all started praying for him. That's something that has stuck with her."

The mother of the rescued child felt terrible because she had been getting hate mail and angry messages saying she and her husband were horrible parents for not watching their children more closely. She and her family had been visiting while on vacation from their home in Florida.

The truth is that had it not been for Alan Hall the mother and her other two children might also have drowned. You have to know that is one family who will never ever forget Alan Hall and his family. They will likely see the face of the man who rescued their daughter every time they look into her eyes.

Alan Hall proved once more that we should never lose hope in the goodness of humanity. I am reminded of a quote from a book about Medal of Honor recipients: "There are no heroes. There are only ordinary people who do extraordinary things in a critical moment."

I suspect the parents of little Ruby, the child Hall saved, might think otherwise. He certainly met the biblical criteria for being a Good Samaritan.

Sheet Rock Installer Michael Patterson

Michael Patterson, 43, died from complications related to injuries he sustained on June 8, 2013 while rescuing a little girl he didn't know from drowning in Euharlee Creek in Cartersville, Georgia.

Patterson, of Rockmart, Georgia, was visiting the Euharlee Creek with his 9-year-old son on June 8 when a four-year old Javea Jones, who had been playing in the creek, stepped into a deep section and was dragged under water.

Patterson immediately tried to save the little girl, but during the rescue he struck his head, breaking his neck in three places, leaving him with a severed spinal cord. He was unconscious in the water for three minutes before being dragged out by bystanders.[130]

Emergency Medical Technicians performed CPR on Patterson before he was taken to the Redmond Regional Medical Center. To complicate matters even further, he had only just started a new job installing sheet rock and didn't have any health insurance.

Unfortunately, Patterson died 20 days later after contracting pneumonia and an infection that left him unable to breath on his own.

While in the hospital he told his mother "I just did what I would hope anybody else would've done for me." His mom said: "He has always been like that, someone else first."

As incredible as it seems, it was the second time in two weeks that Patterson had saved someone's life. He had earlier pulled a truck driver

---

130

Uninsured Good Samaritan paralyzed while rescuing a stranger's child from drowning dies of his injuries three weeks later, by Associated Press and Daily Mail Reporter, June 28, 2013.

to safety when the driver's rig caught on fire.

Strangers were so struck by his heroics and so saddened by his terrible injuries that they pledged thousands of dollars to help pay his huge medical bills. Three friends who did not know him before the accident established a *Friends of Mike Patterson Trust* to help him and his family.

When Patterson died, his fund had already collected more than $90,000 and his Facebook page had amassed more than 65,000 followers.

Some of the comments left on the *Friends of Mike Patterson Facebook* page included:

"A true hero, giving his life to save another. Praying that God will comfort the family during this time."

"A true selfless act of courage. My thoughts and prayers are with the Patterson family. Especially for his son I pray he never forgets that his dad was a real hero."

After he saved Javea Jones, the girl's mother called Michael Patterson a "hero" and an "angel."

"Mike's spirit and selfless actions inspired tens of thousands who sent cards, letters and emails and put posts on his Facebook page. His life and the lives of others were forever changed by his courageous, split-second decision to save another's life.

Mike Patterson was a Good Samaritan by anybody's definition.

Truck Driver Alex Mitchell

Alex Mitchell, 37, of Queens, NY, was alone on the Long Island Expressway when he saw a man in a Chevy Blazer SUV driving erratically, then crash into a tree. The car hit the tree so hard that the rear end flipped upwards. Mitchell pulled over to the shoulder, dialed 911 and ran to the scene.

By the time he got to the car, it was engulfed in flame and smoke, which could have caused a catastrophic explosion. In fact, one of the tires did explode.

Meanwhile, John Bissau, 37, couldn't get free on his own because his foot was pinned down inside the car.

Mitchell reached the man and yanked him up and away from the burning vehicle. "The only thing I was thinking was, 'We have to get out of here before this thing goes up,'" Mitchell said.[131]

The driver Mitchell saved was released from the hospital and was later charged with driving while intoxicated. Mitchell said the man, who has four children, found out Mitchell's name and left a note at his office thanking him.

Mitchell, who was born in Jamaica and served in the U.S. Air Force, downplayed the event, despite police and his family hailing him as a hero. "The best part about it is my mom said she's proud of what I did. That's the best feeling," Mitchell said of the ordeal.[132]

He has no idea what happened to the man after that. That early morning crash could have turned tragic if not for the heroic actions of Alex Mitchell, a gasoline truck driver whose quick reactions saved the life of John Bissau. Four children still have a father because Alex Mitchell cared enough to risk his own life to rescue their dad.

A DIFFERENT KIND OF GOOD SAMARITAN

A new survey conducted by the Mayo Clinic "…shows that support for organ donation is increasing. Eighty-four percent of respondents said they would be very or somewhat likely to consider donating a kidney or a potion of their liver to a close fiend or family member, and 49 percent said they would be very or somewhat likely to consider donating a kidney to a stranger."[133]

---

[131]

Ibid.

[132]

Black Trucker Rescues Man Involved in Drunk Driving Wreck, by D.L. Chandler, NEWSONE For Black America, October 21, 2013.

[133]

Half of Americans would consider donating a kidney to a stranger, Science Daily, April 18, 2013.

Such an organ donation is often referred to as altruistic or "Good Samaritan" kidney donation. The fact that 84 percent of respondents said they would consider donating an organ to a total stranger they had never met is amazing. Dr. Mikel Prieto, surgical director of kidney transplantation at Mayo Clinic in Rochester, Minnesota, said "This is really encouraging news. It is very heartening to hear that the willingness to consider donating a kidney to a stranger has increased so significantly."[134]

Dr. Prieto recommends that people who need a kidney or liver transplant let family, friends and others around them know about the need. More people might be willing to step forward to make a donation if they know that one of their friends or a family member needs a transplant.

The Mayo Clinic survey shows that significantly more people are willing to donate to a close friend or family member than had been found in a similar survey taken in 2001. In fact the willingness to donate to a total stranger more than doubled.

"Organ and tissue donation are generous gifts that save lives and offer hope and healing. At the time of donation, the medical team conducts evaluations to ensure the best possible outcomes for potential recipients," says Susan Gunderson, CEO of LifeSource, Upper Midwest Organ Procurement Organization. "We encourage everyone, regardless of their age, to consider donation and document their wishes on their state's donor registry."[135]

According to the Mayo Clinic, "…it has one of the nation's largest and most experienced transplant practices, with campuses in Minnesota, Arizona and Florida. Over 200 doctors in transplant medicine and surgery perform about 1,800 transplants a year, and have a long track record of excellent outcomes."

---

[134]

Ibid.

[135]

Ibid.

The Mayo Clinic survey was actually conducted March 21-24, 2013 by ORC International, with 1,004 adult Americans questioned by telephone. The survey's overall sampling error is plus or minutes three percentage points. The sample includes 654 interviews among landline respondents and 350 interviews among cellphone respondents.

By almost any definition an organ transplant donor to a total stranger must be considered a Good Samaritan donation.

Kathy Davenport

One such Good Samaritan is Kathy Davenport, a mom who donated one of her kidneys to save the life of a complete stranger.

Dana Rothschild, a South Carolina mother of two young children, had early childhood cancer, survived well into adulthood on three-quarters of a kidney and recovered from aortic bypass surgery thanks to the relentless protection of a fierce mother, strong faith, good doctors, a husband and all that life with two kids brings.[136]

Or so she thought, until she got the latest doctor's report. "At 45, Rothschild faced a terrifying new reality: She was suffering end-stage kidney failure and would need a transplant to save her life." She would face a future connected to a dialysis machine for hours every day, until she could find a kidney donor.

Of course, depending on several factors, the normal wait for a kidney donor was seven to ten years, and with her medical record finding a donor would not be easy.

Her medical ordeal began when she was a four-year-old girl facing neuroblastoma, a cancer that develops from immature nerve cells and often arises in and around the adrenal glands near the kidneys.

At age four, after having one entire kidney and one-quarter of the other removed during a 21-hour surgery, and after six months in the hospital, she beat huge odds against survival.

Then, at age 36, she needed an aortic bypass. That too she survived.

---

[136]

GIVING HOPE: Mom donates kidney to save stranger's life, by Jennifer Berry Hawes, The Post and Courier, January 6, 2014.

But, at age 44, she suffered end-stage kidney failure. She needed a transplant.

Family members and friends stepped forward to see if they could become living donors, but none worked. Jews and Christians all over the world prayed for Rothchild. A Christian radio station held a 24-hour prayer marathon on behalf of her and others needing kidneys. The Post and Courier, a local newspaper, ran a story about her need for a living donor.

People in her daughter, Gussie's, school, as well as people from Israel to North Carolina and Florida were also tested. Nearly 150 people were tested to see if they could be a living kidney donor for Rothschild. One was Kathy Davenport, a 42-year-old Summerville, NC mother.

Davenport had never met Rothschild, but her husband, Kenneth, was a childhood friend of Rothschild's brother. She heard the story through a relative who saw a flier hanging up at her gym.

Davenport prayed. Her husband had battled brain cancer and she knew the horror of looking at a young child and imagining the loss of a mom or dad. A simple blood test confirmed she was a match.

She emailed Rothschild. "I feel honored to be able to do this for you and your family, and I'm thankful I'm a healthy match for you. I can't wait to meet you…and your children…and see you back to the healthy Mama you deserve to be!" she wrote.

By then Rothschild's kidney was working at about eight percent. The day after surgery, wearing matching hospital gowns and exhausted smiles, donor and recipient took a picture together in front of a Tree of Life painting.

During the wait for a donor, Rothschild often asked herself: Would I donate a kidney to save a stranger? When she was honest, the type of honest you don't want to admit out loud, she wasn't sure. Then, just days after turning 46, she teared up with gratitude. Never had she felt so healthy.

"Kathy gave me life," she said.

Could there be any doubt that Kathy Davenport met the biblical standard for being a Good Samaritan? I don't think so!

GOOD SAMARITAN LAWS

There are all kinds of Good Samaritans and all kinds of situations in which they emerge. Unfortunately, not all states protect Good Samaritans. They can be at risk in California, yet protected in some other states. In California, if while carelessly pulling a victim out of a burning car in which the victim would otherwise have burned to death, you do permanent and debilitating damage to the victim's spinal cord, the victim can sue you.

"In a December 2008 case, the California Supreme Court narrowed the application of the Good Samaritans statute. In *Van Horn v. Watson*, the court held that the legislature only intended for the statute to provide immunity to those who rendered emergency medical care at the scene of a medical emergency and not those who provided nonmedical care or assistance.

"In *Van Horn*, the defendant Lisa Torti pulled her friend Alexandra Van Horn out of a car following an accident. Torti claimed she removed Van Horn from the car because she feared it was going to catch on fire or explode. Van Horn suffered serious injuries as a result of the accident, including permanent paralysis. She claimed that by removing her from the car, Torti had exacerbated her injuries and caused the irreversible damage to her spinal cord.

"Torti claimed she was immune from civil liability for Van Horn's injuries under the Good Samaritans law. The trial court agreed. On appeal, however, the court reversed the lower court's decision and found that the statute did not apply to Torti because she provided nonmedical rather than medical care. The California Supreme Court later upheld the appellate court's decision.

"By narrowing the application of the state's Good Samaritans law, the California Supreme Court sent a message to citizens of the state: to provide help following an accident is to risk civil liability."[137]

It raises the question of whether careless rescuers should be subject

---

[137]

California's Good Samaritans Law, Find Law Knowledge Base, September 30, 2009.

to legal liability, and therefore, lawsuits. All 50 states have "Good Samaritan" laws; some protect the rescuer and some do not.

In 1959, California was the first to adopt a "Good Samaritan" law, and the rest of the states followed over the next several decades. Traditionally, at common law, the negligent rescuer might be sued and found libel for hurting the person rescued.

However, because it seems harsh to penalize a well-intended rescuer by putting him or her in jeopardy, Good Samaritan laws in many states immunize negligent rescuers from civil liability. Some, however, only offer limited immunization from prosecution when reasonable care is taken to not injure the person being rescued.

Some laws still protect only medically trained rescuers, while others offer protection to any Good Samaritan. There is not enough room here to review each state's Good Samaritan law; however, it would be well for the reader to become familiar with the laws in the state where he or she resides.

Chapter 6

AMERICANS WHO OVERCAME DISABILITIES

The Americans with Disability Act is a public law that was enacted by the United States Congress in 1990 to prohibit discrimination on the basis of disability.

"Title I of the Americans with Disabilities Act of 1990 prohibits private employers, state and local governments, employment agencies and labor unions from discriminating against qualified individuals with disabilities in job application procedures, hiring, firing, advancement, compensation, job training, and other terms, conditions, and privileges of employment.

The ADA covers employers with 15 or more employees, including state and local governments. It also applies to employment agencies and to labor organizations. The ADA's nondiscrimination standards also apply to federal sector employees under section 501 of the Rehabilitation Act, as amended, and its implementing rules."[138]

The ADA gives civil rights protections to individuals with disabilities that are similar to those provided to individuals on the basis of race, sex, national origin, and religion. It guarantees equal opportunity for individuals with disabilities in employment, public accommodations, transportation, State and local government services,

---

[138]

Facts About the Americans with Disabilities Act, The U.S. Equal Employment Opportunity Commission, September 9, 2008.

and telecommunications.[139]

While protections such as these are well intended, there are individuals who have throughout our history overcome their disabilities by the sheer force of their personalities, their determination, their will to succeed, and their faith in God. They want no special considerations or accommodations. They are highly competitive, strongly motivated, and sharply focused individuals, who often see themselves as no different fundamentally than anyone else.

These individuals succeeded in spite of the overwhelming odds against their success. They serve as an inspiration and as a model for all of us, able-bodied as well as disabled. The following list is inspirational, not exhaustive. There are literally thousands of stories just like these, and would require an entire book to document an account of their legendary accomplishments. These are just a few, a representative sampling.

Albert Einstein (1879 – 1955)

I'm reasonably certain nobody reading this book would ever have expected to find Albert Einstein in a chapter about people who overcame disabilities. But, it's true. He had huge difficulties as a young boy.

Believed to have Asperger's Syndrome, it is documented that the man, for whom the name genius and mad scientist are associated, did not talk fluently until he was nine, failed his college entrance exam and had a hard time remembering simple things such as his phone number or how to tie his shoes.

Nobel Prize winner for Physics, Albert Einstein proved to be one of the most gifted minds in science and history, although he was also rumored to have been dyslexic as a child, which might have accounted for some of his problems with language.

---

[139]

Americans with Disabilities Act, Office of Civil Rights, U.S. Department of Education, GPO: 1990 – 2273-170.

Einstein was known for his energy to mass-light conversion as well as the theory of relativity. Great scientists, including Stephen Hawking, have used his scientific thoughts and theories to create much of the modern world's wonder and new theories.

Truly a gifted mind that was addled by a few kinks, he was remembered as being a genius with a few loose screws. Despite those mental flaws, the man was possibly the greatest mind to walk the earth in centuries and truly deserves to be at the top this list.[140]

At an early age Einstein took music lessons, playing both the violin and piano. He became very proficient on the Violin and developed a love for music, a passion that stayed with him throughout his life.

Moving first to Italy and then to Switzerland, where he attended the Swiss Federal Polytechnic Institute in Zurich, the young prodigy graduated from high school in 1896. The same year he renounced his German citizenship and remained officially stateless before becoming a Swiss citizen in 1901. He accepted a position as a clerk at the Swiss patent office, where he worked until 1909.

"While working at the Swiss patent office, Einstein did some of the most creative work of his life, producing no fewer than four groundbreaking articles in 1905 alone. In the first paper, he applied the quantum theory (developed by German physicist Max Planck) to light in order to explain the phenomenon known as the photoelectric effect, by which a material will emit electrically charged particles when hit by light. The second article contained Einstein's experimental proof of the existence of atoms, which he got by analyzing the phenomenon of Brownian motion, in which tiny particles were suspended in water.

"In the third and most famous article, titled "On the Electrodynamics of Moving Bodies," Einstein confronted the apparent contradiction between two principal theories of physics: Isaac Newton's concepts of absolute space and time and James Clerk Maxwell's idea that

---

140

10 People Who Overcame Their Disabilities, by William O'Dell, People, July 8, 2008.

the speed of light was a constant. To do this, Einstein introduced his special theory of relativity, which held that the laws of physics are the same even for objects moving in different inertial frames (i.e. at constant speeds relative to each other), and that the speed of light is a constant in all inertial frames. A fourth paper concerned the fundamental relationship between mass and energy, concepts viewed previously as completely separate. Einstein's famous equation $E = mc2$ (where "c" was the constant speed of light) expressed this relationship."[141]

In 1913, he became director of the Kaiser Wilhelm Institute for Physics at the University of Berlin. In 1915, he published the general theory of relativity, which he considered to be his masterwork. His was the first major theory of relativity in more than 250 years, and it made him famous.

He began touring the world, speaking to audiences in the United States, Great Britain, France and Japan. In 1921, he won the Nobel Prize in Physics for his work on the photoelectric effect. He built on his theories to form a new science of cosmology, which held that the universe was dynamic instead of static, and was capable of expanding and contracting.[142]

In 1932 he emigrated to the United States and took a position at the Institute for Advanced Study in Princeton, New Jersey. In the late 1930s, his theories, including his equation $E=mc2$, helped form the basis for the development of the atomic bomb. However, he never participated in the Manhattan Project, which developed the Atom bomb.

Einstein became a U.S. citizen in 1940, but also retained his Swiss citizenship. A life long pacifist and Jew, in 1952, he declined an offer extended by David Ben-Gurion, Israel's premier, to become president

---

141

Albert Einstein, www.history.com/topics/albert-einstein, 2014.

142

Ibid.

of Israel. [143] Once Hitler took over Germany, Einstein never returned to the country of his birth.

He was a deeply religious man who argued, "that conflicts between science and religion 'have all sprung from fatal errors.' However, 'even though the realms of religion and science in themselves are clearly marked off from each other,' there are 'strong reciprocal relationships and dependencies' ... 'science without religion is lame, religion without science is blind ... a legitimate conflict between science and religion cannot exist.'"[144]

Over the years Einstein's name became a household word that was synonymous with genius all over the world. In 1999, TIME magazine recognized him as "Person of the Century." He spent much of his life in solitude, played his violin for relaxation, and lived out the remainder of his life in Princeton, New Jersey.

Einstein, who as a young boy had trouble remembering simple things like telephone numbers or how to tie his shoelaces, had an IQ of 160 and was considered to be one of the most brilliant men in history.

On April 17, 1955, he experienced internal bleeding caused by the rupture of an aortic aneurysm. He took a draft of a speech he was preparing for a television appearance commemorating the State of Israel's seventh anniversary with him to the Princeton Hospital, but he didn't live long enough to complete it. He died early the next morning at the age of 76. His remains were cremated and his ashes were scattered.

Before the cremation, however, Princeton Hospital pathologist Thomas Stoltz Harvey removed Einstein's brain for preservation, in hope that the neuroscience of the future would be able to discover what

---

143

Ibid.

144

Albert Einstein, New World Encyclopedia, December 29, 2006.

made Einstein so intelligent.[145]

To this day, Einstein is the man to whom all other geniuses seem to be compared, or contrasted. Few ever measure up to his towering intellect. Everyone knows about his intellect; but, it's doubtful many people know about his early disabilities. A high school student can probably cite E=mc2, but few people know that this man with renowned intelligence couldn't remember how to tie his shoes.

Leon Fleisher (1928 –)

Leon Flsher is a remarkably gifted and versatile musician who managed to succeed despite being struck as a young man by the worst thing that could possibly happen to a pianist. He developed a neurological disorder called "focal dystonia," which adversely affected two fingers on his right hand, nearly ending a flourishing and brilliant career.[146]

Fleisher was born in San Francisco to immigrant parents from Eastern Europe. His father's business was to make hats, while his mother's job was to "make her son a great concert pianist." Fleisher started studying the piano at age four. He made his public debut at age eight and played with the New York Philharmonic at Carnegie Hall under Pierre Monteux at 16; Monteux famously called him "the pianistic find of the century."

In the 1960s, Fleisher lost the use of his right hand, due to a condition that was eventually diagnosed as focal dsystonia. His doctor told him that he would never be able to play again. Undeterred, Fleisher began performing and recording a left-handed repertoire while

---

145

Ibid.

146

How A Great American Pianist Overcame A Devastating Physical Disability – Memoirs of Leon Fleisher, www.blogiversity.org, February 22, 2011.

searching for a cure for his condition. In addition, he took to conducting during this time, serving at one time as Music Director of the Annapolis Symphony Orchestra in Maryland.

He became an inspirational teacher and an inspired conductor, all the while playing, and in fact revitalizing, his left-handed repertory. He underwent brain surgery, grueling experimental treatments, years of trials that certainly would have discouraged any ordinary mortal. Then, against all odds and baffling medical experts, he regained the use of his right hand through a combination of Rolfing and botox injections.

"His comeback," wrote Holly Brubach in *The New York Times* in 2007, "has catapulted him up next to Lance Armstrong as a symbol of the indomitable human spirit and an inspiration to a broader public."[147]

His landmark version of Mozart, Beethoven and Brahms concertos as well as his solo recordings of Schubert and his explorations of the American repertory would become cult classics.

Fleisher was named "Instrumentalist of the Year" in 1994 by Musical America. He has received honorary doctorates from the San Francisco Conservatory of Music, Townson State University, the Boston Conservatory, and the Cleveland Institute of Music. Johns Hopkins University gave him its President's Medal. The filmmaker Nathaniel Kahn's short documentary "Two Hands," chronicling Fleisher's heroic journey, was nominated for an Academy Award in 2007.

"In the end," wrote Anthony Tommasini in *The New York Times*, "his diverse legacy may well prove more pervasive and lasting than if he had simply continued his career as a pre-eminent two-handed pianist."

Still, Fleisher needed to play again, and he has. Returning to Carnegie Hall at 67 for his first two-handed concert there in nearly four decades, Fleisher made history once again.

"The listener was immediately impressed by the pearly beauty of Fleisher's sounds–as gentle as it was firm, ruminative and intensely poetic yet without any smearing of the melodic line," wrote Tim Page in *The Washington Post* in 1996 after the Carnegie Hall concert. "Indeed, I

147

Leon Fleisher, The Kennedy Center, September 2007.

would rather listen to Fleisher, even in his current, delicate shape, than to most other pianists now before the public."[148]

Baltimore philanthropists Robert E. Meyerhoff and Rheda Becker established the Leon Fleisher Scholars Fund for piano students at the Peabody Conservatory, an endowment of over $1,000,000.

"Legendary pianist Leon Fleisher represents the highest standard of musicianship and, at 86 years young, he continues to impart his life-affirming artistry throughout the world, thriving in a sustained career as conductor and soloist, recitalist, chamber music artist, and master class mentor."[149]

Bethany Hamilton (1990 –)

Raised by surfers in Hawaii, Bethany Hamilton was born to be in the water. A natural surfer, she began competing professionally as a young child. However, at 13, she lost her arm and nearly lost her life in a vicious tiger shark attack. One month later she was back on her surfboard with a determined spirit and positive attitude. Two years later she won first place in the Explorer Women's Division of the NSSA National Championships.

Now, the professional surfer shares her inspirational message of hope with millions of people and her story was made into an inspiring major motion picture, *Soul Surfer*, starring Anna Sophia Robb, Helen Hunt and Dennis Quaid.

Hamilton became a source of inspiration to millions through her story of faith, determination, and hope, after losing her left arm to a shark attack in 2003, at age 13.

"The attack left Bethany with a severed left arm. After losing over 60% of her blood, and making it through several surgeries without infection, Bethany was on her way to recovery with an unbelievably

---

148

Ibid.

149

Leon Fleisher, pianist and conductor, Frank Salomon Associates,

positive attitude. Lifeguards and doctors believe her strong water sense and faith in God helped get her through the traumatic ordeal.

"Miraculously, just one month after the attack, Bethany returned to the water to continue pursuing her goal to become a professional surfer. In January 2004, Bethany made her return to surf competition; placing 5th in the Open Women's division of that contest.

With no intention of stopping, Bethany continued to enter and excel in competition. Just over a year after the attack she took 1st place in the Explorer Women's division of the 2005 NSSA National Championships – winning her first National Title. In 2007, Bethany realized her dream and turned pro. "[150]

She is involved in numerous charitable efforts, including her own foundation, Friends of Bethany, which supports shark attack survivors and amputees, and serves to inspire others through her life story.

Born into a family of surfers on the island of Kauai, Hawaii, Hamilton began surfing at a very young age. At the age of eight, she entered her first state-wide surf competition, winning both the short and long board divisions and sparking in herself a love for surf competition.

Despite the trauma of the Shark attack, Hamilton was determined to return to surfing. Less than a month after the incident, she returned to her board. Initially, she adopted a custom-made board that was longer and slightly thicker than standard and had a handle for her right arm, making it easier to paddle, and she learned to kick more to make up for the loss of her left arm. After teaching herself to surf with one arm, on January 10, 2004, she entered a major competition. She now uses standard competitive performance short-boards.[151]

She has since taken second place in the 2003 United States National

---

[150] *Bethany Hamilton – Soul Surfer*, bethanyhamilton.com, The Official Website of Bethany Hamilton.

[151] *Bethany Hamilton*, Wikipedia, The Free Encyclopedia, March 5, 2014.

Championships.

Her personal quote about the shark attack, listed on www.imdb.com web page: "I can't change it. That was God's plan for my life and I'm going to go with it."

On August 18, 2013, she married her boyfriend of a year, Adam Dirks, following a four-month engagement.

Of course surfers are inspired by her story, but anyone who listens to her story will also be inspired by her resilience, determination and grace. She is a fierce, sharply focused, motivated, dedicated and resilient young woman who refused to quit. Bethany Hamilton is unquestionably a champion.

Geraldine "Geri" Ann Jewell (1956 –)

Geri Jewell was born on September 13, 1956 in buffalo, New York. An actress and comedienne, Jewell was the first performer with a life-altering physical disability to hold a regular part on a primetime network sitcom.

Despite a permanent condition of cerebral palsy that affected her speech and physical coordination, Jewell clung to a dream of establishing herself as a stand-up comic, a dream realized with a successful series of engagements at the Los Angeles, California Comedy Store.

"Witnessing great talent and tenacity, producer Fern Field sensed Jewell's potential and introduced her to television mogul Norman Lear, whose work creating such programs as All in the Family, Good Times, Maude and The Jeffersons had put him at the top of his game in the 1970s."[152]

Lear put her in the all-girls prep school sitcom, The Facts of Life. Though not a regular, she appeared occasionally on episodes from 1981 – 1984. In 1984, she turned up on an episode of 21 Jump Street, and in 1991 appeared on the Gail Singer all-female stand-up documentary Wisecracks.

However, Jewell got her biggest audience as a cleaning woman on HBO's 19th century western drama Deadwood from 2004-2006.

---

[152] *Geri Jewell: Biography*, MSN Entertainment, 2014.

"Meanwhile, Jewell continued to tour as a comedienne, a motivational speaker, and a disability trainer for such organizations as the U.S. Army and the CIA. She also opened for musical acts including Robert Goulet and Judy Collins and landed a major role as Aunt Lolly in the 2006 comedy The Night of the White Pants, co-starring Tom Wilkinson and Nick Stahl."[153]

She has received many awards, including the 1992 Founders Award, the 2005 Independent Living Legacy Award, and in 2006 a National Rehabilitation Hospital Victory Award.

Her autobiography, I'm Walking as Straight as I Can was published in 2011. The title refers to the fact that she has cerebral palsy and is a lesbian. Her original autobiography, Geri, published in 1984, was a way for readers to learn more about how to get comfortable dealing with a person who has a disability, and taught them to develop a good sense of humor about it.

Jewell was the first person with a disability to break ground in a TV series, and for that we can all be thankful. She was an inspiration to everyone who has ever suffered a disability of any kind.

Barbara Jordon (1936 – 1996)

Barbara Charline Jordan was a black American politician and a leader of the Civil Rights movement. She was the first black African American elected to the Texas Senate after Reconstruction, the first southern black female elected to the United States House of Representatives, and the first black African-American woman to deliver the keynote address at a Democratic National Convention.[154]

She received the Presidential Medal of Freedom, among numerous other honors. On her death, she became the first black African-American woman to be buried in the Texas State Cemetery.

---

[153]

Ibid.

[154]

Barbara Jordon, Wikipedia, The Free Encyclopedia, February 27, 2014.

Jordon was afflicted with multiple sclerosis and leukemia, but died from viral pneumonia as a complication of leukemia, according to officials of the University of Texas, where she taught.

Multiple sclerosis is an autoimmune disease that affects the brain and spinal cord (central nervous system). It affects women more than men and is most commonly diagnosed between the ages of 20 and 40, but can be seen at any age. The exact cause of multiple sclerosis is not known, but the most common thought is that a virus or gene effect, or both, are to blame.

Multiple sclerosis can affect muscles, cause bowel and bladder problems, cause vision problems, and cause numbness, tingling, or pain. It can also affect speech, cause difficulty swallowing, and generally causes fatigue.[155]

Despite her disabilities, Jordon was an extraordinary lady who would serve equally well as a role model for young men and women. She grew up in a poor black neighborhood in Houston, Texas, the daughter of a Baptist minister. Both of her parents encouraged her to strive for academic excellence, an area in which she excelled.

She had a gift for language and for building persuasive arguments, and she had a voice that was powerful and mesmerizing, which served her well as she became an award–winning debater and orator in high school.

Jordon attended Texas Southern University and the Boston University Law School, after which she returned to Texas and set up a law practice. She also became active in politics, campaigning for John F. Kennedy and Lyndon B. Johnson.

In 1966 Jordon won a seat in the Texas legislature, becoming the first black woman to do so. In 1972 she won election to the U.S. House of Representatives, where she was thrust into the national spotlight during the Watergate scandal. "Jordon stood as a moral compass during this time of crisis, calling for the impeachment of President Richard M.

155

Multiple sclerosis, PubMed Health, U.S. National Library of Medicine, September 25, 2013.

Nixon for his involvement in this illegal political enterprise."[156]

In 1976 she captured the public's attention as the keynote speaker at the Democratic National Convention. However, in 1979, suffering from multiple sclerosis, she finished her final term and left politics to focus on teaching as a professor at the University of Texas at Austin, Texas.

Her disability became progressively worse, as she began to have difficulty climbing stairs and started using a cane and eventually a wheelchair.

While she gave up politics, she never fully stepped away from public life. In 1991, she served as a special counsel on ethics for Texas Governor Ann Richards, and in 1992 she again delivered a speech at the Democratic National Convention, this time from a wheelchair.

When she died in 1996, "…the nation mourned the loss of a great pioneer who shaped the political landscape with her dedication to the Constitution, her commitment to ethics and her impressive oratory skills."

In remembrance of her, Texas Governor Ann Richards said: "There was simply something about her that made you proud to be part of the country that produced her." President Bill Clinton said, "Barbara always stirred our national conscience."

Many of Jordan's speeches have been collected in a 2007 publication from the University of Texas Press, *"Barbara Jordan: Speaking the Truth with Eloquent Thunder."*

In 2011, the U.S. Postal Service issued the Barbara Jordan Forever Stamp. It is the 34th stamp in the Black Heritage series of U.S. stamps.

Barbara Jordan was an extraordinary human being who radiated warmth and passion simultaneously, while reminding us that even with an incurable disability she could still contribute enormously to our society. We all benefited from having Barbara Jordon pass through the American scene.

James E. MacLaren (1963 – 2010)

156

Barbara Jordan biography, BIO True Story, Copyright 2014.

James E. MacLaren was a motivational speaker and author who was noted for his record-breaking performances in the marathon and Ironman triathlon, after having his left leg amputated below the knee, until he was struck by a bus while riding a motorcycle.

He was a standout athlete in football and lacrosse at Yale University. He was 6-foot-5, full of muscle, and had Hollywood good looks. Success seemed to be calling out to him; but, in 1985, at the age of 22, MacLaren lost his left leg below the knee in a fatal motorcycle accident, and had to be defibrillated. He survived, and went on to run the marathon in 3 hours and 16 minutes, and to finish the Hawaii Ironman triathlon in 10 hours and 42 minutes.

Finishing his undergraduate work at Yale University in 1985, McLaren ventured to New York City, to train at the Circle in the Square Theatre School on Broadway. Three weeks later, while leaving a late-night rehearsal session on his motorcycle, he was broadsided by a 40,000-pound city bus. He was rushed to Bellevue Hospital, where he was initially diagnosed as "dead on arrival."[157]

"After 18 hours of surgery doctors stabilized a comatose MacLaren and made a decision that would shape the next eight years of his life. They amputated his left leg below the knee.

"He awoke from his coma, rehabbed diligently, and attempted to resume his graduate studies at the Yale School of Drama. There, he started swimming, and picked up a book on triathlons that sparked his imagination. Soon, MacLaren was ready to resume life as an athlete, as a triathlete. "I felt like I was back in it, back in life," he says. "I didn't compete against other people. I was competing against me."

MacLaren paved the way for a new generation of disabled athletes. He competed and set scores of records in some of the toughest races on the planet, including the New York City Marathon and the Ironman Triathlon in Hawaii, where he routinely finished ahead of 80 percent of the able-bodied athletes, although he ran with a prosthesis.

----

[157]

Jim MacLaren, Keynote Speaker, Life Mentor, Coach, www.jimmaclaren.com/home.htm, 2006.

MacLaren didn't quit. Even though in some ways he wasn't the same, or could have been perceived as limited, he was better than ever.

Then, in 1993, tragedy struck again. MacLaren was hit by a van during the cycling portion of a triathlon and the accident left him a quadriplegic. Complications from that condition ultimately led to his death. But that was 17 years after the accident. During the 17 years since the accident, MacLaren fought back as he always had, and became a renowned motivational speaker and author.

In 2005, MacLaren was presented the prestigious Arthur Ashe Courage Award at the 2005 ESPY Awards. Oprah Winfrey presented the award. He was the star on which everyone focused.

"Truth of the matter is, MacLaren always will be a star, even now that he has died. He will always be known for what he did while he was alive, and for the passion and courage that was so much a part of his life. So maybe making too much of MacLaren's death is inappropriate, because death is something the man continually defied.

"MacLaren accomplished more in his 47 years than most of us could dream of, and that life is sure to find its way to the big screen at some point."[158]

Lazaro Mendez (1971 –)

Lazaro Mendez, better known by his stage name DJ Laz, was born in Hollywood Florida. He is a Cuban–American rapper who had a weekday morning radio program, DJ Laz Morning Show, in Miami on WPOW 96.5 FM for 22 years until he left the company in 2012. He moved to WRMA DJ106.7, a Bilingual Dance/rhymic formatted station.

The "DJ Laz Morning Show, Coast to Coast," airs in both Miami and Los Angeles. Mendez says he is on a mission to become a national sensation. When asked how he appeals to both East and West Coast Latinos, he says: "I'm Cuban Latino, they are Mexican Latinos, but we

---

158

Jim MacLaren story: Triupph over tragedy, by Mike Sullivan, Seacoastonline.com, March 9, 2014.

are all Latinos. So we can relate in one way, shape or form."[159]

But, overcoming obstacles is nothing new to Mendez; he is a man who overcame a serious disability to pursue his American dream. Mendez was born with the bottom of his feet touching his chest. He describes himself as a human "pretzel."

He was diagnosed with Arthrogryposis Multilex. According to the American Association of Neuromuscular and Electrodiagnostic Medicine, Arthrogryposis Multiplex is a disease where newborns suffer decreased flexibility in their joints.

"After 17 surgeries, Mendez went from wheelchair to knee braces, and was able to walk, albeit with a limp, that he now considers normal. 'If I didn't limp or have that disability I wouldn't have the personality or I would not have had the opportunity that I have had in life,' Mendez explains."[160]

Mendez's radio program is very popular. In 2012 President Obama sat with Mendez for an interview. "President Barack Obama put new meaning into the cliche "wide-ranging interview while speaking with DJ Laz of Miami Latin station Romance 106.7 FM..."[161]

When asked how he was, Obama said, "Blessed and highly favored." When Laz said that it was an honor to have Obama on, Obama replied, "I'm the one who should be humbled. You're big time. You've got Pitbull and Flo Rida and all these guys just beating a path to

---

[159]

Coast to coast DJ rules the airwaves after overcoming severe disability, by Victoria Moll-Ramirez, NBC News Miami, February 20, 2013.

[160]

Ibid.

[161]

Obama–DJ Laz Interview: President Talks Flo Rida, Pitbull, Immigratin To Miami Station, by Luke Johnson, The Huffington Post, September 11, 2012.

your door. And so I'm hoping I can get a little of that magic from you in this interview."

Mendez and the President had a very cordial interview "The white House press corps in Washington has griped that Obama does not spend enough time speaking to its reporters, instead going to non–news outlets like swing-state radio stations, Entertaiment Tonight and *People* magazine."

Nevertheless, DJ Laz has a huge following and overcame enormous disabilities to reach a level of success that might not have been possible for anyone who was less motivated or less dedicated. Mendez may not be everybody's "cup of tea," but he is certainly someone who has shown Americans what is possible if you are persistent and stay focused —even when you suffer from unimaginable difficulties.

Aron Lee Ralston (1975 –)

Aron Lee Ralston is an American outdoorsman, engineer and motivational speaker who survived a canyoneering accident in southeastern Utah in 2003, during which he amputated his own right forearm with a dull multi-tool knife to extricate himself from a dislodged boulder, underneath which he had been trapped for five days and seven hours.

Ralston was born on October 27, 1975, in Marion, Ohio. He and his family moved to Denver when he was age 11. He is a graduate of Cherry Creek High School in Greenwood Village, Colorado. He received his college degree from Carnegie Mellon University in Pittsburgh, finishing with degrees in mechanical engineering and French, with a minor in piano. At Carnegie Mellon, he served as a resident assistant, studied abroad, and was an active intramural sports participant. He left his job as a mechanical engineer with Intel in Phoenix, Arizona, in 2002 and moved to Aspen, Colorado to pursue a life of climbing mountains.[162]

---

[162]

Aron Ralston, Wikipedia, The Free Encyclopedia, March 4, 2014.

His goal was to climb all 59 of Colorado's peaks over 14,000 ft. high, as a solo climber, during the winter (a feat that had never before been recorded).

"In April 2003, while he was on a hiking trip in Blue John Canyon in Canyonlands National Park, a boulder became dislodged, crushing his right forearm and pinning it against the canyon wall. Ralston had not told anyone of his hiking plans and knew no one would be searching for him.

"Assuming that he would die, he spent five days slowly sipping his small amount of remaining water while trying to extricate his arm. His efforts were futile, as he could not dislodge his arm. He eventually ran out of water, carved his name, date of birth and presumed date of death into the sandstone canyon wall, and videotaped his last goodbyes to his family.

"After five days of trying to lift and break the boulder, the dehydrated and delirious Ralston prepared to amputate his trapped right arm below the elbow in order to escape. Although he never named the manufacturer of the tool other than to say it was not Leatherman, he did describe it as "what you'd get if you bought a $15 flashlight and got a free multi-use tool".

"After freeing himself, he was still seventeen miles from his vehicle, and he had no mobile phone. He had to rappel down a 65-foot sheer wall, and then hike out of the canyon in the hot midday sun. While hiking out, he encountered a couple on vacation from The Netherlands, Eric and Monique Meijer, and their son, Andy, who gave him water and then alerted the authorities.

"He was ultimately rescued by a helicopter search team six hours after amputating his arm. His arm was removed from under the boulder and retrieved by park authorities. Ralston then cremated his arm. He subsequently returned to the accident scene with Tom Brokaw six months later, on his birthday, for two reasons: to film the Dateline NBC episode of his accident, and to scatter the ashes of his arm where, he says, "they belong"..[163]

---

[163]

Aron Ralston and the Blue John Canyon Accident ,

Once he realized his only option was to cut off his forearm or die trapped under the boulder, he first had to break two bones in his arm, after which he could cut through skin, muscle, arteries, and nerves to get free.

Describing the amputation to Tom Brokaw for NBC–TV, Ralston said the process took over an hour. He said it didn't really hurt much until he had to cut the nerves. His blades were bent and dull, but they were all he had to use. He cut through muscle, two arteries, and tendons. Then he had to cut the nerves. When he cut the nerves it sent a horrible burning sensation all the way up to his shoulder; but, at that point, he was free of the boulder.

After escaping from the boulder, he encountered the couple on vacation from The Netherlands. They gave him water and alerted the authorities. A helicopter search team ultimately rescued him six hours after he amputated his arm, which was retrieved by park authorities.

He returned with Tom Brokaw six months later to scatter the ashes of his cremated arm. He said freeing himself from the boulder was at once his most powerful experience and the happiest moment in his life.

The story was documented in his autobiography, "Between a Rock and a Hard Place," and became he basis for the 2010 film "127 Hours," which starred James Franco. Ralston says that, except for a few early scenes, the movie is very accurate. "It's as close to a documentary as you can get and still be a drama." The film received six Academy Award nominations: Best Film, Best Director, Best Actor, Best Adapted Screenplay, Best Cinematography, Best Editing, Best Song and Best Sound. It's main theme song, "If I Rise" won the Critics Choice award for Best Song.

There were eight production companies involved, but 20th Century Fox distributed the film.

Ralston is still a passionate climber and his disability or the unfortunate accident did not stop him from doing what he likes best, climbing mountains. In 2005, he became the first person to climb all 59 ranked and/or named Colorado's 'fourteeners' solo in winter, a project he started in 1997 and resumed after the amputation in Blue John

---

Canyonlands National Park, NP Ranger.com,

Canyon.

David Ring (1953 –)

David Ring is a Christian evangelist and motivational speaker who has cerebral palsy. Few individuals have felt the crushing blows that have besieged David Ring since birth. He was born to lose, but became a huge success. His story is inspirational and heart warming.

On October 28th, 1953, in Jonesboro, Arkansas, Ring was born with Cerebral Palsy. His doctor says Ring was born dead for 18 minutes. Ring says they put him on a table in the corner and left him for dead. He had no oxygen to the brain during that 18 minutes, but a miracle occurred…he lived! He says that is because "it's not over until God says it's over."

Cerebral Palsy is caused by damage to the motor control centers of the developing brain and is considered a disability that alters speech and body movement skills. As a child his speech was impaired and his bodily movements, such as writing, walking and even just sitting down were quite challenging.

He hated school because the kids in school teased him about the way he talked and walked.

"Orphaned at age 14, he was cast about from family to family with nowhere to call home. He endured constant physical pain, humiliating public ridicule and constant discouragement. Yet in the face of these seemingly insurmountable obstacles, David emerged not victimized… but victorious!"[164]

Both of his parents died while he was very young. He struggled with their death, his disability and depression, and tried to commit suicide many times over a two-year period. However, with the encouragement of his sister, he straightened out his life, became a Christian, earned a Bachelor of Arts degree from William Jewell College in Liberty, Arkansas, and became an evangelist and motivational speaker.

164

David Ring: Reach Out & Touch Ministries, www.davidring.org, Copyright 2007.

Because of his Cerebral Palsy, he is difficult to understand at first, but his audiences are rapidly captured by his quick wit and warm personality.

Whether giving a motivational message at a sales convention, or inspiring church leaders, David always focuses on an individual's need to conquer the personal challenges and adversities of life.

"As a nationally known speaker, David shares his story with over 100,000 people each year at churches, conventions, schools and corporate events. He has been featured on numerous occasions on several nationally televised programs."

In 1994 he wrote a book, titled: *Just As I Am: The Life of David Ring*. He has since written a second book, *Ring*, which will be out in book stores in the Fall of 2014.

His greatest "liability" (his hard to understand speech), became his greatest asset. He has spoken in over 6,000 venues for 37 years. He's now 61 years old and travels all over the United States because God told him to tell his story. Since 1973, he has challenged thousands of people with his signature message – "I have cerebral palsy…What's your problem?"

While growing up he was constantly told he would never have a wife or kids. "Life is not fair," he said, "but God is Good." He currently resides in Nashville, Tennessee, with his wife and four children: April, Ashley, Nathan and Amy Joy.

David Ring knows better than anyone that life is not finished until God says it is.

Maria Runyan (1969 –)

Maria Runyan was the first legally blind athlete to compete in the Olympics. The three–time national champion in the women's 5,000 meters was born in Santa Maria, California on January 4, 1969. At the age of nine, she developed Stargardt's Disease, which is a form of macular degeneration that left her legally blind.

Her doctors had very low expectations for her future, predicting that she would never get above a "C" in school, learn to drive, or go to college. At that time she was very active in soccer and gymnastics, but eventually had to drop them when her vision made it hard for her to see the soccer ball.[165]

Despite her disability she attended San Diego State University, where she received a B.S. in Education of the Deaf and a M.S. in Education of Deaf–Blind Children in 1994.

While attending San Diego State she also began competing in several athletic events: the heptathlon, 200–meter dash, high jump, shot put, 100–meter hurdle, long jump, javelin throw, and the 800–meter run. She also participated in gymnastics and soccer, until she could no longer see the ball.

Runyan began to make her mark as a world–class runner in 1999 at the Pan American Games. The following year Runyan became the first legally blind person and Paralympian to compete in the Olympic Games in Sydney, Australia. She finished eighth in the 1,500–meter, the highest finish by an American woman in that event. In 2002, Runyan finished as the top American, with the second–fastest debut time by a woman, in the New York City Marathon. She also holds several American records for various running events: 20k Road (2003), All–female marathon (2002), 500m (2001), and Heptathlon (1996).[166]

Being legally blind she initially focused on competing in events for visually impaired athletes. She was highly successful, winning three sprint events and the long jump at the 1992 Paralympics, while also competing in cycling. She added a fifth title at the 1996 Atlanta Paralympics, winning the pentathlon and a silver medal in the shot put.

But Runyan also aspired to compete in the Olympics, and had tried to qualify for the heptathlon at the US Olympic Trials, placing 10th. Her good 800 meters in that competition convinced her to switch to middle distance running. This switch proved a good choice, and in 1999

165

Sports Hero: Marla Runyan, by Jane from Grand Rapid, Michigan, Sports Heroes, September 10, 2008

166

Marla Runyan (1969-), National Women's History Museum, Spring 2006.

Runyan won the 1500 meters at the Pan American Games, and reached the World Championship final in the same event. She repeated that performance in Sydney, placing 8th in the Olympic final. She then turned her attention to long distance running, eventually competing in the 2004 Olympic 5 km, and placing 4th in the 2002 New York Marathon.

Unfortunately, Runyan's vision worsens as time passes. She is no longer able to see the large "E" on the eye exam chart; her vision is measured at 20/400 in both eyes. However, she has not allowed her worsening condition to affect her career. She plans to continue competing in running events. In 2001, she co-wrote and published her autobiography, *No Finish Line: My Life As I See It*.

Maria Runyan was and is an authentic sports hero, but more than that, she is a role model and an inspiration to everyone who needs to see beyond their disabilities. She actively educates the public as an ambassador for the Perkins School for the Blind.

Runyan lives in Eugene, Oregon, with her husband and coach Matt Lonergan, whom she married in August 2002, and their daughter Anna Lee, who was born on September 1, 2005.

Wherever she goes, Runyan inspires people to look beyond their disabilities and focus on the things they can still do.

Chapter 7

AMERICANS WHO BEAT
THE ODDS AGAINST THEM

One of the hallmarks of the American version of democracy is that everyone is pretty much guaranteed to have an equal opportunity to succeed, but there is no guarantee of an equal outcome from effort.

A huge key to equality in America has traditionally been education. Education has generally been considered to be the pathway out of poverty.

Access to higher education for poor students was helped dramatically around 1965, with the passage of the Higher Education Act of 1965, the creation of the Pell Grant, the development of federally sponsored low interest loans, and work–study programs.

However, there have been and are some extraordinary individuals who represent strong exceptions to this formula. Some folks rise out of poverty through hard work and diligent effort alone, living frugally, saving religiously, taking advantage of unique opportunities, and building on each success as a stairway to the middle class and above.

This chapter highlights people who overcame poor backgrounds that often lead to failure and a perpetuation of poverty. These people overcame great odds against success to become beacons of hope to millions of indigent citizens who desperately need role models to prove there is a way out of poverty.

"Time and again, talented, enterprising and hardworking Americans have shown that great success can come from humble beginnings. The belief that everyone has the opportunity to make it big if they work hard enough, regardless of their background or connections, is a shared

American value dating back to our country's beginnings."[167]

These are examples of Americans who illustrate the axiom that perseverance is often the most essential element leading to success. A person who perseveres may succeed, while other more talented or more skilled people fail because they give up and quit.

These individuals are unique, but their path to success is not. Hard work, perseverance, and good fortune (luck), in no specific order, appears to be a common thread that runs through their lives and connects them to the stereotypical "rags to riches" story.

Sheldon Adelson (1933 –)

Sheldon Adelson, born August 4, 1933, is an American business magnate who started out poor. He is now the chairman and chief executive officer of the Las Vegas Sands Corporation, parent company of The Venetian Resort Hotel Casino and the Sands Expo and Convention Center. Today he has an estimated worth of $40.8 billion. Forbes places him as the 8th richest person in the world, but he came from humble origins.[168]

The son of Ukrainian immigrants, he grew up in a poor Boston neighborhood. As a young boy at the age of 12, he sold newspapers on the street. Even at that young age, he had an entrepreneurial spirit that would stay with him throughout life and lead him to enormous wealth.

Over the course of his business career, he created over 50 companies and became a multi-millionaire in his 30s. However, he is best known as the CEO of the Las Vegas Sands, which operates casinos throughout the world.

In 1988, he and his partners bought the Sands Casino for $128 million. The Sands Casino was famous for being the hangout of Frank

---

[167]

5 Super-Rich Americans Who Started Out Super-Poor, by Brian Reed, Investing Answers, October 21, 2011.

[168]

Sheldon Adelson, Wikiedia, The Free Encyclopedia, March 8, 2014

Sinatra and the Rat Pack.

In 1991, he met his wife Miriam, an Israeli-born physician specializing in drug abuse treatment. "While honeymooning in Italy, he was inspired by the canals and architecture of Venice and began to envision a mega-resort hotel.

In 1995, "Adelson shed his partnerships with Interface and ventured out on his own to build his $1.5 billion Venetian Resort Hotel Casino and the Sands Expo and Convention Center. Despite legal and contractual battles with unions and contractors, the resort opened in 1999 and was wildly successful."[169]

Adelson subsequently opened a Venetian casino resort on the Chinese island of Macao, and in 2006 he was awarded a license to construct a casino resort at Singapore's Marina Bay. The Marina Bay Sands Hotel and Casino opened in 2010 at a rumored cost of $5.5 billion.[170]

In March 2014, Forbes said about Adelson, he "…returns to the top 10 richest in the world…after making an average of $32 million a day over the last year, third-most of anyone on the planet. Shares of his Las Vegas Sands, worth more than all other U.S. casino companies combined, continued climbing thanks to booming business in Asia, where he plans to continue expanding.

"Adelson, who spent $100 million trying to get a republican in the White House in 2012, is now using his vast fortune to fight internet gambling in America, pitting himself against some of the biggest names in finance, private equity and gambling. He told Forbes he is willing to "spend whatever it takes" to win."[171]

The Adelsons have also given millions of dollars to charitable organizations. Adelson is a member of the board of directors of the

---

[169]

Sheldon Adelson. Biography, bio true story, 2014 A+E Netorks.

[170]

Ibid.

[171]

#8 Sheldon Adelson, Forbes, March 2014.

United States Holocaust Memorial Museum in Washington, D.C. In 2007, Sheldon Adelson established the Adelson Family Charitable Trust, which is expected to donate $200 million to Jewish and Israeli causes.

At age 80, Sheldon Gary Adelson represents the classic American "rags-to-riches" story.

John Paul DeJoria (1944 –)

John Paul DeJoria was born April 13, 1944, the second son of an Italian immigrant father and a Greek immigrant mother in the Echo Park neighborhood of Los Angeles, California. His parents divorced while he was only two-years-old and his single mother was not able to support he and his brother. Consequently, they were both sent to an East Los Angeles foster home.[172]

DeJoria graduated from John Marshall High School in 1962 and spent two years in the United States Navy, after which he held a series of jobs. He did everything he could to make ends meet, from selling encyclopedias and photocopying machines to repairing bicycles, pumping gasoline and working as a janitor.

Eventually he broke into the hair care industry as an employee of the Redken Laboratories, then the leading professional hair salon product company in the U.S.. "Within 18 months, he was promoted to national manager, overseeing their schools and chain salons, eagerly learning everything there was to know about the hair business."[173]

In 1980 he secured a $700 loan to start John Paul Mitchell Systems, with hairdresser Paul Mitchell. The company was a smashing success and today its annual revenues exceed $900 million.

DeJoria also owns 70 percent of The Patron Spirits Company, which makes premium tequila. In 2011 they sold approximately

---

[172]

John Paul DeJoria, Wikipedia, The Free Encyclopedia, January 21, 2014.

[173]

John Paul DeJoria – From Homeless to Multi-Millionaire, by Kaya Morgan, Millionaire Magazine, 2004.

2,450,000 cases of tequila. He is also a founding partner of the House of Blues nightclub chain and has interests in Pyrat Rum, Ultimat Vodka, Solar Utility, Sun King Solar, Touchstone Natural Gas, Three Star Energy, Diamond Audio, a Harley Davidson dealership, a diamond company (DeJoria), mobile technology developer ROK AMERICAS, the John Paul Pet company, which does hair and personal grooming for animals, and J&D Acquisitions LLC, the parent company for the Larson, Striper, Triumph, Marquis and Carver boat companies formed with Minneapolis-based investor Irwin L. Jacobs.[174]

"So, what is the secret to this tremendous success? DeJoria's golden rule of "Success unshared is failure," runs true throughout the company. Sources from within say that it is a place where people joyfully show up for work as opposed to merely showing up to collect a paycheck. And, he has gone to great lengths to create an atmosphere of success by hiring only the very best people, asking for them to give 110%, and then compensating them higher than what the industry normally pays to let them know their work is valued."[175]

DeJoria has also been active in the film industry as an executive producer and actor, and has appeared on the television show, *Shark Tank*, as a guest investor. As a philanthropist he is a supporter of Food4Africa.

In 2008, he traveled to sub-Saharan Africa to join Nelson Mandela in an effort to help feed over 17,000-orphaned children. In the same year, his company Paul Mitchell, helped provide over 400,000 life-saving meals for the children.

With six homes scattered around the U.S., one as big as a shopping mall, environmentalist, philanthropist, and entrepreneur, DeJoria has an estimated net worth of $3 billion.

When asked what ranked so high on his list that without it, life wouldn't be worth it, he quickly replied, "Happiness....because if

---

[174]

Ibid.

[175]

Ibid.

you're not happy with what you're doing, life just isn't worth living."

What else would you expect from a guy who started out with nothing and overcame huge odds to become wealthy?

Lawrence Ellison (1944 –)

Lawrence Joseph "Larry" Ellison was born on August 17, 1944 in the Bronx, New York. He is an American businessman, best known as the genius co-founder and chief executive officer of the Oracle software company. Ellison started life dirt poor but now has a net worth estimated to be close to $48 billion.

Ellison was born to a single, unwed, 19-year-old, mother who gave birth to Ellison in the Bronx. When he was just nine months old, his mother sent him to live in Chicago with his aunt and uncle, who later adopted him. Ellison was raised in a two-bedroom apartment on the city's South Side, and did not know he was adopted until he was 12-years-old. He did not meet his biological mother again until he was 48.[176]

As a youngster, Ellison was thought to be a bright but inattentive student. He left the University of Illinois at Urbana-Champaign after his second year, after not taking his final exams because his adoptive mother had just died. After spending a summer in northern California, Ellison attended the University of Chicago for one term, where he first encountered computer design. In 1966, aged 22, he moved to northern California where he bounced from job to job, working as a technician for Fireman's Fund and Wells Fargo bank. As a programmer at Amdahl Corporation, he participated in building the first IBM-compatible mainframe system.[177]

In 1977, Ellison and two colleagues Robert Miner and Ed Oates

---

[176] *Larry Ellison*, Wikipedia, The Free Encyclopedia, March 10, 2014.

[177] *Prophet of Software*, www.achievement.org, October 15,

founded a company called Software Development Labs, where they came across a paper called "A Relational Model of Data for large Shared Data Banks, which became the basis of their soon-to-be-found fortune with establishment of Oracle, which is now one of the world's biggest software companies.[178]

Ellison is known as a multi-faceted businessman and a marketing genius who has a voracious appetite for new properties. "He follows a simple approach, 'Buy the best, without compromise'. The scores of properties he has includes two holdings in Woodside, California, a hotel and two restaurants in Malibu along with two other homes, a 249-acre estate in Palm Springs, which he got for $49 million and a garden property in Kyoto Japan worth at least $86 million."[179]

Ellison is also known for his enthusiastic support of outdoor activities. In 1998, Ellison and his 78-foot yacht, *Sayonara,* won the Sydney to Hobart race, overcoming near-hurricane winds that sank five other boats, drowning six participants. Ellison is a principal supporter of the BMW Oracle Racing team, which has been a significant force in America's Cup competition. His yacht, Rising Sun, over 450 feet long, is one of the largest privately owned vessels in the world.

After many years of pursuing a victory in the America's Cup yacht race, Ellison triumphed at last in 2010, bringing the oldest trophy in international sports back to the United States for the first time in 15 years. Just as Ellison revolutionized the world of business software, so has he transformed the sport of yacht racing.[180]

2013.

[178]

Larry Ellison, BornRich.com, Home of Luxury, 2014

[179]

Ibid.

[180]

Prophet of Software, www.achievement.org, October 15, 2013.

"In August 2010, it was reported that Ellison is one of the 40 billionaires who has signed "The Giving Pledge." Ellison wrote: 'many years ago, I put virtually all of my assets into a trust with the intent of giving away at least 95 percent of my wealth to charitable causes. I have already given hundreds of millions of dollars to medical research and education, and I will give billions more over time. Until now, I have done this giving quietly because I have long believed that charitable giving is a personal and private matter.'"[181]

By almost any standards, Ellison would have to be listed among those individuals who began life super poor, but became super rich. Starting with nothing, he now ranks fifth on the list of the world's richest people.

Christopher Gardner (1954 –)

Christopher Gardner was born on February 9, 1954 in Milwaukee, Wisconsin. He is an American entrepreneur, author, inspirational speaker, investor, stockbroker, philanthropist and single parent.

His childhood was marked by poverty, domestic violence, alcoholism, sexual abuse and family illiteracy. His life story was chronicled in an autobiography, *The Pursuit of Happyness*, which became a *New York Times* and *Washington Post* bestseller that was translated into more than 40 languages.[182] He published his autobiography to shed light on those universal issues and show they do not have to define you.

Gardner never knew his father, and lived with his mother, Bettye Jean Triplett (nee Gardner), when not in foster homes. His mother provided him with strong "spiritual genetics" and taught him that in spite of where he came from, he could chart another path and attain

---

[181]

Larry Ellison, Wikipedia, The Free Encyclopedia, March 10, 2014.

[182]

Biography, Chrisgardnermedia.com,.

whatever goals he set for himself.[183]

"Gardner joined the Navy out of high school and after discharge moved to San Francisco where he worked as a medical research associate and for a scientific supply distributor. In 1981, as a new father to son Christopher Gardner Jr., he was determined to find a career that would be both lucrative and fulfilling. Fascinated by finance, but without connections, an MBA or even a college degree, Gardner applied for training programs at brokerages, willing to live on next to nothing while he learned a new trade. Chris Jr.'s mother left and Gardner, despite his circumstances, fought to keep his son because, as he says, "I made up my mind as a young kid that when I had children they were going to know who their father is, and that he isn't going anywhere.""[184]

Gardner also determined from his early experiences that alcoholism, domestic abuse, child abuse, illiteracy, fear and powerlessness were all things he wanted to avoid in the future. During the late 1960s and early 1970s he developed a deep sense of black pride and expanded his worldview beyond the black African/American experience.

During his time in the Navy, he was stationed at Camp Lejeune in North Carolina for four years, where he was a hospital corpsman. He met a San Francisco cardiac surgeon, Dr. Robert Ellis, who offered him a position assisting with innovative clinical research at the University of California Medical Center and Veterans Administration Hospital in San Francisco.[185]

Gardner got out of the Navy and took the position, moving to San Francisco, where in a few short years he had been given full responsibility for a laboratory and had co-authored several articles with

---

[183]

Ibid.

[184]

Ibid.

[185]

Chris Gardner, Wikipedia, The Free Encyclopedia, March 6, 2014.

Dr. Ellis that were published in medical journals.

However, in 1977 Gardner married Sherry Dyson, a Virginia native and an educational expert in mathematics. The marriage did not last and Gardner had a son, Christopher Jarrett Medina Gardner, Jr., with a dental student named Jackie Medina. He quit his job and became a medical equipment salesman until he met a stockbroker who introduced him to the world of finance.

He was accepted into a training program at E.F. Hutton and dedicated his time exclusively to training as a stockbroker. He later gained a position in Dean Witter Reynolds' stock brokerage training program.

Eventually Jackie Medina deserted him and left him with his son. He didn't make enough money to support them both and his rooming house did not allow children; so, although gainfully employed, he and his son secretly struggled with homelessness, while he saved money for a rental house.

Gardner stayed with the new found career as a stockbroker and entrepreneur and in 1987, he established the brokerage firm, Gardner Rich & Co., in Chicago, Illinois.

In 2006 he sold his stake in Gardner Rich in a multi-million dollar deal and became chief executive officer and founder of Christopher Gardner International Holdings, with offices in New York, Chicago and San Francisco. His firm has become very successful, and today Gardner is thought to be worth approximately $60 million.[186]

Gardner is also a philanthropist who sponsors many charitable organizations, primarily the Cara Program and the Glide Memorial United Methodist Church in San Francisco, where he and his son received desperately needed shelter.

"He has helped fund a $50 million project in San Francisco that creates low-income housing and opportunities for employment in the area of the city where he was once homeless.

---

[186]

Christopher Gardner Net Worth is $60 Million, Get Net Worth, March 10, 2014.

"Dedicated to the well-being of children through positive paternal involvement, Gardner serves on the board of the National Fatherhood Initiative(NFI). He is also a board member of the *National Education Foundation* and sponsors two annual education awards: the *National Education Association's National Educational Support Personnel Award* and the *American Federation of Teachers' Paraprofessionals and School-Related Personnel Award.*"[187]

Gardner also had the honor of receiving the *25th Annual Humanitarian Award* and the *2006 Friends of Africa Award*, presented by the *Los Angeles Commission on Assaults Against Women* (LACAAW) and by the *Continental Africa Chamber of Commerce*, respectively.

Gardner's personal struggle with establishing himself as a stockbroker while managing fatherhood and homelessness is portrayed in the 2006 motion picture The Pursuit of Happyness, directed by Gabriele Muccino, and starring Will Smith.

According to Box Office Mojo, the movie was very successful. It had a production budget of $55 million and grossed over $307 million worldwide.

David Geffen – (1943 –)

David Geffen was born February 21, 1943 in Brooklyn, New York. He grew up poor in Brooklyn, living in a one-bedroom apartment with his family and sleeping on the couch. Geffen did poorly in high school, attended Santa Monica College, Brooklyn College and the University of Texas at Austin, but didn't finish college. However, his natural gift in spotting and developing musical talent – along with business sense that he learned from his mother - made him a millionaire by the time he was 26.

At 71, he is a renowned art collector and philanthropist and is worth an estimated $4.6 billion - making him one of the richest behind-the-

---

[187]

Chris Gardner, Wikipedia, The Free Encyclopedia, March 6, 2014.

scenes players in showbiz. He is widely regarded as the wealthiest man in the American film industry.

Geffen is considered to be an ambitious, energetic music and movie executive who established a vast Hollywood-based empire, featuring Geffen Records and DreamWorks, which he cofounded with Steven Spielberg and Jeffrey Katzenberg. His interest in DreamWorks will likely ensure he will continue to shape the entertainment landscape well into the 21st Century.[188]

One of his first jobs in Hollywood was in the mailroom at the William Morris Talent Agency, where he was paid $55 a week for sorting letters. A year and a half later he became a junior agent. Soon he was managing the careers of such up-and-coming stars as Laura Nyro, Joni Mitchell, Crosby, Stills, Nash, & Young, and Janis Joplin.

In 1969, at age 26, Geffen made his first million dollars by selling out the music publishing operation that he had started with Nyro. In 1970, he cofounded Asylum Records with Elliot Roberts. He signed up some of the hottest rock and roll acts of the early 1970s, including Linda Ronstadt, Jackson Browne, and the Eagles. In 1971, he sold Asylum Records to Warner Communications, but stayed on as president of Asylum Records.

In 1980, he founded Geffen Records and began signing up new and established talent, such as John Lennon, Elton John, and Donna Summer. Two years later he branched out into the movie business. His film company's initial release was the highly successful *Risky Business*, which starred Tom Cruise. He later expanded his portfolio to include Broadway and off-Broadway theater. He helped bankroll such successful productions as *Dreamgirls, Little Shop of Horrors*, and the hugely profitable *Cats*.[189]

His business enterprises have become hugely successful and he is

---

[188] *David Geffen*, biography, bio.true story, 2014 A+E Networks.

[189] Ibid.

widely influential in the entertainment business and beyond. "He donates much of his annual salary to the David Geffen Foundation, a charitable organization devoted to his favorite causes. These include AIDS research, a crusade he has backed avidly since publicly announcing his homosexuality in the early 1980s. Beyond making financial contributions, Geffen has lobbied Washington tirelessly on behalf of funding AIDS research and gay rights. In 1993, he took out full-page newspaper ads protesting President Clinton's policy on gays in the military. Yet Geffen continues to support Democratic politicians, hosting a 1999 Hollywood bash that raised about $1.5 million for Democratic congressional candidates."

In 2001, the Los Angeles School of Medicine at the University of California, an accredited medical school, was renamed the David Geffen School of Medicine at UCLA in honor of David Geffen, who donated $200 million in unrestricted funds.[190]

In 2006, he donated $1.6 million to the David Geffen Foundation. In December 2012, he established a $100 million scholarship fund for students of the Geffen School of Medicine.

Geffen, who is described as the world's fifth richest billionaire bachelor lives in Malibu, California, near Los Angeles.[191] By almost any definition Geffen must be among the very top of any list of Americans who have beaten the odds against climbing out of poverty to reach the pinnacle of success.

Steven Jobs (1955 – 2011)

Steven Paul "Steve" Jobs was born February 24, 1955 in San Francisco, California. He was an American entrepreneur, marketer, and inventor, who was the co-founder, chairman, and chief executive

---

[190]

David Geffen School of Medicine at UCLA, Wikipedia, The Free Encyclopedia, February 19, 2014

[191]

The World's 10 Richest Billionaire Bachelors, by Susanna Kim, ABC News, December 4, 2013.

officer of Apple Inc. His parents were two unmarried University of Wisconsin graduate students who gave him up for adoption almost immediately after he was born.

His biological father was a Syrian-born student, who later taught at the University of Wisconsin, and his biological mother was a Swiss American Roman Catholic, whose parents objected to her relationship with the Syrian, which is why they gave the baby up for adoption.

Shortly after they placed Jobs up for adoption, they married and had another child Mona Simpson, who became a novelist and who Jobs knew nothing about. He was 27-years-old before he was able to uncover information about his biological parents.[192]

His adoptive parents were Paul and Clara Jobs, who Steve later in life emphatically declared, "were my parents." He stated in his authorized biography that they "were my parents 1,000 percent."

As Steve Jobs was growing up, his adoptive dad showed him how to work on electronics in the family garage, demonstrating to his son how to take apart and rebuild electronics such as radios and televisions. His adoptive mother was an accountant who taught him to read before he was old enough to go to school.

Jobs had always been an intelligent and innovative thinker, and Jobs tested so well in the fourth grade that administrators wanted to skip him ahead to high school, but his parents vetoed that idea.

Not long after Jobs enrolled at Homestead High School in 1979, he was introduced to his future partner, Steve Wozniak. Wozniak was attending the University of Michigan at the time.

In a 2007 interview with *ABC News*, Wozniak spoke about why he and Jobs clicked so well: "We both loved electronics and the way we used to hook up digital chips," Wozniak said. "Very few people, especially back then had any idea what chips were, how they worked and what they could do."

In 1974, Jobs took a position as a video game designer with Atari.

192

Steve Jobs.biography, Facts, Birthday, Life Story, Biography.com.

Several months later he quit Atari and went to India, traveling the continent and experimenting with psychedelic drugs.

In 1976, at age 21, he and Wozniak started Apple Computers. To finance the effort Jobs sold his Volkswagen bus and Wozniak sold his scientific calculator. Together, they built their new company in the Jobs family garage, revolutionizing the computer industry by making their computers smaller, cheaper, intuitive and accessible to everyday consumers.

"Wozniak conceived a series of user-friendly personal computers, and—with Jobs in charge of marketing—Apple initially marketed the computers for $666.66 each, and the Apple I earned the corporation around $774,000. Three years after the release of Apple's second model, the Apple II, the company's sales increased by 700 percent, to $139 million. In 1980, Apple Computer became a publicly traded company, with a market value of $1.2 billion on its very first day of trading."[193]

However, in 1985, Jobs resigned from Apple and spent the next 12 years workinf at NeXT, Inc. and Pixar Animation Studios, both of which became very successful. Pixar Studios produced wildly popular animation films such as *Toy Story, Finding Nemo* and *The Incredibles*. Eventually NeXT faltered and Jobs returned to his post as Apple's chief executive officer.

Taking an annual salary of $1, Jobs revitalized Apple. His ingenious products such as the iMac, iPods, iPhones, iPads, and iTunes caught on big time with consumers. Although Jobs earned only $1 a year as CEO of Apple, he held 5.426 million Apple shares worth $2.1 billion, as well as 138 million shares in Disney (which he received in exchange for Disney's acquisition of Pixar) worth $4.4 billion. Forbes estimated Jobs' net wealth at $8.3 billion in 2010, making him the 42nd-wealthiest American.

However, in 2003, Jobs discovered that he had a neuroendocrine tumor, a rare but operable form of pancreatic cancer.

---

[193]

Ibid.

In 2004, he had a successful surgery to remove the pancreatic tumor. True to form, in subsequent years he disclosed to the public very little about his health. He remained a very private man to the end.

He had fathered a daughter when he was age 23, but denied paternity until his daughter, Lisa, turned age 7. When she was a teenager, she came to live with him. On March 18, 1991, he married Laurene Powell, who he had met at Stanford business school, where she was an MBA student. They lived together in Palo Alto, California, with their three children.

On October 5, 2011, Apple Inc. announced that its co-founder had died, after battling pancreatic cancer for nearly a decade. He was 56 years old.

He is almost certain to be remembered as a technological innovator, a superb marketer, and an excellent corporate manager. He is also sure to be remembered as a pioneer American corporate executive who started his successful climb in his family garage and rose from "rags to riches" during the 20th Century. For many years he was the iconic image of Apple computers.

George W. McManus, Jr. (1921 – 2013)

George W. McManus, Jr. was born on May 13, 1921, in Baltimore, Maryland. He was born into a poor family, but through education, hard work and perseverance he became an extraordinarily wealthy lawyer and philanthropist.

Through the years McManus gave millions of dollars to help schools. He also defended indigent citizens through the Legal Aid Bureau of Maryland. When he died at age 92, of congestive heart failure, he was a multi-millionaire who had already notified local charities that he planned to leave $8.5 million to the Baltimore Community Foundation. Officials expected his bequeath to generate about $400,000 annually for the local charity, an amount that will be distributed by the foundation in McManus' name in perpetuity.[194]

---

[194]

George W. McManus, Jr., by Jacques Kelly, The Baltimore

Education was his escape from poverty. "Catholic schools in Baltimore propelled George W. McManus, Jr., from poverty to success as a lawyer...providing him a solid education," said a Baltimore Sun articled. "And years later, when the legal tables turned and he needed defense witnesses, priests and school officials were there as character witnesses."

"My mother died when I was six, and I never had any money for my tuition," he said in an interview with The Baltimore Sun. Even when he attended Harvard Law School on the GI Bill after World War II, McManus could not afford a suit to wear. Instead, he had a tailor remove the shiny buttons and trim from his Navy uniform. "That was the only clothes I had," McManus said.

McManus said he only earned $50 a week on his first job, but by the late 1970s he was making hundreds of thousands of dollars a year at a practice he started by taking on wills, deeds and estates – "whatever came in the door."

Dubbed by a Legal Aid Bureau colleague "the Godfather of pro bono" because of his indigent defense work, McManus rose to prominence in Baltimore as a lawyer and philanthropist in the 1970s and 1980s, frequently giving to Catholic causes. He claimed Catholic schools in Baltimore propelled him from poverty to success as a lawyer.

Several weeks before his death, McManus, in a wheelchair and in failing health, attended a two-hour board meeting at his company. "He was someone who felt strongly about remembering where he came from and about giving back," said Frank P. Bramble Sr., interim president of the Calvert Hall College High School, which McManus had attended. [195]

Mr. Bramble speculated that the Christian Brothers, the founders of Calvert Hall, and other religious orders had given Mr. McManus free or minimal tuition as a student in the 1930s.

After Calvert Hall, McManus attended Loyola University, where he

---

Sun, November 4, 2013.

195

    Ibid.

attracted the attention of its president, the Jesuit priest Edward Bunn. McManus later credited Father Bunn's intervention with Harvard University admissions officials for helping him gain entrance. McManus graduated from Harvard Law School after his military service in World War II.

Herbert "Garten, a Baltimore attorney, said McManus was a magnet who attracted people and clients. "He could draft a will or work in very complex litigation."

McManus was clearly someone who epitomized the concept of "lifting yourself up by the bootstraps." He overcame huge odds against success, rising from near poverty to extreme wealth, garnering respect and praise from peers and indigent citizens alike. He was simply an American who beat the odds, and felt a personal obligation to share his wealth with other people and organizations.

Oprah Winfrey (1954 –)

Oprah Gail Winfrey was born in Kosciusko, Mississippi on January 29, 1954. She is an American media proprietor, talk show host, actress, producer, and philanthropist. She is best known for her multi-award-winning talk show *The Oprah Winfrey Show* that was the highest-rated program of its kind in history and was nationally syndicated from 1986 to 2011.

Dubbed the "Queen of All Media", she has been ranked the richest black African-American of the 20th century, the greatest black philanthropist in American history, and is currently North America's only black billionaire. Some people believe she is currently the most influential woman in the world. In 2013, she was awarded the Presidential Medal of Freedom by President Barack Obama and an honorary doctorate degree from Harvard.[196]

What some people may not know is that Winfrey was the daughter of an unwed teenage mother from rural Mississippi, and that she

---

[196]

The Oprah Winfrey Show, Wikipedia, The Free Encyclopedia, March 12, 2014

conquered poverty, sexual abuse and her own teenage pregnancy to become one of the biggest American media moguls of all time.

"After a troubled adolescence in a small farming community, where she was sexually abused by a number of male relatives and friends of her mother, Vernita, she moved to Nashville to live with her father, Vernon, a barber and businessman.[197]

She won a scholarship to Tennessee State University and would go on to work as a television news anchor in Baltimore and Nashville. In 1976, she moved to Baltimore, Maryland, where she hosted the TV chat show *People Are Talking*. The show became a hit and Winfrey stayed with it for eight years, after which she was recruited by a Chicago TV station to host her own morning show, A.M. Chicago. Her biggest competitor in the time slot was Phil Donahue, who she beat with 100,000 more viewers than he had. Within a few months, Winfrey had transformed A.M. Chicago from one of the city's lowest rated shows to the highest.

Her success led to nationwide fame and a role in Steven Spielberg's 1985 film The Color Purple, for which she was nominated for an Academy Award for Best Supporting Actress.

Her television popularity increased through syndication, making her show a welcome addition in millions of American households. Her sustained high ratings and ability to launch other people and products into guaranteed success stories by merely mentioning their name led some to call her the most influential woman in the world. Her empire goes beyond television and includes publishing producing, and creating a new television network, OWN.[198]

When Winfrey started *Oprah's Book Club* in 1996, it was an instant success and became one of the most influential forces in publishing. When she mentioned a book club selection on her show, the book's

____

[197]

5 Super-Rich Americans Who Started Out Super-Poor, by Brian Reed, Investing Answers, October 21, 2011.

[198]

Ibid.

sales often reached into the millions and pushed the book to the top of best selling lists.

Winfrey is also very active as a philanthropist. According to Forbes magazine, Oprah was the richest black African American of the 20th century and the world's only black billionaire for three years running. *Life* magazine hailed her as the most influential woman of her generation. In 2005, Business Week named her the greatest black philanthropist in American history. Oprah's Angel Network has raised more than $51,000,000 for charitable programs, including girls' education in South Africa and relief to the victims of Hurricane Katrina.[199]

In 2002, Winfrey was named the first recipient of the Academy of Television Arts & Sciences' Bob Hope Humanitarian Award, and in 2003 she became the first black female billionaire in the United States.

The Oprah Winfrey Show ended on September 9, 2011, but Winfrey has remained in the rapidly shifting and converging media field through The Oprah Winfrey Network (OWN), which launched on January 1, 2011.

In November 2013, Winfrey received the nation's highest civilian honor, the Presidential Medal of Freedom. President Barack Obama gave her this award for her contributions to her country.

Oprah Winfrey is truly a sterling example of someone who overcame herculean odds to move from poverty to wealth. She may be the best example in modern times of someone who escaped her draconian and dehumanizing environment to reach the pinnacle of success, accompanied by great wealth. She is truly a sterling example of someone who achieved the American dream of rising from poverty to extreme affluence.

---

[199]

Oprah Winfrey. Biography, bio. true story, 2014 A+E Networks.

Chapter 8

ORGAN DONORS AND RECIPIENTS

An organ donation represents one of the most selfless and considerate acts of human empathy imaginable. To offer someone else, in all likelihood someone else you don't even know, a chance at life that would otherwise not be possible, is the ultimate in compassion for another human being.

People of all ages, from newborns to senior citizens have been organ donors. There is no age limit. In fact, people in their 90s have even been donors. The important thing about a donor is not age, but the health of the donor. Certain diseases, such as HIV/AIDS, can make a person ineligible as an organ donor, but those cases are very rare.

By deciding to be a donor, you give the gift of hope. and sometimes the gift of life, to individuals awaiting an organ transplant. According to the U.S. Department of Health and Human Services, 14,631 organ donors provided 28,464 organs in the U.S. in 2009. As impressive as those figures are, they are far fewer organ donations than are needed. As of April 2010, there were 106,759 people in the U.S. on waiting lists for organ transplants.

The U.S. Government Information on Organ and Tissue Donation and Transplantation, from the Department of Health & Human Services, says that while an average of 79 people receive organ transplants every day, an average of 18 people die each day waiting for an organ transplant that isn't available because of the shortage of donated organs.

In 2012, 28,052 people received organ transplants. Many people would probably assume that all of those organ transplants came from donors who were deceased. They would be wrong. Nearly 6,000 of them came from living donors.

In 2012, 62% of living donors were women and 38% were men. The statistics are nearly reversed for deceased donation: 40% were women and 60% were men.

In 2012, 66% of all deceased donors were Caucasian, 17% were Black African/American, 13% Hispanic/Latino and 3% Asian, Native Hawaiian and other Pacific Islander.

As of May 2013, the national waiting list was made up of 44% Caucasian, 30% Black African/American, 18% Hispanic/Latino, and 7% Asian, Native Hawaiian and other Pacific Islander.

As of May 4, 2009, the percentage of recipients who were still living, five years after their transplant is noted below for kidney, heart, liver, and lung:

Kidney: 69.3%
Heart: 74.9%
Liver: 73.8 %
Lung: 54.4%

In 2010, (the most recent data) almost 2.5 million people died in the United States. Imagine the lives that might have been saved if every one of those persons had donated their organs for transplant.

Keep in mind that every number in these statistics represents an individual person. Each number represents a life: a mom, a dad, a brother, a sister, or a child, someone who is loved and cherished by someone else.

Unfortunately, the number of candidates waiting for an organ donation dwarfs the number of donor organs available. Right now there are more than enough people waiting for an organ donation to fill a large football stadium twice over. Donors are desperately needed.

As of October 2013, there were over 120,000 men, women and children awaiting organ transplants in the United States. Of these, 96,645 await kidney transplants. Each of us has two kidneys and it is possible to live with just one. My mother lost a kidney to disease when she was very young, but she lived to age 92 on one kidney. It is not unusual for a living donor to sacrifice one kidney to save the life of another.

More than one million tissue transplants are done each year and the surgical need for tissue has been steadily increasing. In 2012 more than 46,000 corneas were transplanted.

There are currently more than 100 million Americans signed up to be an organ donor. If everyone who reads this book signs up, the list could be even more impressive and the gap could be closed considerably.

Despite continuing efforts at public education, misconceptions and inaccuracies about donation persist. Here are some important facts to help you better understand organ, eye and tissue donation:

Fact: Anyone can be a potential donor regardless of age or race.

Fact: All major religions in the United States support organ, eye and tissue donation and see it as the final act of love and generosity toward others.

Fact: If you are sick or injured and admitted to the hospital, the number one priority is to save your life. Organ, eye and tissue donation can only be considered after you are deceased.

Fact: When you are on the waiting list for an organ, what really counts is the severity of your illness, time spent waiting, blood type, and other important medical information, not your financial or celebrity status.

Fact: An open casket funeral is possible for organ, eye and tissue donors. Through the entire donation process the body is treated with care, respect and dignity.

Fact: While some countries allow for the sale of organs, and there is a "black market" for organ sales in a few others, the National Organ Transplant Act of 1984 made it illegal to sell organs in the United States.

Fact: There is no cost to the donor or their family for organ or tissue donation.

Signing up to be an organ donor is one of the most generous, compassionate and empathetic things you can do — especially when you consider that a single donor can potentially save *eight* lives. Eight people will not have to spend agonizing months or years on the transplant waiting list. Eight people who will get a second chance, because you made the selfless decision to be a donor.

What follows are incredible examples of organ donations that saved the lives of recipients. Some of them are quite well known celebrities; however, except perhaps for Dick Cheney, it is unlikely that most Americans have ever heard of their organ transplants. For some unknown reason, organ transplant recipients don't seem to generate a lot of publicity.

In come cases, it may be because they don't want the publicity, which is unfortunate because more people need to know about the need for donors, and the only way they are likely to hear about that need is if we promote successful transplant stories to inspire other potential donors.

Hopefully, one day the number of donors will match the number of potential recipients on waiting lists for organs. Please join the growing number of people who are committed to giving the gift of life.

The National Network of Organ Donors is committed to preventing the needless deaths of people who need transplants, by establishing a system that guarantees that a person's expressed wishes to donate organs will be honored without exception, and by educating the country about the vital importance of organ donation to save lives

Representatives of The National Network of Organ Donors will be happy to provide you with information about their program. You can reach them by telephone at (866) 755-9798 or by E-mail at: info@tnnod.org.

Cheynne Arnold and Harrison Black – Heart Transplant Recipients

The story of Cheynne Arnold and Harrison Black, both of St. Louis, Missouri, is unusual because theirs was a double blessing. They are granddaughter and grandfather and received heart transplants within three years of each other.

At only four months old, Cheyenne developed cardiomyopathy from an unknown source. Medicines helped stabilize her for a period; but, in February 1999, her parents were told that she was slowly dying from heart failure. She was hospitalized until the following April, when a suitable heart became available for transplant.

"Ironically, during the same time that Cheyenne was diagnosed with cardiomyopathy, physicians had also informed her grandfather, Harrison

Charles Black, that he had developed cardiomyopathy.

It was as if lightening had struck twice. Doctors thought a viral infection might be responsible. But, whatever the cause, the previously healthy grandfather suddenly needed a heart transplant.

With a family history of deaths from this disease, Mr. Black, at age 58, began to "get his business in order" in preparation for his death. Married for thirty-eight years, and with five children, Mr. Black began to pay off all of his debt so that his family would not be left with that burden."[200]

Transplantation was not unfamiliar to Black, since his granddaughter had gone through this same procedure just three years earlier. He was willing to try it stating, "If Cheyenne made it through it, surely I can make it through it."

So, he was placed on the heart transplant waiting list. Black had always been active, healthy and strong. He lifted weights for years. He regularly babysat for his 11 grandchildren.

Riding Harley-Davidson motorcycles had been a lifelong passion. But heart failure robbed him of energy. As he waited for a new heart, he relied on the Washington University heart failure program at Barnes–Jewish Hospital to help him make it to transplant.[201]

Six weeks later, a suitable heart became available and on September 20, 2002, Black received a heart transplant and fully recovered. In December 2005, Harrison and Cheyenne, then a healthy, bubbly nine-year-old, helped Barnes–Jewish Hospital celebrate the 20th anniversary of its heart transplant program by lighting candles to honor the organ donors and transplant staff who gave them a second chance at life.

Black credits his granddaughter's strength and courage with helping him survive. "She is my heart," he said.

---

[200]

Memories & Miracles, A Double Blessing, Cheyenne Noel Arnold, Mid-"America Transplant Services, October 4, 2011.

[201]

Harrison Black Heart Transplant Patient, Transplant Center, Barnes Jewish Hospital,

The Black family wants everyone to know that "…transplantation works! We are most grateful to the families who chose organ donation as an option during the loss of their loved ones. Two lives in our family were saved as a result of decisions made during difficult times in their lives. Our prayers are with them."

May Chen – Tissue Transplant

May Chen, from Harlingen, Texas, is world–class martial arts competitor and teacher, who relies on her physical skills and mobility to compete in her sport.

As she neared age 60, her knees began to swell after workouts. She tried physical therapy and steroid injections with very little lasting relief from the effects of the swollen knees. Her doctor suggested an allograft transplant.

A meniscal allograft transplantation is a type of surgery in which a meniscus -- a cartilage ring in the knee -- is placed into the knee. The new meniscus is taken from a person who has died (cadaver) and donated his or her tissue. Other surgeries, such as ligament or cartilage repairs, may be done at the time of the meniscus transplant or with a separate surgery.

General anesthesia is generally administered before the surgery, which means the patient is asleep and unable to feel pain. Sometimes, patients are given regional anesthesia instead and medicine to make them feel very sleepy during the operation. The affected area will then be numbed so the patient does not feel any pain.

The meniscus transplant is usually performed using knee arthroscopy, after which an incision is made in the front of the knee to insert the new meniscus. Screws or other devices may be used to hold the meniscus in place. [202]

This procedure is only done in cases of meniscus tears that are so severe that all or nearly all of the meniscus cartilage is torn or has to be

---

[202]

Meniscal allograft transplantation, MedlinePlus, U.S. National Library of Medicine, April 16, 2013.

removed. The new meniscus can help with knee pain and possibly prevent future arthritis.

"Meniscus allograft transplantation is technically a difficult surgery, because it must be placed accurately and secured to the tibial plateau. The recovery can be very difficult as well. But for persons who are missing the meniscus and have pain, it can be very successful."

Recovery can take four to six months generally, but can take as much as a year to fully return to activities and sports.

At first, Chen felt strange about donated tissue, but decided it would be her best chance of resuming a normal life. She had the surgery as soon as tissue became available and made a remarkable recovery. "My knee is almost 100% where it was before," explains May. "It does not limit me in competition."

Only one year after her surgery, Chen won two world championship medals in China. When she returned home, she sent her medals to Allosource, the tissue recovery agency, and requested that they be sent to her tissue donor's family. Chen recognizes that without their kindness, she would have never been able to compete again.

She has since continued to win tournaments, and views her new knee as a gift. Her story is courtesy of the California Transplant Donor Network, Oakland, California.

Richard Bruce "Dick" Cheney – Heart Transplant Recipient

Perhaps the most famous heart transplant recipient in recent years was Richard Bruce "Dick" Cheney, an American Republican politician and businessman who served as the 46th Vice President of the United States, under President George W. Bush from 2001 to 2009.

Previously, he had been the youngest White House Chief of Staff in history, after gaining the position in the Gerald R. Ford administration. Cheney served four Republican presidents and spent six terms in the U.S. House of Representatives. He specialized in national defense, energy and the Middle East.

Cheney was born on January 30, 1941 in Lincoln, Nebraska and was raised primarily in Sumner, Nebraska and Casper, Wyoming. He enrolled at the University of Wyoming, where he received a Bachelor of Arts degree in political science in 1965 and a Master of Arts degree in political science in 1966.

Over the span of his 73 years, he survived five heart attacks, was the recipient of several angioplasties and stent procedures, had a quadruple bypass surgery, had a cardioverter defibrillator implanted in his chest, and then in 2010 he had a left ventricular assist device commonly known as an LVAD installed. Finally, in 2012 he received a heart transplant.

Two years after his transplant, Cheney and his cardiologist, Jonathan Reiner, MD, wrote a book about his history of heart ailments, *Heart: An American Medical Odyssey.*

It appears that over the years Cheney has taken advantage of every new technology, innovation and development in the field of heart medicine. A heart transplant was the last and only option left to him.

When interviewed by Paul Costello for a February 25, 2014 cardiovascular medicine, podcast, Cheney commented on his "spiritual" experience:

"It's the gift of life itself… After you've been through all of the procedures and so forth and then anticipating death and finding your life has been extended that it's miraculous… You have a sense that after you've been through all of that, everything else is small. You don't sweat the small stuff… A friend of mine asked me when I told him it was a spiritual experience: "Does that mean now, that you're a Democrat?" I told him, "Well, not that spiritual."

Cheney's long history of cardiovascular disease and periodic need for urgent health care raised questions of whether he was medically fit to serve in public office. Having smoked approximately 3 packs of cigarettes per day for nearly 20 years, Cheney sustained the first of five heart attacks in 1978, at age 37. Subsequent attacks in 1984, 1988, 2000, and 2010 resulted in moderate contractile dysfunction of his left ventricle.

He underwent four-vessel coronary artery bypass grafting in 1988, coronary artery stenting in November 2000, urgent coronary balloon angioplasty in March 2001, and the implantation of an implantable cardioverter-defibrillator in June, 2001.[203]

On March 24, 2012, Cheney underwent a seven-hour heart transplant procedure at Inova Fairfax Hospital in Falls Church, Virginia, at the age of 71. He had been on a waiting list for more than 20 months before receiving the heart from an anonymous donor.

Cheney's principal cardiologist, Dr. Jonathan Reiner, advised his patient that "it would not be unreasonable for an otherwise healthy 71-year-old man to expect to live another 10 years" with a transplant, saying in a family-authorized interview that he considered Cheney to be otherwise healthy.[204]

From his first heart attack at age 37 to a full transplant in 2012, Cheney says he is proud to have lived an active life, despite battling heart disease. None of his heart attacks seemed to have slowed down his work or the pace of public speaking and writing. Even in retirement, he stays active writing, speaking to live audiences and engaging in television interviews.

Cheney is the quintessential example of a grateful organ recipient, whose life has been extended beyond what it might have been without the benefit of a donor.

Kenneth Joseph "Ken" Howard, Jr. – Kidney Transplant Recipient

Ken Howard is an American actor who was born on March 28, 1944 in El Centro, California, but grew up in the Long Island, New York community of Manhasset. At 6'6" tall he had basketball in his blood. In 1961 he was given the nickname "The White Shadow" by the Long Island press because he was the only white starter on the Manhasset High School varsity basketball team. He was also called

---

[203] *Dick Cheney*, Wikipedia, The Free Encyclopedia, March 24, 2014.

[204] Ibid.

"Stork" and "The Big K."

Howard turned down several basketball scholarships in favor of a more focused academic education. He graduated from Amherst College, which is consistently ranked one of the top liberal arts colleges in the United States. He also attended the Yale School of Drama, but left before completing his master's degree to make his Broadway debut in *Promises, Promises* with Jerry Orbach.[205]

In 1970, he won a Tony Award as Best Supporting or Featured Actor (Dramatic) for *Child's Play*. Howard later starred on Broadway as Thomas Jefferson in *1776* and reprised the role in the 1972 film of the same name. Other Broadway appearances included the *Seesaw* in 1973 and *The Norman Conquests*. He also portrayed several US presidents in the 1975 Broadway musical *1600 Pennsylvania Avenue* and in 1976, appeared as Warren G. Harding in *Camping with Henry and Tom* in 1995.

Howard is probably best known for his role as a basketball coach and former Chicago Bulls player Ken Reeves in the television show *The White Shadow*. The hit show was the first ensemble drama on prime-time television with a predominantly black African–American cast, and ran on the CBS network from November 27, 1978 to March 16, 1981.

The show's title came from a comment by Morris Thorpe, a black student played by Kevin Hooks, in response to a statement by Reeves in the final scene of the pilot episode. Reeves told the members of the team that he would support them and be right behind them, every step of the way, to which Thorpe replied, "Yeah. Like a white shadow." It is ironic that *The White Shadow* was Howard's nickname in high school.

In 2011, ESPN Classic began re-airing all 54 episodes of the *White Shadow*. Howard went on to have an illustrious acting career on Broadway, in television and the movies, and his voice can be head on more than 30 best-selling books on tape.

In July 2000, Howard's kidneys were failing as the result of a

---

[205]

Ken Howard, Wikipedia, The Free Encyclopedia, March 11, 2014.

misdiagnosed urinary blockage, and he was in urgent need of a kidney transplant. His wife, Linda, had already been rejected as a possible donor, and Howard was facing biweekly dialysis treatments while waiting for a donor kidney. "I felt like I was running out of time," he said.[206]

There was a blockage in his urethra that was causing toxins to build up in his blood system, effectively poisoning him. The level of infection was so high that both his kidneys had been damaged. He could have died.

That's when Jeannie Epper happened to call the Howards' L.A. home. Epper, a professional stuntwoman, was a longtime friend of Howards. "Linda had just found out she couldn't be a donor and she was quite hysterical," recalls Epper. "I didn't think twice about it. I said, 'Well, I'll do it.' It just came out." [207] She later said she had done a lot of praying about it and knew God wanted her to do it.

Seven weeks later, both she and Howard checked into UCLA Medical Center, and on July 26th her right kidney was transplanted into his abdomen.

After the successful transplant, Howard was appointed Chancellor of the National Kidney Foundation. He works diligently with the foundation to promote and encourage people to donate their organs.

He is also a member of the Board of Directors of the Los Angeles Alzheimer's Committee and, along with his wife, retired stunt-woman Linda Fetters Howard, serves as a Board member of Shambala Animal Preserve.

On Sepember 24, 2009, Howard was elected National President of the Screen Actors' Guild for a two-year term. He has been a working member of the Screen Actors Guild for more than 40 years.

Howard and his wife live in Los Angeles, California. No one can

---

206

A Friend in Deed, by Julie K.L.Dam, People, October 2, 2000.

207

Ibid.

doubt Howard's gratitude for the organ donation; however, when asked about her donation she is reported to have said, "Maybe giving this kidney is the greatest stunt I've ever done."

Luke Maeding – Double–lung Transplant Recipient

Heather Maeding and her seriously ill 9–year–old son, Luke, had just made the six-hour drive from Children's Hospital of Pittsburgh of UPMC back to Nazareth, Pa., home when she received a phone call from the hospital transplant coordinator that would require their immediate return to the hospital. Luke needed a double–lung transplant.

Luke's life had been difficult from the very beginning. He was born at 26 weeks gestation and spent three months in the neonatal intensive care unit of St. Luke's Hospital in Bethlehem, Pennsylvania, before going home on oxygen with the Maedings as a foster child. They later adopted Luke.[208]

Because he had been born prematurely, his lungs had failed to mature and he had abnormalities of formation of or damage to his lungs that would plague him throughout his young childhood development.

Over the years doctors tried many treatments, but his lungs did not keep up with his growth. He became wheelchair-bound and was in constant need of oxygen support. His mother said: "Even though he was alive, he wasn't really living and he could only watch his brothers and sisters play."

Eventually it became clear that Luke would need a double–lung transplant to have any chance of a reasonably normal life. After the six-hour procedure to remove his diseased lungs and implant donor lungs, Luke spent seven weeks recovering.

Successful transplantation will not end Luke's need for heavy medication and regular visits to the Children's Hospital. He will need to continue taking medication to stave off rejection and will need biopsies and close surveillance of his lung function. He will also need to

---

208

A Double–lung Transplant Gave Luke His Life, Children's Hospital of Pittsburgh of UPMC, 2014.

condition his body after so many years of inactivity. But his prognosis is good.

"Today, Luke walks around his neighborhood, weather permitting, and works out on a treadmill when it doesn't. He hikes with his family, has resumed his baseball career, and can play hide-and-seek with his brothers and sisters without leaving a trail of oxygen tubing behind. "Luke is an amazing patient. He's a strong boy," says his doctor.

"Luke is adjusting to living the active life of a child. In fact, less than two months after his transplant, he was playing baseball with his Miracle League of the Lehigh Valley team, the Pirates. "He made it to his last game and he ran to first base," says his mother. "He was so happy."[209]

Luke's story is only possible because another human being was compassionate and empathetic enough to become an organ donor.

James Thrston "Jim" Nabors – Liver Transplant Recipient

"Jim" Nabors was born on June 12, 1930 in Sylacauga, Alabama. A graduate of the University of Alabama, where he earned a degree in business administration, Nabors moved to southern California because of his asthma.

While working at a Santa Monica nightclub, The Horn, he was discovered by Andy Griffith and later joined The Andy Griffith Show, playing Gomer Pyle. The character proved popular, and Nabors was given his own spin-off show, Gomer Pyle, U.S.M.C.

Though best known for his portrayal of Gomer Pyle, Nabors became a popular guest on variety shows in the 1960s and 1970s (including two specials of his own in 1969 and 1974), which showcased his rich baritone voice. He subsequently recorded numerous albums and singles, most of them containing romantic ballads.[210]

On TV, Nabors became a frequent singing/comedy guest performer on all the top prime-time variety and late night shows, including "Sonny

---

[209]

Ibid.

[210]

Jim Nabors Biography, IMDb, 2014.

& Cher," "The Tonight Show," "The Dean Martin Show," "The David Frost Show" and "The Joey Bishop Show." He also became the annual "good luck charm" opening season guest on close friend Carol Burnett's TV variety series during her twelve-year run.

It was enough for CBS to entrust Nabors with his own TV variety series The Jim Nabors Hour (1969), which ran for two seasons, featured his "Gomer Pyle" co-stars Frank Sutton and Ronnie Schell, and earned him a Golden Globe nomination.

In the late 1970s, Nabors made Hawaii his permanent home. For a time, he even stepped away from the stage, television and entertainment industry completely and concentrated his time on managing his 500-acre Maui ranch and his more than 20,000 macadamia trees.

A decade later he returned to the format hosting The Jim Nabors Show (1978), which was short-lived but earned him a daytime Emmy nomination. Nabors was seen on a limited basis in the early 1990s and his life took a serious hit in 1994 when, after years of ill health, he was forced to have a liver transplant.

"The realization was as grim and alien as the emaciated face that stared back at him in his bathroom mirror. 'It was like a bad B movie,' he says, "where you're looking at your reflection and your eyes have become sunken, your face is gray, and your skin is just hanging off your bones.

"My legs and arms began to swell, and my stomach blew up so big I looked like I was pregnant." His doctor ordered him to fly at once to the renowned Mayo Clinic in Rochester, Minn. "That's when I knew I was in deep trouble," he says.[211]

Nabors told Carol Burnett, a close friend who sprang into action, searching for a top liver specialist and finding Dr. Gary Gitnick of the UCLA School of Medicine in Los Angeles, who submitted Nabors' name to a list of transplant hopefuls.

But Nabors' destiny was largely in the hands of a computer

---

[211]

Preserving Mr. Pyle, by Tim Allis, People magazine, April 25, 1994.

programmed to match transplant patients with suitable donor organs. "Everybody thinks you move to the head of the line because you're famous," Nabors says. "But the computer doesn't know what [Gomer's] 'Well, gaahhly!' is." Adds Gitnick: "There's no weight given to a person's position or philanthropic background. A person cannot force himself onto the list." And even a place high on the list is no guarantee that a matching organ will become available in time. Nabors' call came at 9 p.m. on Sunday, Feb. 6, 1994.[212]

Near death, Nabors underwent transplant surgery to replace a liver being destroyed by hepatitis B. Nabors, at age 61, was listed in critical but stable condition after a seven-hour operation at the University of California, Los Angeles Medical Center.

He remained hospitalized for a month, after which he recovered and basically retired to his Hawaii residence. Nabors said he contracted hepatitis B in the early 1990s after cutting himself shaving while traveling in India.

Nabors is not altogether out of the woods. Hepatitis B will remain in his system and could at some point infect his new liver. To keep that from happening, he receives large doses of gamma-globulin serum, as well as drugs to ward off rejection, which he will have to take for the rest of his life.

At 84 he says he feels good, is positive about his future and he is very grateful for this extension to his life that has been granted by an organ donor.

Mandy Patinkin – Corneal Transplant Recipient

Millions of Americans know Mandy Patinkin from his Emmy-winning role as Dr. Jeffrey Geiger on the hit television show, *Chicago Hope*, or his more recent role on the hit television show *Homeland*, or for his all time favorite role of "Inigo Montoya" from the popular 1987 movie, *The Princess Bride*. What his fans probably do not know is that Patinkin almost lost his sight during the 1990s.

Patinkin had two corneal transplants between 1997 and 1998, which

---

212

    Ibid.

he says "…not only saved my sight, they gave me an entire new perspective on the enormous generosity of those who understand the value of giving."[213]

Patinkin, known as much for his singing as for his multi-talented acting performances, was on the way to New York's La Guardia Airport in 1982 to meet his mother when, "suddenly, for the first time, I realized I couldn't read the exit signs.

"Patinkin immediately consulted an eye professional and was given prescriptive lenses. 'The very next day I was disconcerted to find they no longer worked. I was given a different pair, but within days they didn't help either.'

"Patinkin and his doctors quickly discovered that he was suffering from Keratoconus (KC), an eye disease that over time creates a malformed or "cone-shaped" cornea."

Following a doctor's advice, he wore hard contacts for 15 years and had his eyes checked every six months to treat the condition. But his eyes worsened. In 1997 he got a speck of dust under his contact and couldn't open his eye for 20 minutes. He realized he was in trouble.

He needed an immediate corneal transplant and was placed on an emergency donor list. Shortly thereafter, he received a cornea from the family of a deceased 13-year-old boy. By the next morning he could see better than he had been able to see for the previous 15 years. Then, a year and a half later, he needed a transplant on his left eye. That time the donor was a 14-year old-girl.

"There is no way to begin to describe the kindness of families who, in the midst of their own tragedies, find a way to help others," says Patinkin. "I pray for these children and their families every day — and through their example, I want to share the miraculous impact we can all have on others' lives."[214]

213

Mandy Patinkin saves sight with corneal transplants, by W. Reed Moran, Spotlight Health, USA Today, March 6, 2001.

214

According to the Eye Bank Association of America, corneal transplants are the most successful of all tissue transplants. More than 46,000 sight-restoring transplants are performed every year in the United States. Over 700,000 of them have been performed since 1960, restoring sight to more than 90% of the patients.

Patinkin is devoted to focusing a spotlight on the importance of continued corneal donations. "We lucky recipients simply depend upon the kindness of strangers," he says. He looks forward to the day when organ donation is presumed under law, unless a person stipulates to the contrary a preference to not donate.

"Until that time, fill out the organ donation form on your driver's license" he says. "Tell your family members of your intentions while you are still young and healthy. It's immeasurably rewarding to be part of a community that can both offer and receive the gift of sight."

Kelly Perkins – Heart Transplant Recipient

Kelly Perkins is an American heart transplant recipient known for climbing mountains to inspire others and promote organ donation.

Perkins has selected peaks of many famous mountains, with both personal and cause related significance, since her heart transplant operation in 1995. A good example is her climb of El Capitan in Yosemite National Park, with its natural heart shaped cut-out, where she was recently quoted as saying, "We thought, how great would that be to climb straight through the heart of El Capitan... in a symbolic way we are tugging on the heart strings of people to be educated about organ donation".[215]

At age 53 Perkins is an inspiration to many Americans, especially folks who are active outdoors, particularly climbers. College sweethearts Kelly and Craig Perkins share a longtime love for the outdoors. They

---

Ibid.

[215]

Kelly Perkins, Wikipedia, The Free Encyclopedia, January 10, 2014.

consider themselves to be a team, which is why Craig feels Kelly's illness and subsequent transplant happened to both of them.

According to her biography, Perkins was going about the business of creating a good life with her husband in Southern California, when their happy life came to an abrupt stop. Kelly found herself in the hospital with virally induced idiopathic cardiomyopathy and, after an intense life or death struggle over a period of three years, her heart lost its battle with congestive heart failure.

It got so bad, Perkins couldn't even walk up the stairs of her own house and was in danger of dying.

"In November of 1995, while at UCLA Medical Center, she was the fortunate recipient of donor blood and a donor heart. This was huge, life changing! She said goodbye to any kind of normal life. Life was redirected; she found her purpose intention, and ultimately...a story!

"Since her transplant, she has gained international recognition for her remarkable courage and landmark accomplishments in climbing mountains—the first ever with a donor heart. Kelly's accomplishments set her apart from other climbers because physically her heart functions different than her native heart.

Her donor heart is denervated, meaning the brain cannot automatically send messages to hasten the supply of blood to the body during strenuous activity. Therefore, Kelly's heart does not 'know' immediately when to start beating faster to match the exertion of her body and therefore has to rely on adrenaline."[216]

Nevertheless, after receiving a lifesaving heart transplant at the age of 34, Perkins decided to keep doing what she loved most—mountain climbing! Against incredible odds, she became the first heart transplant survivor to climb some of the world's tallest peaks, including Mount Fuji, the Matterhorn, Mount Kilimanjaro and Mount Whitney.

216

The Climb of my Life, by Kelly Perkins, www.craigandkelly.com, 2014.

"For heart patients, the Kelly Perkins story suggests that people with a donor heart can, in most cases, push their cardiovascular system to the limit," says Timothy Gardner, a transplant surgeon at the University of Pennsylvania–Philadelphia and a spokesman for the American Heart Association.

"If you've got a donor heart, you can do just about anything," he says. "In fact," he says, "he and other cardiologists encourage heart transplant patients to get regular exercise, which improves the heart's ability to pump blood to the rest of the body."[217]

Some of the mountains Perkins has climbed since her heart transplant operation include:

. Half Dome, California, USA, 1996

. Mt. Whitney, California, USA, 1997

. Mount Fuji, Japan, 1998

. Mount Kilimanjaro, Tanzania, 2001'

. Matterhorn, Zermatt, Switzerland, 2003

. El Capitan, California, USA, 2005

. Cajon de Arenales, Argentina, 2007

. Half Dome, California, USA, 2008

. Teton Range, Wyoming, 2009

Kelly's post transplant activities are enough to inspire the most unenthusiastic individuals. The former president of the American Heart Association, Dr. Donald Harrison, said "Perkins' biography is 'a gripping story' that many will enjoy . . . particularly patients, relatives, and friends who are experiencing the ravages of heart disease--giving them hope."

Kelly and Craig are not just passionate about mountain climbing. They are also passionate about spreading the word about organ donation. They encourage people to discuss this issue with family members and become educated about organ transplants. "If you're fully

---

217

Mountain climb is personal peak after transplant, by Kathleen Fackelmann, USA Today, March 12, 2003.

educated on it and you really do look at it in its entirety, then you will feel compelled to be a donor."

Haden Thomas – Liver Transplant Recipient

On January 28, 1997, 38-year-old Lynn Thomas and his 18-month-old son, Haden, made organ transplant history in Pittsburgh, Pennsylvania. Haden received a portion of his father's liver during the area's first living-related pediatric liver transplant.

Thomas' ordeal began when he was only two months old. After many tests, he was diagnosed with biliary atresia, a disease that prevents bile ducts from properly eliminating bile from the liver, causing the organ to malfunction. If untreated, the disease leads to liver failure and eventually death.

According to the Children's Hospital of Pittsburgh, the survival rates for patients who have undergone related living donor liver transplants are approximately 85 percent.

In Thomas' case, the liver transplant was successful and became "a modern day miracle", said his mother, Nanette Thomas.

"Children's Hospital of Pittsburgh of UPMC pioneered pediatric liver transplantation. The hospital's transplant teams have performed more pediatric liver transplants than any other center in the United States and are regarded as experts in the pediatric transplant community because of their experience, the high liver transplant survival rate of their patients, and their years of working with Prograf, the anti-rejection drug therapy.[218]

Two months after surgery, both Haden and Lynn were in good condition. The father's liver had completely regenerated itself and Haden's body accepted his dad's liver section. When asked for his thoughts after the procedure was over and everyone was recovering, the father said, "I can't tell you how good it makes me feel to look at him and know that there is a piece of me inside of him that helped keep him

---

218

Living Donor Liver Transplant for Biliary Atresia, Children's Hospital of Pittsburgh of UPMC, 2014.

alive. I thank God I was able to help."

A living-related pediatric liver transplant involves extracting a section of a relative's liver--normally a parent--and transplanting it into a child. A healthy adult does not need an entire liver for it to function properly, a fact that gives hope to families of children who have end-stage liver disease and anxiously await the bittersweet notification that another child has died and a liver is available. Unfortunately, some families never receive that call, and the child dies while waiting.

The Children's Hospital of Pittsburgh of UPMC has been performing liver transplants for children since Thomas E. Starzl initiated the hospital's pediatric liver transplantation program in 1981. Since then, they have performed more than 1,600 liver transplants, improving the quality of life for countless children whose lives were affected by metabolic diseases, hepatitis and liver disease.[219]

Myra de la Vega – Kidney Transplant Recipient

Dan Coyne of Evanston, Illinois didn't know anything about Myra de la Vega, a Filipina immigrant and single mother of two, except that she was his favorite cashier at the grocery store where he had shopped for over 18 years.

One day he noticed her growing thin and asked about her health. She broke down in tears and explained that her kidneys were failing. She was on daily dialysis. When he heard that she had renal failure, needed dialysis eight hours a night, and was constantly exhausted, he decided to give her one of his kidneys.

De la Vega didn't know if he was serious, but when her sister turned out to be a poor match for a transplant, Coyne insisted on being tested. Some might say, as luck would have it, he was a match. Others might choose to believe God orchestrated the organ donation.

After the test, which proved he was a match, Coyne said, "I came from around the counter where I was hiding, held her hand and told her

---

219

Ibid.

I was a match. De la Vega said she was speechless. "I was hugging him and thanking him." Coyne said, "She just busted out crying with joy. Her knees buckled, and I had to get her off the floor she was so happy."[220]

Whether one chooses to believe it was luck or the hand of God, the operation was a success and, since Coyne was a Chicago Public Schools social worker, the principal of his school, Pershing Magnet School on the near south side of Evanston, declared March 23, 2010 "Dan Coyne Day" and incorporated his organ gift into the teaching curriculum.

Students learned about the kidney donation, while Coyne and de la Vega told their extraordinary story. Coyne, who has been described as "a deeply religious man," said he'd prayed about it, knew it was the right thing to do, and wasn't afraid. On the other hand, de la Vega said: "It still makes me cry. It gives me chills because of his generosity."[221]

Coyne and De la Vega forged a unique friendship; their families shared many meals together, including Thanksgiving. Coyne also helped fix De la Vega's roof, trimmed her trees and drove her daughter to Knox College for her freshman year of school.

De la Vega returned to her job as a cashier at Jewel-Osco two months after the transplant. She said, "the kidney was my early Christmas gift." Meanwhile, when Coyne talks with school children he reminds them that the most important gift can't be bought or even made. "The most precious gift is what your teacher gives you every day. That gift is knowledge."

Both Coyne and De la Vega hope their story will inspire others to help the 84,000 American waiting for kidney donations.

220

Saving Lives in the Checkout Line, by Michael Milberger, ABC News Good Morning America, April 4, 2010.

221

Dan Coyne, Kidney Donor: Giving Kidney to his Favorite Jewel-Osco Cashier, Huffington Post, Chicago, March 28, 2014.

Chapter 9

TOPICS NOT ADEQUATELY COVERED BY THE NEWS MEDIA

When I wrote this first story, the topic seemed so obvious to me, and it garnered a lot of reader responses, mostly supportive, but only one newspaper ran it and the responses were internet responses—not letters to the editor. It was as though people were afraid to address the subject publicly.

Nevertheless, I still think it merits consideration on a national scale, but don't think there is much chance it will be taken seriously by politicians for fear of a negative reaction from parents of school age children among their constituents.

Education costs seem to be spiraling out of control, and no school districts anywhere appear to have enough money to meet their needs, so no approaches may become necessary. My approach may seem unreasonable to some, particularly parents of children in school. However, mine is only a suggestion. There are no doubt other possibilities too, if we think about ways in which money could be spent differently, while still providing a quality education.

Another topic rarely discussed nationally, except when someone in Congress introduces a bill to address it is our national language. Does it make any sense that we have been a nation for 238 years and we don't officially have a national language? Everyone knows English is our national language, but it has never been officially designated as such. Isn't it about time for our Congress to bite the bullet and make English our official national language?

The topic of immigration reform always seems to jump to the top of political discussions around election time; but, over the years, it has never become a settled issue. The national news media covers it whenever it becomes a political hot button, but it never seems to reach the point of a settled issue.

Perhaps that's because we are somewhat of a divided nation when it comes to immigration. Some people believe it's not possible to deport millions of undocumented workers who are here illegally, and think we need to put together a plan that will give them a path to citizenship. Others believe that would serve as a magnet to draw even more illegals across our border. They think we should first find a serious answer to our porous borders. They believe securing our borders should be our first and most important priority, so we don't have to revisit this topic every few years.

A topic of great importance that is not covered very well by the mainstream news media and, frankly, doesn't seem to get the attention it deserves from anyone, is the technically amazing commercial spinoffs from NASA's space programs.

There is an almost endless list of spinoffs that we as a society take for granted, that are a direct result of the research and development associated with our space programs, and some of those are covered in this chapter. But, why don't we hear more about them?

We tend to get excited when we think about astronauts and space travel, especially when we speculate about sending a space vehicle and crew to Mars, but what about all the wonderful discoveries and inventions that will benefit the average American citizen as a result of that research? Why don't we see more media focus on the wonders of things that make everyday living easier or more enjoyable for regular citizens in places like Cairo, Illinois or Paducah, Kentucky? These things deserve more attention nationally than they get.

Each of these topics could fill a book, but space only allows a brief discussion of them. I hope it will be enough to stimulate further discussion at dinner tables around our wonderful country. There are answers to all of our problems if we stay focused and persevere in the face of seemingly insurmountable odds.

America is a Christian Nation

In Turkey on April 6th and again in Egypt on June 4[thf] of 2009

President Barrack Obama said we do not consider ourselves to be a Christian nation, a statement that is demonstrably not true. According to a recent CNN report over 75 percent of Americans call themselves Christian.

That figure has changed rather dramatically over the years. "In 1948, 91% of Americans identified with a Christian faith. Twenty years ago, in 1989, 82% of Americans identified as Christian. Ten years ago, it was 84%. This year, as noted, 78% of all American adults identify with a Christian faith."[222] That means that just over 245 million Americans claim to be Christian in 2014.

Even though that figure is less than it was 20 years ago, we are still the largest Christian population in the world—larger than Brazil, which has the largest Roman Catholic population in the world. Catholics and Protestants make up 86.6 percent of the Brazilian population, which is just over 200 million, which would make their Christian population roughly 173 million. However, the president's speech does reflect an evolving secularization of America that flies in the face of our religious heritage.[223]

For the first two hundred years of our existence, we were universally recognized as a nation founded on Judao/Christian principles, with freedom to practice our religious beliefs unfettered by any kind of government intrusion or restriction.

According to *Florida Today*,[224] a Gannett Company newspaper, there is a movement in Missouri to display "In God We Trust" at local

---

[222]

This Christmas 78% of Americans Identify as Christian, by Frank Newport, Gallup Well-being, December 29, 2009.

[223]

Catholic World Population Center Shifts to South, America, *The National Catholic Review*, March 11, 2013.

[224]

"In God We Trust" movement grows, *Florida Today*, Melbourne, Florida, March 8, 2013.

government sites. "Raised letters spelling out the national motto will be installed in St. Peters Municipal Court, the city's aldermanic meeting room and three other city buildings.

Bakersfield, California councilwoman Jacquie Sullivan has been promoting the idea since 2002. She says she wants to show respect for the nation's heritage."

All fifty states acknowledge God in their state constitutions. It is customary for the president of the United States to place his hand on a Bible while being sworn into office. The United States Congress begins each day with a prayer, and many of our federal buildings, including the U.S. Supreme Court, have engravings that recognize God as our creator. There are bible verses etched in stone all over the federal buildings and monuments in our nation's capitol.

For instance, there is an aluminum cap on top the Washington Monument that says Laus Deo, which is Latin for "Praise Be To God." The Lincoln Memorial includes an inscription that says: "This nation under God shall have a new birth of freedom." The Jefferson Memorial includes an inscription that says: "God who gave us life, gave us liberty."

The U.S. Capitol building declares our Christian heritage throughout. Church services were held there for over fifty years. When the President of the United States delivers his State of the Union address in the House Chamber, he stands before an inscription that reads, "In God We Trust." In the Capitol's Chapel a prayer is inscribed in the window that says, "Preserve me, God, for in Thee do I put my trust."

It is ironic that in 2005 members of the United States Supreme Court declared in a 5-4 ruling in the case of McCreary County v. ACLU, that the Ten Commandments could not be displayed in court buildings or indoors anywhere else on government property, even though an engraving of Moses holding the Ten Commandments is displayed prominently on the front of the Supreme Court building.

"They are more than just symbols, they are history," said Catherine Millard, founder of Christian Heritage Tours, which shows tourists where they can find such government depictions of religion in

Washington.[225]

The court said that Kentucky displays of the Ten Commandments violated the Establishment clause of the First Amendment, which prohibits the government from endorsing or supporting one religion above others. For many, that was an indefensible ruling that has repeatedly been unsuccessfully challenged over the years.

The ruling continues to raise the ire of committed and dedicated Christians who see the ruling as a violation of the intent of the First Amendment to the United States Constitution, which says that "Congress shall make no law respecting an establishment of religion, or prohibiting the free exercise thereof." It does not say Congress may make some laws or occasional laws restricting the freedom of religion. The founders were also careful to say freedom of religion, not freedom from religion.

The Supreme Court ruling essentially established a law that prohibits the display of the Ten Commandments, which violates that part of the First Amendment that clearly states that Congress shall "make no law" prohibiting the free exercise of religion.

The Supreme Court justices need to be reminded that the establishment clause was not intended to protect the government from the citizens, but to protect the citizens from the government. No law, means just that—no law!

While it's true that all religious beliefs are welcomed in the United States, in almost every religious poll of Americans, the overwhelming majority claims to be Christian. A small cadre of atheists and agnostics, supported by court rulings, try desperately to deny our basic religious freedoms.

They haven't succeeded completely, but they have made huge strides toward removing God and prayer from the public square, even though Christmas is still a national holiday.

225

In the Supreme Court itself, Moses and his law on display, by Andrea James, *The Christian Index*, March 3, 2005

It is ironic that as a nation we can celebrate the birth of Jesus Christ, which is the purpose of the national holiday. But, while the government gives employees a paid holiday to celebrate that day, we can't display a crèche, representing His birth on public property.

It is also ironic that there has been no call for elimination of Christmas as a national holiday. Atheists and Agnostics do not plead for the right to go to work on Christmas. They gratefully accept their time off with pay to honor the birth of Jesus Christ, whether or not they share any of the beliefs that are represented by this national holiday.

Contemporary spiritual warfare began in 1963 when Madalyn Murray O'Hair successfully challenged prayer in public schools. Her mysterious death in 1995 ended her attacks on the Christian churches, and her son has become a Christian. However, others have since taken up the mantle of atheistic challenger to all things religious.

Michael Newdow, a California atheist who spent four years in an unsuccessful effort to ban the Pledge of Allegiance from being recited in public schools, has also challenged the national motto printed on U.S. currency.

That motto has been challenged by three federal lawsuits and each time has been found to be constitutional. Still, the motto is under constant challenge from fringe elements of the secular movement in an effort to remove God from our society.

There is yet another challenge to Christian prayers. A 2013 article by Gary DeMar in *Political Outcast* said this time the challenge came from an atheist who does not like to have prayers open a city council meeting.[226]

His claim was that "...people of other faiths or no faith shouldn't have to endure a Christian prayer at a government meeting." DeMar suggested the best approach to such a challenge is to point out that public references to our Lord is only following "... what the Constitution itself acknowledges."

---

[226]

Another Atheist Wants the Constitution Violated, by Gary DeMar, *Political Outcast*, March 7, 2013.

"The Year of our Lord" is part of the Constitution. You can read it just above George Washington's signature. This is an obvious reference to Jesus because of the use of "Lord" and the dating from the supposed time of Jesus' birth which is also part of the Constitution: "one thousand, seven hundred and eighty seven."

Military Stifling of Religious Expression

In our increasingly secularized society, the United States government is attempting to muzzle our military, despite 1st Amendment rights to free speech. There is considerable evidence of this!

Historically, men and women in uniform have been expected to give up some of their basic rights. For instance, the government says they cannot participate in partisan politics while in uniform, because it implies government sanction of whatever party they indorse.

Confusing government pronouncements in 2013 suggested those in uniform can't share their religious beliefs with anyone. A Pentagon policy stated, "...religious proselytization is not permitted within the Department of Defense." Another statement said, "Members are free to express their personal beliefs as long as it does not make others uncomfortable."

Yet, the government does not explain where the line is between proselytization and sharing one's beliefs. Uncomfortable is a very subjective word and in 2013 Tony Perkins' Washington Update said evangelism is not included in the government's definition of proselytization.

How is a service member to know what is permissible and what is not? Perkins said "the concerns stated by Christians in the military are the result of an environment of increasing religious hostility that has been created by restrictive regulations at the behest of activists like Mikey Weinstein.

Weinstein is the founder and president of the Military Religious Freedom Foundation, who is believed to be a Pentagon consultant helping them develop new policies on religious tolerance, including a policy for court-martialing military chaplains who share the Christian Gospel during spiritual counseling of American troops.

In a speech at a National Day of Prayer observance in Washington, DC, Rear Admiral William Lee, a Coast Guard officer, spoke about the growing religious hostility in the military and the restrictive religious liberty regulations. He said: "I want you to know right up front, I am not a chaplain. I wouldn't even describe myself as a religious man. I am nothing more than a sinner in a sailor's suit. But I am a man of deep and abiding faith, who happens to be wearing a uniform."

He went on to explain that men and women who put on a military uniform do not give up their Constitutional right to express their religious beliefs. "They expect us to check our religion at the door." When faced with the need to counsel a young man who had earlier considered committing suicide, Lee said: "the rules said, send him to the chaplain. My heart said, give this young man a bible."

Senior leaders like Admiral Lee are highly vulnerable to political attacks for expressing their faith, for crossing an invisible line that makes them vulnerable to such attacks. Admiral Lee said he is so glad he has crossed that line so many times. "I will not run from my right under the Constitution to tell a young man that there is hope." He further explained that the Bible provides that hope.

He finished by asking the audience to pray for the right of military members to continue expressing their religious beliefs. He said it is not a religious issue; it is an American issue.

Strong secular anti–Christian movement

Each year Christians face increasing secular efforts to deny a basic tenet of our Declaration of Independence: "We hold these truths to be self–evident, that all men are created equal, that *they are endowed by their Creator with certain unalienable rights*, that among these are life, liberty and the pursuit of happiness."

Yet, in the face of overwhelming evidence to the contrary, in Turkey on April 6th and again in Egypt on June 4[thf] of 2009 President Barrack Obama said we do not consider ourselves to be a Christian nation, a statement that is demonstrably not true.

In this author's opinion, he was pandering to Middle–eastern audiences, by telling them what he thought they wanted to hear. Hopefully in future speeches he will change that impression by acknowledging that we have been a Christian nation since 1776.

President Obama could take a lesson from our sixteenth president, Abraham Lincoln. How did he feel about this issue? On April 30, 1863, he issued a proclamation for a national day of fasting, humiliation and prayer, in which he said: "We have been the recipients of the choicest bounties of heaven. We have been preserved, these many years, in peace and prosperity. We have grown in numbers, wealth and power, as no other nation has ever grown. But we have forgotten God.

"We have forgotten the gracious hand which preserved us in peace, and multiplied and enriched and strengthened us; and we have vainly imagined, in the deceitfulness of our hearts, that all these blessings were produced by some superior wisdom and virtue of our own.

"Intoxicated with unbroken success, we have become too self-sufficient to feel the necessity of redeeming and preserving grace, too proud to pray to the God that made us!

"It behooves us, then to humble ourselves before the offended Power, to confess our national sins, and to pray for clemency and forgiveness."

Abraham Lincoln was prescient. His proclamation could have been issued yesterday. As I read newspapers every day, I am mindful that they include stories covering an almost unimaginable range of problems that demand constant attention from our leaders.

We forget too often that we have a benevolent, generous and compassionate God, who has singled out our country for greatness. Oh sure, some folks who don't believe in God will claim we are great because of our own efforts; but, like Abraham Lincoln, I think we are Great because God has blessed our country with so much that is good.

Instead of arrogantly showing contempt for God by puffing out our chests and boasting of our own accomplishments, we need to humble ourselves and regularly thank Him for the blessing that is the United States of America.

That blessing is said so well in America the Beautiful! "America! God shed His Grace on thee and crown thy good with brotherhood from sea to shining sea!"

According to the U.S. Census Bureau and the Pew Forum on Religion and Public Life, Christians make up about seventy-eight percent of the U.S. population. Those with no particular religious affiliation or belief make up sixteen percent of the population. The remaining six percent are represented by a large variety of other religions.

Jesus Christ is the Reason for the Season

Meanwhile there is a growing annual attack on Christmas. Bill O'Reilly, host of The Factor on the Fox News Network, does a yeoman's job of defending our traditional national holiday, but still Christmas is attacked each year.

The annual assault on Christmas begins earlier each year, sometimes even before Halloween. The big debate seems to be whether or not the traditional Christmas tree should be called a Holiday tree and whether or not stores should return to the use of a Merry Christmas greeting instead of Happy Holidays.

In 2012 Rhode Island governor Lincoln D. Chaffee, insisted on calling it a Holiday Tree. Perhaps he will yet rethink his position. Wal-Mart rethought its position on season greetings. According to CNN, after an outpouring of customer criticisms, Wal-Mart abandoned the Happy Holidays greeting and restored its Merry Christmas greeting, as have other retail outlets.[227]

What is surprising is that these attacks on Christmas are in a predominately Christian nation. According to the Central Intelligence Agency there are approximately 2.3 billion Christians in the world. More than 245 million of those Christians live in the United States. That's about 78 percent of our population.[228]

---

[227]

Wal-Mart: We're not afraid to say Merry Christmas, *CNN Fortune & Money,* November 9, 2006.

[228]

Numbers of adherents of major religions, theirgeographical distribution, date founded, andsacred texts, *ReligiousTolerance.org,* Religions of the World, September 28, 2011

We have been celebrating the birth of Jesus Christ since before the founding of our country, and Christmas has been a federal holiday since June 26, 1870. The federal government, many local governments, and commercial companies give their employees a paid holiday to celebrate Christmas, whether or not the employees are Christian.

I can find no statistics anywhere that suggest non-Christians refuse to accept this holiday. They take the day off with pay, even as some of them debunk the celebration.

Equally perplexing, local governments honor the national holiday, but often forbid public display of anything calling attention to the reason for the season. Oddly enough, a government organization can pay its employees to take the day off to celebrate Christmas and then forbid them from doing so on public property.

According to biblestudies.suite101.com, "Saint Francis of Assisi is credited with creating the first Christmas Nativity scene in 1223 to commemorate the birth of Christ at Bethlehem. Since then it has been a familiar sight in Christian homes all over the world."

Yet, increasingly, communities in the U.S. are forbidding the traditional display of a crèche on government owned property. Other countries don't seem to be offended by the crèche and there don't seem to be any limitations on the celebration of other religious observances.

According to the Union for Reformed Judaism, Chanukah, meaning "dedication" in Hebrew, refers to the joyous eight-day celebration during which Jews commemorate their victory of the Maccabees over the armies of Syria in 165 B.C.E. and the subsequent liberation and "rededication" of the Temple in Jerusalem. [229]

While www.holiday.net says Chanukah is not a major holiday in the Jewish calendar,[230] it often coincides with the Christmas season and some Jewish families celebrate both so their children won't feel left out

---

[229]

Hanukkah, Jewish Life in Your Life, *Reformed Judaism.org*, no date provided,

[230]

The Story of Chanukah, *www.holiday.net*, December 20, 2011.

during the national focus on Christmas.

In Islam, Muslims do not celebrate Christmas. Their major religious celebration is Ramadan, which occurs during the ninth month of the Muslim year. It is a month long observance in which Muslims must fast during daylight hours. It is a time of inner reflection and devotion to their God.

Everyone seems to respect the Jewish and Muslim observances, yet many of our citizens disrespect the Christian celebration of the birth of Jesus. Even so, despite these differences, Christmas is a joyous period, universally celebrated around the world. Peace on earth and goodwill towards men is still the operative phrase during this season.

Mel Gibson's Movie Was Unique

Mel Gibson's movie, "The Passion of the Christ opened nationwide at 2,000 movie theaters on February 25, 2004.

It was a powerful depiction of the last twelve hours in the life of Jesus Christ. According to newspaper and magazine accounts, public reactions were nearly unanimous. Except for a few people who thought it was anti-semitic, screening audiences were profoundly moved by it's message of love.

What was most unique, however, was its graphic depiction of the crucifixion. After attending a private showing, Pope John Paul II is reported to have said: "It is what it was."

Audiences witnessed the most brutal account of the crucifixion ever filmed.[231] Crucifixions typically began with a flogging. The Romans used a whip called a flagrum, consisting of small pieces of bone and metal attached to leather strands. During the scourging, the skin was ripped from the back, exposing a bloody mass of tissue and bone. Jesus was also beaten severely and tormented by the Roman soldiers, including the piercing of His scalp with a crown of thorns.

After the flogging, the victim was often forced to carry his own crossbar, or patibulum, to the execution site. The patibulum could

---

[231]

The Crucifixion of Jesus, *Our Catholic Faith*, Ordinary Time, March 5, 2013.

easily weigh 100 pounds.

Once the victim arrived at the execution site, he was nailed to the patibulum using spikes about 7 inches long and 3/8 of an inch in diameter driven into his wrists, not in his hands as is traditionally depicted in photographs. These would hit the area of the median nerve, causing shocks of pain to run up the arms to the shoulders and neck.

A seven-foot post, called a stipes was already standing at the crucifixion site. In the center of the stipes was a crude seat to provide "support" for the victim. The patibulum was then lifted on to the stipes, and the victim's body was awkwardly turned on the seat so his feet could be nailed to the stipes.

This caused tremendous strain on the wrists, arms and shoulders. The placement of the body held the victim's rib cage in a fixed position, which made it difficult to exhale, and impossible to take a full breathe. By that time, Jesus was described as extremely weak and dehydrated, probably also suffering from severe cramps and spasmodic contractions.

Ultimately, Jesus died of suffocation or heart failure. To breathe, he was forced to push up on his feet to inflate his lungs. As the body weakened and pain in the feet and legs became unbearable, he was forced to trade breathing for pain and exhaustion, eventually lapsing into unconsciousness. Because he could no longer lift his body off the stipes and inflate his lungs, he probably suffered from hypoxia and respiratory acidosis, which eventually causes the heart to fail.

Regardless of the actual medical cause of death, the historical record is very clear -- Jesus suffered hours of horrible and sustained torture on the cross of Calvary, to a degree never before shown in a movie.

Mel Gibson had the courage to finance, produce and direct the film, knowing that religious movies do not traditionally do well at the box office. His film was an exception to that rule!

Most Hollywood executives predicted the movie would be a financial disaster; but, it made over $611 million worldwide.[232] Since

---

232

The Passion of the Christ Total Lifetime Grosses, *Box Office Mojo*, February 25, 2004.

Mel Gibson financed it himself, most of that money went into his pocket.

Religious conclusion

While it is true that we have many religious faiths expressed side by side in our country, the United States is and always has been predominately a Christian nation, despite President Obama's public remarks claiming the contrary. Statistically, that is unlikely to change any time soon.

Nevertheless, since Christianity represents three quarters of the population of the United States, is it not logical to expect the national news media to occasionally come to the defense of Christianity when challenged by secularists? It seems like every radical secularist can attract media attention on a moment's notice, without the press corps feeling any need to bring balance and objectivity to the public discussion.

While it may not be appropriate for the news media to take sides, it seems rational to expect it will present both sides whenever it covers a religious event in which secularists try to demean Christians.

You may notice that Muslims don't have such a problem. Could it be that reporters are intimidated by the image of chaos caused by Muslims in Europe whenever Islam is challenged or denigrated?

Whatever the reason, Muslims appear to be treated much differently than Christians by the mainstream news media.

All that is asked here is a sense of fairness by the news media whenever secularists attack Christianity.

America is Still a Land of Opportunity

Not enough is written about the fact that, with all our problems, the United States is still a land of opportunity for Americans and legal immigrants who come to this country, especially for those graduating from high school.

High school graduation is a special day in a student's life--a defining moment that can open a lifetime path to success. Not success in the narrowly defined commercial sense, but the kind that comes from having inner peace; the kind that comes from finding excitement and satisfaction in the pursuit of excellence; the kind that comes from knowing you are doing the very best you can at whatever you choose to do.

The present generation is the beneficiary of incredible technological advances in communications, transportation and medicine--advances that already bring the world into living rooms nightly, make it possible to fly from London to New York in just over two hours and have already extended life expectancy to 79 years for men and 82 for women.

Despite all the violence and terrorism, all the hunger and disease, all the evil and stupidity in the world, there is also beauty and love, rewarding work and personal satisfaction.

For those who want to fly airplanes, design automobiles, be a doctor, lawyer or teacher, or work in any number of highly specialized professions, more education is the key that unlocks those doors. That doesn't mean everyone needs to attend an Ivy League school. An excellent curriculum is available at every state university or community college.

It does mean to succeed one must stay focused. A tragically high percent of college freshmen never graduate--not because they are intellectually deficient, but because they don't stay focused or they let someone else define success for them.

But, college is not for everyone. We also need people to work in the guilds, crafts and trades. We need merchants and shopkeepers, service people and clerks. We need a whole range of specialties that don't require a college education.

Success is not just for the privileged few. It is available to everyone. The real trick is to have the intelligence, the heart, the courage, the discipline and perseverance to succeed, even when there are outrageous odds against success.

Of these, perseverance is probably the most important. Many people who persevere succeed when other more talented and skilled competitors lose heart and quit.

The United States is still the most exciting country in the world, and young people here inherit as a birthright opportunities that are the envy of citizens around the world. As a nationally syndicated talk show hosts says: "There is no trying. There is doing and there is not doing." For those who are really serious in their pursuit of success, there is only doing! And doing is possible for everyone who stays focused and perseveres even in the face of long odds against success.

My advice for high school graduates is simple: don't let negative people turn you away from your shot at success and don't let someone else define success for you. Take heart in the certain knowledge that you are surrounded by opportunities, no matter where you live. Now, go face the challenges with a strong sense of purpose and carve out your own niche in this world.

A Perspective on Poverty

I thought my family was poor, because we wore hand me down clothes, ate catsup and lard sandwiches and often relied on bags of groceries donated by neighbors. Most people who knew us thought we were poor. Today much of the world would laugh at such a conclusion.

Our government defines poor by how much income a family has. For instance, an American family of four, making under $21,000 per year qualifies as poor and is entitled to certain public benefits, such as food stamps, low rent housing, Medicaid, etc.

Yet, the average American homes, even those which qualify for government assistance, have indoor toilets, kitchen sinks, running water, electricity, gas heat, televisions, cell phones, a pantry of food, cigarettes, comfortable clothing, shoes, sometimes cars, and access to grocery stores, welfare and government sponsored health care.

If you contrast our poor with conditions in Pakistan, India, Cambodia, Darfur and the slums of Venezuela, you might find some resentment over cataloging folks as poor when they have so many things to make life easier and so much governmental help.

For instance, in Pakistan 74 percent of its people live on less than $2.00 per day, while 17 percent live on less than $1 per day. Nine percent of their children die before their first birthday. In India 40 percent of the population is illiterate and 350–400 million Indians live below their poverty level. That's more than our entire population. The per capita rate spent per month is 356 Rupees or about $9.

Measured by income and broader human development indicators, Cambodia is among the poorest countries in the world. The per capita income is $256 per year. One Cambodian citizen defined poverty in her country as "…having no land, buffalo, hoe, rake, plow, transport, mosquito net, cooking pots or even plates to eat from and a spoon and fork to pick up the food…"

The tragedy in Darfur and much of Africa has been labeled by the UN as the 'world's worst humanitarian crisis." It is one of the poorest regions of Africa. Citizens daily face the possibility of dying from hunger, lack of safe drinking water and disease. They live in squalor, with outdoor toilets, no indoor water, meager clothes, no shoes, and no modern conveniences.

Yet there are bright spots among the world's misery. On April 13, 2008, 60 Minutes aired a piece showing how a Venezuelan program called "The System" leads children out of their slums by teaching them how to play musical instruments in a symphony orchestra. It was an incredible lesson in a unique communal effort to lead children out of poverty and crime by providing them with a dramatic new focus on their future, even as they live with pain and suffering every day.

The point of this article is not to denigrate poor people in our own country, but to point out that there are literally hundreds of millions of people around the world for whom existence is far more threatening, desperate and more difficult than life is for folks who live under our welfare system. And, while we should not be satisfied with our system, we should be immensely grateful that it is so much better than programs in most third world countries.

This is a topic that could use a significantly greater share of national attention. Politicians often talk about "income inequality," without bothering to define what that term actually means. Since no two individuals are equal in almost any respect, it might be rather difficult to explain the concept of "income inequality" in any literal sense that would be widely applicable to our general population.

Does anyone actually believe that a highly educated, talented and skilled employee who works 50–60 hours per week, should be paid the same as a high school drop out working an unskilled task 40 hours per week? Should a custodian be paid the same as a corporate president?

I suspect "income inequality" has more political relevance than workplace relevance, and I doubt it can ever be defined in a way that would satisfy everyone.

Educational Costs

I've lived in Melbourne, FL for over 20 years and each year I've read about how difficult it is to run the school system on it's existing budget. In 2013 the Brevard County School Board voted to close three public schools. This year they are threatening to cut even more schools if they don't get a one-half cent sales tax increase.

Over the years I've lived in twelve states and everywhere I've lived school boards have pleaded for more money. No matter how big their budget, they never seem to have enough money. My memory might be a bit fuzzy, but I don't recall a constant shout out for more money when I was in high school during the 1950s. Perhaps it's because we pay for so much more now than we paid for then.

Consider this: in the 1940s and 1950s, in my home town, students, were either driven to school by their parents, rode a public bus, rode bicycles, or walked to school. There were no school buses to pick up students and deliver them to the front door of the schools.

Today, the American School Bus Council says "Some 480,000 school buses carry 25 million children — more than half of America's schoolchildren – each day, making the school bus industry the largest form of mass transit in the United States." The council says the United States spends $17.5 billion per year on school bus transportation at an average cost of $692 per student transported. That is a huge amount of money sucked right out of our tax base.

Admittedly, there are enormous benefits from school busing. It is safer, more eco-friendly, more reliable, and cheaper than having every parent drive their children to school; however, it is one of the contributors to the huge costs of running school systems.

Next, is the cost of feeding students. When I was in school, even though we were very poor, I carried a sack lunch with a peanut butter and jelly sandwich and a piece of fruit. Today, the cost of providing breakfast and lunch for students is astronomical.

According to the Journal of Agricultural and Resource Economics, the U.S. Department of Agriculture reimburses schools for meals provided to students participating in the National School Lunch and School Breakfast Programs. In fiscal year 2009, the USDA provided about 42 million lunches and breakfasts, with a national average meal cost of $2.36. Simple arithmetic makes the cost for meals nearly $100 million a year. It is difficult to teach hungry children, but is that really a proper education cost?

Even someone with modest math skills should be able to see that busing students to school and feeding them breakfast and lunch eats up a lot of education money (no pun intended). But I rarely see those items even mentioned in discussions about education.

While there are definite advantages from both programs, there is little direct benefit to childless couples, single adults and senior citizens. Perhaps it's time to reconsider the cost/benefit ratio from these expenditures and consider new approaches.

One approach might be to quit charging education for expenses that are not directly tied to teaching. For instance, the $17.5 billion it costs us every year to bus students to school could be charged to parents directly by instituting a bus fee based on community needs. Each parent should have to pay to have their children bused to school, instead of taxing citizens who do not have children to cover the cost.

It might also make sense to charge welfare programs for the expense of providing reduced cost meals for lower income families. After all, it's quite a stretch of the imagination to consider the cost of breakfast and lunch as an educational expense.

While it's true that hungry students are more difficult to teach, it's also true that providing nutritional meals should be considered a family expense, or at least welfare cost, not a logical educational expense.

The costs associated with these two programs will undoubtedly be the same, but accounting for the costs would be radically different. And reimbursement for the costs would stifle the drain on tax dollars.

Establishing a National Language

Press one for English. Does that make sense in an English speaking country? We may be the only place in the world where citizens have to press one to hear a message in their own language. Isn't it time we establish English as our national language and quit diluting our culture with other languages? Isn't learning English one of the requirements for citizenship in the United States?

For 236 years English has been the principal language spoken in the United States. President Theodore Roosevelt once said, "We have one language here, and that is the English language…" English has replaced French as the international business language and the international language of aviation.

According to *Charles Krauthammer*, Fox News commentator, 31 states have made English their official language, and official English bills are pending in a dozen more. But, English has never been designated as our national language. In almost every session of Congress someone introduces legislation to make English the official language of the United States. However, none of those efforts have been successful, and special-interest lobbies have been laboring for years to undermine that concept.

According to The Phyllis Schlafly Report, the billion-dollar boondoggle called bilingual education has "…always been a fraud because, contrary to the term bilingual, it doesn't teach two languages; instead it keeps immigrant children languishing in Spanish-speaking classes for six years or more."

California and Arizona decisively rejected bilingual education, and test scores in 2007 indicated that children progressed faster in California schools after they started immersing students in English.

Historically our nation was forged out of millions of immigrants from all over the world, who assimilated into our country and proudly learned English so they could meld into our culture as quickly as possible.

Now record numbers of non-English speaking immigrants are flooding into our country and, instead of assimilating into our culture, insist on bringing their culture with them and sometimes refuse to learn English. This attitude is literally encouraged by our government, which promotes diversity by increasingly operating in languages other than

English.

In recent years our government has provided bilingual ballots, education, publications, and similar services at public expense. That would seem to discourage new immigrants from learning English.

However, we have a linguistic paradox in our country. According to the *Language Policy* web site, "While the number of minority language speakers is increasing, so is the rate of linguistic assimilation. All available evidence suggests that today's newcomers are learning English – and losing their native tongues – more rapidly than ever before."

The 1990 census claimed at least 323 separate languages are spoken in the United States. However, the *Pro English* web site claims that learning to speak English empowers immigrants. "By more than 2-1 immigrants themselves say the U.S. should expect new immigrants to learn English and by a 9-1 margin Hispanic immigrants believe learning English is essential to succeed in the U.S."

Charles Hulse, in a New York Times article, claimed that designating English as our official national language would be "… equivalent to establishing a formal national anthem or motto and that it would simply affirm the pre-eminence of English without overturning laws or rules on bilingualism."

Even so, no legislation has ever been passed to establish English as our national language. As strange as it seems, in this 21st century, we have no official national language.

Isn't it time we recognize that English is the national language, make it official, and quit catering to every diverse group that migrates to the United States?

Commercial Spinoffs from NASA Research

It's very romantic to imagine astronauts when we think of the space program. Many young men and women dream of having a career in space. But, in reality, there is a lot more to the space program than astronauts and space travel.

Space is as much about research and development as it is about putting astronauts into orbit or taking them to the International Space Station. There are impressive benefits to our society from NASA research, although we don't discuss them as much as we probably should.

Commercial spinoffs from our space program exist everywhere. They are in our environment, in our bedrooms, in our bathrooms, in our toothpaste, in our showers, in our kitchens, in our refrigerators, in our baby food, in our shoes, in our tennis rackets, in our paints, in our freeze dried products, in our airports, in our medicine, and in our carbon footprint. They're everywhere we look.

According to the Ultimate Space Place, technical applications needed for space flight have produced thousands of "spinoffs" that contribute to improving national security, the economy, productivity and lifestyle. It is almost impossible to find an area of everyday life that has not benefited from these spinoffs.

Spin-off benefits embrace areas of multiple disciplines, such as: health and medicine, transportation, public safety, consumer, home and recreation, environmental and agricultural resources, computer technology, and industrial productivity, just to name a few.

In 1957, notable science fiction author Robert A. Heinlein was asked to appear before a joint committee of the House and Senate after recovering from one of the earliest known carotid bypass operations to correct a blocked artery that was causing transient ischemic attacks; in his testimony, reprinted in the book *Expanded Universe*, he characterized the technology that made the surgery possible as merely one of a long list of spinoff technologies from space development.[233]

One of the truly remarkable benefits is the ability to digitally image breast biopsies, which can detect minute differences between a malignant or benign tumor without the need for a surgical biopsy — at a fraction of the cost and with a much shorter recovery time.

NASA also developed a water purification system that uses iodine rather than chlorine to kill bacteria, and a swimming pool purification system that can kill bacteria and algae without chemicals.

---

[233]

NASA spin-off technologies, Wikipedia, The Free Encyclopedia, March 27, 2014.

Other consumer home/recreation spinoffs, according to Ultimate Space Place, include: the "dustbuster vacuum, shock-absorbing helmets, home security systems, smoke detectors, flat panel televisions, high-density batteries, trash compactors, food packaging and freeze-dried technology, cool sportswear, sports bras, hair styling appliances, fogless ski goggles, self-adjusting sunglasses, composite golf clubs, hang gliders, art preservation, quartz crystal timing equipment, a non-toxic coating for aluminum, advanced lubricants, cordless power tools, and automotive insulation that protects NASCAR drivers from extreme heat coming through the engine area."

Other health and medicine spinoffs include: arteriosclerosis detection, ultrasound scanners, portable X-ray devices, invisible braces, dental arch wire, palate surgery technology, clean room apparel, implantable heart aid, MRI, bone analyzer, cataract surgery tools, a transportable oxygen system for air rescue, a cancer detection device, laser angioplasty, a digital cardiac imaging system, an infrared thermometer, kidney dialysis machines, and implantable and external insulin pumps.

One might argue that all of these things could have been invented or discovered by direct research and development, unrelated to the space program, at a fraction of the cost of space exploration. But who would suggest that we not take advantage of the spinoff wonders inherent in the R&D that made space travel possible?

The kind of imaginative minds that took us to the moon and back are already planning for trips to asteroids and distant planets. We don't know what kind of spinoffs will be available to future generations; but, so long as there is a space program there will be technical benefits that make our life better.

I just wish those in the space program would toot their horns a bit more. I suspect this may be the first time you've heard about some of these spinoff benefits. The truth is we all benefit from the space program in ways that are sometimes difficult to imagine.

Fathers Missing in Action

For most of the past century it has been assumed the best environment for raising children is a two-parent family. That is, a mother and father is the ideal family nucleus in which a child should be raised.

It is pretty much conceded that mothers have a unique role in raising young girls, but not enough is written on the role fathers fill in raising young sons. Ask any young man who was raised without a father if he missed out on much by not having a male role model and you might be surprised by the answer: a resounding yes! I can vouch for that because my father abandoned my mother and our family of four children while my mother was eight months pregnant with her fifth child.

Chief among the many threats to the current generation of young people is the disintegration of the family. According to the latest national statistics "…72 percent of black babies, 53 percent of Hispanic babies and 29 percent of white babies in the United States are born out of wedlock. Most will never know their fathers. Only 34 percent of all children born in America will live with both biological parents through age eighteen."

Dr. William Pollock, Harvard psychologist and author of *Real Boys*, concludes that divorce is difficult for children of both sexes but it is devastating for males. He says the basic problem is the lack of discipline and supervision in the father's absence and his unavailability to teach what it means to be a man. Unfortunately what boys don't learn at home they often pick up on the streets, which sometimes is mythological and not based on Judeo/Christian ethics.

"Boys are in trouble today primarily because their parents, and especially their dads, are distracted, overworked, harassed, exhausted, disinterested, chemically dependent, divorced, or simply unable to cope.

"Involved fathers find the time to attend their children's games and recitals. They pull themselves away from the TV to show their children how to change a tire and balance a checkbook. They set firm limits and encourage their kids to do their best — even when they fail."

What boys need most from fathers is a healthy balance between love and limits, along with lots of one on one quality personal time. They need guidance, spiritual as well as physical. They need to see a rock solid foundation for their father's life, which can then be used as a model for their own maturing life.

Of course, a young son also needs to know the guidance he gets from his dad will be tempered with love and realistic expectations. While the apple doesn't fall far from the tree, one must start with healthy apples, which rarely come from a poisoned tree.

A healthy Judeo/Christian foundational relationship between a father and son sets the stage for developing a mature set of values that are enduring, with lifetime ideals that never change. That is increasingly important as the 21st Century family dynamics continue to change.

Of course, it would help if there was more of a national focus on this problem from the mainstream news media and the entertainment industry, especially movies and television.

Federal Income Tax

A political mantra heard endlessly from politicians almost every year is that the rich don't pay their fair share of federal income taxes. What does that mean? Who decides what is fair? How does our nation benefit by beating up on successful entrapaneurs who become wealthy? And do people in the bottom of our economic scale really benefit by denigrating those on the top?

We have a regressive income tax system. The more money you make the higher the percentage of it must be paid to the government, and if you don't make enough the government will give you some in the form of welfare.

A 2011 Gallup Poll found that 60 percent of respondents believe the income tax they themselves pay is fair. It seems nobody wants to pay any more income tax, except perhaps Warren Buffet.

A very small percentage of rich Americans pay most of our income taxes. The latest data, provided by The Journal of the American Enterprise Institute, shows that "the wealthiest 1 percent of the population earns 19 percent of the income but pays 37 percent of the income tax.

The top 10 percent of earners pay 68 percent of the tab. Meanwhile, the bottom 50 percent—those below the median income level—now earn 13 percent of the income but pay just 3 percent of the taxes."

Even more surprising, according to Fox news, nearly 50 percent of American income earners paid no income tax at all in 2010. Where do they fit into the scheme when people talk about paying a fair share of taxes? What should their fair share be? We all get roughly the same benefits: roads, schools, government, security, etc., but some pay for those things in the form of taxes and some do not.

Nevertheless, CNN Money reports that Americans of both parties believe the rich should pay more taxes. Of course, "the rich" always means somebody making more than the person being quoted. Rich is a relative term that pundits and politicians seem reluctant to define beyond some generality.

For awhile, some politicians mentioned increasing the tax rate for couples making over $250,000 per year; but when you are talking about millionaires and billionaires, a quarter of a million doesn't really qualify as "rich." That is especially true when you consider that it includes small business owners.

Article 16 of the U.S. Constitution gives Congress the power "…to lay and collect taxes on incomes, from whatever sources derived…." It doesn't say who should pay or how much the government should collect.

One could argue that Congress should collect taxes from everyone who earns income from any source, including those below the poverty line.

That would amount to what some people call a flat tax, which would require everyone to pay the same percentage of their income no matter how much or how little they earn, with no allowable deductions.

On the other hand, former Arkansas Governor Mike Hukabee would replace all federal income and payroll based taxes with a consumption tax, sometimes called the Fair Tax.

Hukabee's approach would eliminate the present tax system completely, including all the deductions and loopholes. He would also repeal the 16th Amendment to the U.S. Constitution, and abolish the Internal Revenue Service.

In fact, he would replace all federal taxes on personal and corporate income with a single broad national tax on retail sales. It would be a consumption tax, rather than a regressive income tax. However, under his fair tax there would be no federal taxes on spending for those who live at or below the poverty level.

The fair tax plan would benefit from collecting sales taxes from such people as foreign visitors, criminals who don't declare their income, folks who get paid in cash under the table, people who don't make enough income to be required to pay income taxes under the current tax system, and anyone else who purchases goods or services in the United States.

Under the fair tax approach, everyone who buys anything would pay a "fair tax," including the richest Americans, the poorest Americans who nevertheless live above the poverty line, and everybody in between. That would tie our tax revenues to the purchasing power of consumers. Obviously, the rich would pay more than the poor, because they buy and spend more on expensive items. But, since we all shop, everybody would pay something.

Unfortunately many people believe the flat tax is not flat and the fair tax is not fair. However, none of these plans define what is fair, and we don't seem to be able to reach a national consensus on how best to approach federal income taxes.

Besides, none of these programs would solve our problems, because generating income is not the real issue, although it seems to be what we focus on the most.

As a nation, we are addicted to spending. As long as we continue to spend more money than we take in we will continue to increase the national debt, which will eventually coke us to death.

George Will pointed out on "This Week with Christiane Amanpour" on Oct. 2, 2011, that in 1919, the wealthiest man in America, John D. Rockefeller, could write a personal check big enough to wipe out our national debt. Today, Bill Gates, the richest man in America, could write a check for the total amount of his entire personal wealth and it would pay only for two months of interest on our national debt.

We simply must quit spending money we don't have and quit borrowing money from China and other countries to cover interest on the money we borrow.

And, if we continue to print ever-increasing amounts of money that is backed by nothing more than an American IOU, we will eventually create hyperinflation that could destroy our economy beyond repair.

Changing the tax system is an excellent beginning, but we will not get well until we treat our addiction to spending. To be fiscally responsible, we simply cannot continue to spend more than we take in. That is a prescription for disaster.

Meanwhile, our present tax code is far too complicated for a lot of people. According to finance.townhall.com, on February 17, 2013, "… it now takes 73,954 regular 8 ½" x 11" sheets of paper to explain the complexity of the U.S. federal tax code!" What is truly amazing is how anyone can stay abreast of the changes in our federal income tax code from year to year.

Nobody likes to pay income taxes, but few people really oppose paying the taxes. Everyone recognizes federal income taxes are necessary. Many would just rather they didn't have to pay taxes themselves. Taxes are OK for you and me, but not for them.

What escapes logic, however, is how irrational and unreasonable it us for those who pay nothing into the system to tell the wealthiest citizens they don't pay their fair share, especially since the wealthiest already pay the lion's share of our income taxes.

No matter how many statistics reporters and columnists quote to the contrary, raising taxes on the rich will not solve our problems. Many of those articles leave me feeling like I've eaten an appetizer, instead of an entrée.

Even if we confiscated all the money wealthy people make, it wouldn't begin to be enough to pay for all of the benefits we need as a nation. As long as we have entitlement and welfare programs, we will have to collect taxes in some form to cover the costs of these programs. It is not unreasonable to expect everyone to contribute something, however small, to offset the burden.

This topic raises its ugly head every year, especially leading up to April 15th, when federal income taxes become due. There is always a lot of media attention to this issue for a brief period, but it never seems to sustain itself. Once the tax season is over, we seem to go to sleep on this topic until the next politician raises it once more as a national issue.

Fair is a relative thing and it isn't likely we will agree on a national definition any time soon. But, for sure, this is one topic that could use a sustained national focus by the mainstream media and our politicians.

Immigration Reform

The only people who will win with the immigration bill slowly moving through Congress are illegal immigrants and politicians. No matter how you cut it, and despite what Senator Marco Rubio claims, the immigration bill grants amnesty to people euphemistically called "undocumented immigrants."

Senator Rubio regularly claims it is not amnesty because the illegal immigrants will have to go to the back of the line. That is ridiculous! Making them learn English, pay a fine, comply with E-verify, and wait a long time is not "going to the back of the line." They will still be able to wait out their time working in the United States.

The back of the line is in the country they came from, behind all those immigrants patiently waiting to come here legally. It is customary for politicians to say there is simply no way we can break up families and deport between 10 and 20 million people. That is rubbish. Of course we can!

Three times in the last 85 years U.S. presidents sent illegal immigrants packing. Presidents Hoover, Truman and Eisenhower deported millions of illegal immigrants to preserve jobs for American workers.

In 1949 the Border Patrol seized nearly 280,000 illegal immigrants. By 1953, the numbers grew to more than 865,000, and the U.S. government felt pressured to do something about the onslaught of illegal immigration. What resulted was President Eisenhower's program, euphemistically called "Operation Wetback."

Sixty-one years ago, "…when newly elected Dwight Eisenhower moved into the White House, America's southern frontier was as porous as a spaghetti sieve. As many as three million illegal migrants had walked and waded northward over a period of several years for jobs in California, Arizona, Texas, and points beyond.

"President Eisenhower cut off this illegal traffic. He did it quickly and decisively with only 1,075 United States Border Patrol agents – less than one-tenth of today's force. The operation is still highly praised among veterans of the Border Patrol."[234]

Of course, nobody really knows the number of illegal immigrants or undocumented migrant workers that were actually deported under these three presidents. Many of the numbers have been wildly distorted or inflated over the years to support political positions. Claims run as high as 15 million, but the figures are probably more like six or seven million.

Nevertheless, it isn't a question of what's possible. It's a question of whether or not we have the national will to do it.

There is the rub. Deporting them is not politically correct or expedient. Democrats don't want to deport illegals because they see them as a huge voting block ready made for democrat candidates. Republicans don't want to deport them because they know if they don't cater to the Hispanic vote they will soon become the forgotten party.

On June 19, 2013 Reuters reported that "Prospects for U.S. Senate passage of an immigration bill with strong bipartisan support brightened on Wednesday when a group of Republican and Democratic negotiators reached a tentative deal on ways to shore up border security..."

Of course, it doesn't seem to matter that many blacks and Hispanics believe passage of this bill will effectively take jobs away from them so that companies can profit off of the sweat of illegal immigrants who are willing to work for slave wages.

So, I predict this bill will eventually pass and be signed by President Obama. Then this bill, like most immigration bills, will become a stopgap measure. In a matter of years we will face the same issues all over again.

It was only a few years ago that President Ronald Reagan granted amnesty to millions of illegal immigrants, promising to secure the border, which never happened. The reason is simple; it is almost impossible to secure the border. The distance from Texas to California is over 2,000 miles.

234

How Eisenhower solved illegal border crossings from Mexico, by John Dillin, The Christian Science Monitor, July 6, 2006.

We can't or won't put enough troops on the border to keep illegals out and even if we built a 2,000-mile fence from Texas to California illegals will climb over it or burrow under it. So, we will delude ourselves into believing we have secured the border and grant amnesty to between 10-20 million illegals (nobody actually knows the real number)—which will serve as a magnet to attract more illegals for our next round of hand wringing.

Politicians will take credit for solving an unsolvable problem and we will move on for a period, until the next influx of illegals swamps our borders again.

In 2013, Hispanics overtook Black African-Americans as the largest minority in the United States. Hispanics now account for approximately 17 percent of our population. Demographers are estimating that by the year 2050 they will account for 30 percent of our population. They are already a prominent portion of the California population.

No other nation has our immigration problems. People from all over the world want to migrate to the United States and often are willing to do so by whatever means possible, sometimes legally and sometimes illegally. This issue will be with us for the foreseeable future, unless or until we get serious as a nation about sealing our southern borders.

A comprehensive immigration reform package might one day work its way through our Congress; but, if it doesn't address these issues in depth and provide realistic answers to the serious problems, we could be revisiting this topic over and over in the years to come.

Chapter 10

INSPIRATIONAL, HUMOROUS AND ENCOURAGING STORIES

From time to time I run across interesting items in obscure places that strike me as incredibly inspirational, humorous or just very encouraging, and I wonder why they don't receive wider attention.

It's kind of the flip side of wondering why there is so much negative news reported by the national media, with seemingly little effort to balance it with positive stories.

Why is it that a story that makes everyone feel good doesn't have the same appeal as one that shocks the reader? Why is it that a story that tickles the fancy doesn't merit as much attention as the theme of "if it bleeds it leads? I've never found a suitable answer to that question.

What follows are stories that I think are very interesting, yet I had to work hard to ferret them out or to create them from scratch.

A Glass of Milk, Paid in Full[235]

One day, a poor boy who was selling goods from door to door to pay his way through school, found he had only one thin dime left, and he was hungry. He decided he would ask for a meal at the next house. However, he lost his nerve when a lovely young woman opened the door.

Instead of a meal he asked for a drink of water. She thought he

---

[235]

A glass of Milk, paid in Full, by Stephen, Excerpt from Moral Stories, www.academicTips.org, September 15, 2008.

looked hungry so brought him a large glass of milk.

He drank it slowly, and then asked, "How much do I owe you?"

"You don't owe me anything," she replied. "Mother has taught us never to accept pay for a kindness."

He said, "Then I thank you from my heart."

As Howard Kelly left that house, he not only felt stronger physically, but his faith in God and man was strong also. He had been ready to give up and quit.

Year's later that young woman became critically ill. The local doctors were baffled. They finally sent her to the big city, where they called in specialists to study her rare disease.

Dr. Howard Kelly was called in for the consultation. When he heard the name of the town she came from, a strange light filled his eyes. Immediately he rose and went down the hall of the hospital to her room.

Dressed in his doctor's gown he went in to see her. He recognized her at once. He went back to the consultation room determined to do his best to save her life. From that day he gave special attention to the case.

After a long struggle, the battle was won. Dr. Kelly requested the business office to pass the final bill to him for approval. He looked at it, then wrote something on the edge and the bill was sent to her room.

She feared to open it, for she was sure it would take the rest of her life to pay for it all. Finally she looked, and something caught her attention on the side of the bill. She began to read the following words:

"Paid in full with one glass of milk"

Signed, Dr. Howard Kelly.

Unfathomable Beauty of the Bible

The symmetry and irony of this will probably interest most people, even if they hold few or no religious beliefs.

It is pretty strange how this works out, even for a non-believer. The bible is made up of 66 books, 39 books in the Old Testament and 27 books in the New Testament. They were written in three different languages, on three different continents, on the most controversial of subjects, by 40 different authors, whose education and backgrounds varied greatly, over a period of 1,500 years. Yet, though it seems inconceivable, the 66 books maintain harmony, and do not contradict each other.

Ask anyone who has ever been to a courtroom and listened to witnesses testify to events they each had viewed at the same time, and remember how dramatically different was their memory of those events —often contradicting each other.

Yet the bible reads as though it was written by one great mind. Christians and Jews would say it was: men of God who were inspired to write as they were moved to do so by the Holy Spirit.

Let's continue with more evidence of the bible's symmetry:

The shortest chapter in the Bible is Psalm 117. The longest chapter in the Bible is Psalm 119. The absolute center of the Bible is Psalm 118. There are 594 chapters before Psalms 118 and 594 chapters after Psalms 118. Add these numbers and you get 1188. The center verse in the Bible is Psalm 118:8.

Psalm 118:8 says: "It is better to trust in the Lord than to put confidence in man."

Even an Atheist or Agnostic, who refuses to acknowledge that God is in the center of this symmetry and the divine inspiration for the bible in its entirety, would have to agree these are profoundly interesting facts that have to be more than happenstance.

For a non-believer, I suggest you try to find any other work, anywhere in the world, made up of 66 books, with 1,188 chapters, written in three different languages, on three different continents, by 40 different authors, covering the most controversial of subjects, over a period of 1,500 years, with no one chapter contradicting another. It will undoubtedly be the most difficult task you will have in your lifetime.

Now, let's look at some more interesting facts about the Bible:

. The Bible has been partially or totally translated into more than 1,200 languages and dialects.

. The Bible is believed to be the most shoplifted book in the world.

. One Bible fun fact is that the phrase "do not be afraid" is repeated 365 times in the Bible, which suggests that God is available to guide us 24/7.

. The Bible is the only book that states the origin of the world, birth of man, journey of man's life to the present time, and even foretells what is going to happen in the future.

.The Bible was first printed in 1454, making it the first book ever to be printed.

. The entire Bible, divided into chapters and verses, first appeared in the Geneva bible of 1560.

. The Bible is the largest and best seller of all the books ever published.

. The last word in the Bible is Amen.

. About 50 bibles are sold ever minute of every day.[236]

. Dogs are mentioned 14 times in the bible, and lions 55 times, but domestic cats are not mentioned at all.

. The word "Christian" only appears three times in the Bible: Acts 11:26, 26:28; 1 Peter 4:16.

. Esther and Song of Solomon are the only books in the bible that do not contain the word "God."

. The tallest man in the bible was Goliath, who was 9'6" tall.

. A Biblical chariot would cost the equivalent of $77,000 in today's dollars.

. Ezra 7:21 Contains all the letters of the alphabet except "J."

. Daniel 4:37 Contains all the letters of the alphabet except "Q."

. The words, eternity, reverend and grandmother occur in the Bible only once.

An 87 Year Old College Student Named Rose

"The first day of school our professor introduced himself and challenged us to get to know someone we didn't already know.

"I stood up to look around when a gentle hand touched my shoulder. I turned around to find a wrinkled, little old lady beaming up at me with a smile that lit up her entire being.

236

Interesting Facts About the Bible – Did You Know That?, Christian Talk, August 8, 2013: Isaiah 57:15, Psallm 111:9 & 2 Timothy 1:5.

"She said, "Hi handsome. My name is Rose. I'm eighty-seven years old. Can I give you a hug?"

"I laughed and enthusiastically responded, "Of course you may!" and she gave me a giant squeeze.

"Why are you in college at such a young, innocent age?" I asked.

"She jokingly replied, 'I'm here to meet a rich husband, get married, and have a couple of kids…'

"No seriously," I asked. I was curious what may have motivated her to be taking on this challenge at her age.

"I always dreamed of having a college education and now I'm getting one!" she told me.

"After class we walked to the student union building and shared a chocolate milkshake. We became instant friends. Every day for the next three months, we would leave class together and talk nonstop. I was always mesmerized listening to this "time machine" as she shared her wisdom and experience with me.

"Over the course of the year, Rose became a campus icon and she easily made friends wherever she went. She loved to dress up and she reveled in the attention bestowed upon her from the other students. She was living it up.

"At the end of the semester we invited Rose to speak at our football banquet. I'll never forget what she taught us. After she was introduced, she stepped up to the podium.

As she began to deliver her prepared speech, she dropped her three by five cards on the floor. Frustrated and a little embarrassed she leaned into the microphone and simply said, 'I'm sorry I'm so jittery. I gave up beer for Lent and this whiskey is killing me! I'll never get my speech back in order so let me just tell you what I know.'

"As we laughed she cleared her throat and began, "We do not stop playing because we are old; we grow old because we stop playing. There are only four secrets to staying young, being happy, and achieving success. You have to laugh and find humor every day.

"You've got to have a dream. When you lose your dreams, you die. We have so many people walking around who are dead and don't even know it! There is a huge difference between growing older and growing up.

"If you are nineteen years old and lie in bed for one full year and don't do one productive thing, you will turn twenty years old.

"If I am eighty-seven years old and stay in bed for a year and never do anything I will turn eighty-eight.

"Anybody can grow older. That doesn't take any talent or ability. The idea is to grow up by always finding opportunity in change. Have no regrets.

"The elderly usually don't have regrets for what we did, but rather for things we did not do. The only people who fear death are those with regrets."

"She concluded her speech by courageously singing 'The Rose.'

"She challenged each of us to study the lyrics and live them out in our daily lives.

"At the year's end Rose finished the college degree she had begun all those years ago. One week after graduation Rose died peacefully in her sleep.

"Over two thousand college students attended her funeral in tribute to the wonderful woman who taught by example that it's never too late to be all you can possibly be. When you finish reading this, please send this peaceful word of advice to your friends and family, they'll really enjoy it!

"These words have been passed along in loving memory of ROSE.

"REMEMBER, GROWING OLDER IS MANDATORY. GROWING UP IS OPTIONAL.

"We make a Living by what we get, We make a Life by what we give."[237]

Laus Deo... **A History Lesson**
Author Unknown
In Washington DC, there can never be a building of greater height than the Washington Monument... this is a LAW. On the

---

[237] *An 87 Year Old College Student Named Rose*, Short Inspirational Stories, www.livelifehapy.com/stories, 2014.

aluminum cap, atop the Washington Monument in Washington DC, are two words: Laus Deo. No one can see these words. In fact, most visitors to the monument are totally unaware they are even there and for that matter, probably couldn't care less.

These words have been there for many years; they are 555 feet, 5.125 inches high, perched atop the monument, facing skyward to the Father of our nation, overlooking the 69 square miles which comprise the District of Columbia, capital of the United States of America.

Laus Deo! Two seemingly insignificant, unnoticed words. Out of sight and, one might think, out of mind, but very meaningfully placed at the highest point over what is the most powerful city in the most successful nation in the world.

So, what do those two words, in Latin, composed of just four syllables and only seven letters, possibly mean? Very simply, they say... **"Praise be to God**!"Though construction of this giant obelisk began in 1848, when James Polk was President of the United States, it was not until 1888 that the monument was inaugurated and opened to the public. It took twenty-five years to finally cap the memorial with a tribute to the Father of our nation, "Laus Deo... Praise be to God!"

From atop this magnificent granite and marble structure, visitors may take in the beautiful panoramic view of the city with it's division into four major segments. From that vantage point, one can also easily see the original plan of the designer, Pierre Charles L'Enfant... a perfect cross imposed upon the landscape, with the White House to the north. The Jefferson Memorial is to the south, the Capitol to the east and the Lincoln Memorial to the west.

A cross you ask? Why a cross? What about separation of church and state? Yes, a cross; separation of church and state was not, is not, in the Constitution. So, read on. How interesting and, no doubt, intended to carry a profound meaning for those who bother to notice.

Praise be to God! Within the monument itself are 898 steps and 50 landings. As one climbs the steps and pauses at the landings the memorial stones share a message! On the 12th Landing is a prayer offered by the City of Baltimore; on the 20th is a memorial presented by some Chinese Christians; on the 24th a presentation made by Sunday School children from New York and Philadelphia quoting Proverbs

10:7, Luke 18:16 and Proverbs 22:6. Praise be to God!

When the cornerstone of the Washington Monument was laid on July 4th, 1848, deposited within it were many items, including the Holy Bible, presented by the Bible Society. Praise be to God! Such was the discipline, the moral direction, and the spiritual mood given by the founder and first President of our unique democracy." One Nation, Under God." Also included was a prayer by our nation's first president.

George Washington's Prayer – have you ever read it? If not, do so now

"Almighty God; We make our earnest prayer that Thou wilt keep the United States in Thy holy protection; that Thou wilt incline the hearts of the citizens to cultivate a spirit of subordination and obedience to government; and entertain a brotherly affection and love for one another and for their fellow citizens of the United states at large." And finally that Thou wilt most graciously be pleased to dispose us all to do justice, to love mercy, and to demean ourselves with that charity, humility, and pacific temper of mind which were the characteristics of the Divine Author of our blessed religion, and without a humble imitation of whose example in these things we can never hope to be a happy nation. Grant our supplication, we beseech Thee, through Jesus Christ our Lord. Amen."

When one stops to observe the inscriptions found in public places all over our nation's capitol, he or she will easily find the signature of God, as it is unmistakably inscribed everywhere you look.

You may forget the width and height of "Laus Deo," it's location, or the architects... but no one who reads this will be able to forget it's meaning, or these words: ***"Unless the Lord builds the house its builders labor in vain. Unless the Lord watches over the city, the watchmen stand guard in vain."*** -- Psalm 127:1[238]

<u>**The pledge of allegiance "meaning"**</u> As told by Red Skelton

---

[238]

Laus Deo... A History Lesson, American Inspiring Stories, Inspire21.com, 2012.

The late Red Skelton spoke the following words on his television program as he related a story about his teacher, Mr. Laswell, and how his students felt about the Pledge of Allegiance.

Mr. Laswell, Red Skelton's teacher, felt that his students had come to think of the Pledge of Allegiance as merely something to recite in class each day. Here is the text of that story.

"I've been listening to you boys and girls recite the Pledge of Allegiance all semester and it seems as though it is becoming monotonous to you. If I may, may I recite it and try to explain to you the meaning of each word?"

I -- me, an individual, a committee of one.

Pledge -- dedicate all of my worldly goods to give without self pity.

Allegiance -- my love and my devotion.

To the Flag -- our standard, Old Glory, a symbol of freedom. Wherever she waves, there's respect because your loyalty has given her a dignity that shouts freedom is everybody's job!

United -- that means that we have all come together.

States -- individual communities that have united into 48 great states. Forty-eight individual communities with pride and dignity and purpose; all divided with imaginary boundaries, yet united to a common purpose, and that's love for country.

And to the republic -- republic... a state in which sovereign power is invested in representatives chosen by the people to govern. And government is the people and it's from the people to the leaders, not from the leaders to the people.

For which it stands, **one nation** -- one nation... meaning "so blessed by God"

Indivisible -- incapable of being divided.

With liberty -- which is freedom... the right of power to live one's own life without threats, fear or some sort of retaliation.

And Justice -- the principle or qualities of dealing fairly with others.

For all -- for all... which means, boys and girls, it's as much your country as it is mine.

And now, boys and girls, let me hear you recite the Pledge of

Allegiance...

I PLEDGE ALLEGIANCE TO THE FLAG OF THE UNITED STATES OF AMERICA, AND TO THE REPUBLIC FOR WHICH IT STANDS, ONE NATION, INDIVISIBLE, WITH LIBERTY AND JUSTICE FOR ALL.

(then Mr. Skelton went on to say...)

Since I was a small boy, two states have been added to our country, and two words have been added to the Pledge of Allegiance... UNDER GOD. Wouldn't it be a pity if someone said that is a prayer and that would be eliminated from schools, too?

God Bless America... and God bless Red Skelton!

Don't Mess with Momma–– Author Unknown

My son came home from school one day, with a smirk upon his face.He decided he was smart enough, to put me in my place.

"Guess what I learned in Civics Two, what's taught by Mr. Wright? It's all about the laws today, The "Children's Bill of Rights."

It says I need not clean my room, don't have to cut my hair. No one can tell me what to think, or speak, or what to wear.

I have freedom from religion, and regardless what you say,I don't have to bow my head, and I sure don't have to pray.

I can wear earrings if I want, And pierce my tongue & nose.I can read & watch just what I like, and get tattoos from head   to toes.

And if you ever spank me, I'll charge you with a crime.I'll back up all my charges, with the marks on my behind.

Don't you ever touch me, My body's only for my use,not for your hugs and kisses, that's just more child abuse.

Don't preach about your morals, like your Mama did to you.That's nothing more than mind control, and it's illegal too!

Mom, I have these children's rights, so you can't influence me,or I'll call Children's Services Division, better known as C.S.D.

Of course, my first instinct was to toss him out the door.But the chance to teach him a lesson made me think a little more.

I mulled it over carefully, I couldn't let this go.A smile crept upon my face, he's messing with a pro.

The next day I took him shopping at the local Goodwill Store.I told him, "Pick out all you want, there's shirts & pants galore.

I've called and checked with C.S.D. who said they didn't care if I bought you K-Mart shoes instead of those Nike Airs.

And I've canceled that appointment to take your driver's test. The C.S.D. is unconcerned, so I'll decide what's best.

I said "No time to stop and eat, or pick up stuff to munch. And tomorrow you can start to learn to make your own sack lunch."

Just save the raging appetite, and wait till dinner time. We're having liver and onions, favorite dish of mine.

He asked "Can I please rent a movie, to watch on my VCR?" "Sorry... but I sold your TV, for new tires on my car.

I also rented out your room, you'll take the couch instead. All the C.S.D. requires is a roof for over your head.

Your clothing won't be trendy now, and I'll choose what we eat. That allowance that you used to get, will buy me something neat.

I'm selling off your jet ski, dirt-bike & roller blades. Check out the "Parents Bill of Rights," it's in effect today!

Hey hot shot, are you crying, and why are you on your knees? Are you asking God to help you out, instead of C.S.D.?

Carrot, Egg, and Coffee... – Author unknown

After you read this you will never look at a cup of coffee the same way again...

A young woman went to her mother and told her about her life and how things were so hard for her. She did not know how she was going to make it and wanted to give up. She was tired of fighting and struggling. It seemed as one problem was solved, a new one arose.

Her mother took her to the kitchen, where she filled three pots with water and placed each on a high fire. Soon the pots came to a boil. In the first she placed carrots, in the second she placed eggs, and in the last she placed ground coffee beans. She let them sit and boil, without saying a word.

In about twenty minutes she turned off the burners. She fished out the carrots and placed them in a bowl. She then pulled the eggs out and placed them in another bowl. Then she ladled out the coffee and placed it in a bowl.

Turning to her daughter, she asked, "What do you see?" The daughter replied, "Carrots, eggs, and coffee."

Her mother brought her closer and asked her to feel the carrots. The daughter felt the carrots and noted they were soft. The mother then asked her daughter to pick up an egg and break it.

After pulling off the shell, the daughter observed the hard boiled egg. Finally, the mother asked her daughter to sip the coffee. The daughter smiled as she smelled its rich aroma and tasted its flavor.

The daughter then asked, "What does it mean, mother?" Her mother explained that each of the objects had faced the same adversity —boiling water—but each had reacted differently.

The carrot went in strong, hard and unrelenting. However, after being subjected to the boiling water, it softened and became weak. The egg had been fragile. Its thin outer shell had protected its liquid interior, but after sitting through the boiling water, its inside became hardened. However, the ground coffee beans were unique. After they were in the boiling water, they had changed the water.

"Which are you?" she asked her daughter. "When adversity knocks on your door, how do you respond? Are you a carrot, an egg or a coffee bean? Think about it. Are you the carrot that seems strong, but with pain and adversity do you wilt and become soft and lose your strength? Are you the egg that starts with a malleable heart, but changes with the heat? Do you have a fluid spirit, but after a death, a breakup, a financial hardship or some other trial, have you become hardened and stiff? Does your shell look the same, but on the inside you are bitter and tough with a stiff spirit and hardened heart?

Or are you like the coffee bean? The bean actually changed the hot water, the very circumstance that brought the pain. When the water gets hot, it releases the fragrance and flavor. If you are like the bean, when things are at their worst, you get better and change the situation around you. When the hour is the darkest and trials are the greatest, do you elevate yourself to another level? How do you handle adversity?

Are you a carrot, an egg or a coffee bean? May you have enough happiness to make you sweet, enough trials to make you strong, enough sorrow to keep you human and enough hope to make you happy.

The brightest future will always be based on a forgotten past; you can't go forward in life until you let go of your past failures and heartaches.

The happiest of people don't necessarily have the best of everything; they just make the most of everything they have.

How'd You Break Your Arm?-- Author Unknown[239]

A friend just got back from a holiday ski trip to Utah with the kind of story that warms the cockles of anybody's heart.

Conditions were perfect, 12 below, no feeling in the toes, basic numbness all over, the "tell me when we're having fun" kind of day. One of the women in the group complained to her husband that she was in dire need of a restroom.

He told her not to worry, that he was sure there was relief waiting at the top of the lift in the form of a powder room for female skiers in distress.

He was wrong, of course, and the pain did not go away. If you've ever had nature hit its panic button in you, then you know that a temperature of 12 below zero doesn't help matters.

So, with time running out, the woman weighed her options. Her husband, picking up on the intensity of her pain, suggested that since she was wearing an all white ski outfit, she should go off in the woods. No one would even notice, he assured her. The white would provide more than adequate camouflage.

So she headed for the tree line, began disrobing and proceeded to do her thing. If you've ever parked on the side of a slope, then you know there is a right way and a wrong way to set your skis so you don't move.

Yep, you got it... she had them positioned the wrong way. Steep slopes are not forgiving, even during embarrassing moments. Without warning, the woman found herself skiing backward, out of control, racing through the trees, somehow missing all of them and onto another slope.

239

How'd you break your arm? Author Unknown, www.Inspire21.com, 2012.

Her derriere and her reverse side were still bare, her pants down around her knees, and she was picking up speed all the while. She continued on backwards, totally out of control, creating an unusual vista for the other skiers. The woman skied, if you define that verb loosely, back under the lift, and finally collided violently with a pylon.

The bad news was that she broke her arm and was unable to pull up her ski pants. At long last her husband arrived, putting an end to her nudie show, then went to the base of the mountain and summoned the ski patrol, who transported her to a hospital.

In the emergency room she was regrouping when a man with an obviously broken leg was put in the bed next to hers. "So, how'd you break your leg?" she asked, making small talk.

"It was the darndest thing you ever saw," he said. "I was riding up this ski lift, and suddenly I couldn't believe my eyes. There was this crazy woman skiing backward out of control down the mountain with her bare bottom hanging out of her clothes and her pants down around her knees. I leaned over to get a better look, and I guess I didn't realize how far I had moved. I fell out of the lift. So, how'd you break your arm?"

Pick up a Penny – Author Unknown[240]

Several years ago, a friend of mine and her husband were invited to spend the weekend at the husband's employer's home. My friend, Arlene, was nervous about the weekend. The boss was very wealthy, with a fine home on the waterway, and cars costing more than her house.

The first day and evening went well, and Arlene was delighted to have this rare glimpse into how the very wealthy live. The husband's employer was quite generous as a host, and took them to the finest restaurants. Arlene knew she would never have the opportunity to indulge in this kind of extravagance again, so was enjoying herself

---

[240]

Pick up a penny, by Author Unknown, www.Inspire21.com, 2012.

immensely.

As the three of them were about to enter an exclusive restaurant that evening, the boss was walking slightly ahead of Arlene and her husband.

He stopped suddenly, looking down on the pavement for a long, silent moment.

Arlene wondered if she was supposed to pass him. There was nothing on the ground except a single darkened penny that someone had dropped, and a few cigarette butts. Still silent, the man reached down and picked up the penny.

He held it up and smiled, then put it in his pocket as if he had found a great treasure. How absurd! What need did this man have for a single penny? Why would he even take the time to stop and pick it up?

Throughout dinner, the entire scene nagged at her. Finally, she could stand it no longer. She causally mentioned that her daughter once had a coin collection, and asked if the penny he had found had been of some value.

A smile crept across the man's face as he reached into his pocket for the penny and held it out for her to see. She had seen many pennies before! What was the point of this?

"Look at it." He said. "Read what it says."

She read the words "United States of America."

"No, not that; read further."

"One cent?"

"No, keep reading."

"In God we Trust?"

"Yes,"

"And?"

"And if I trust in God, the name of God is holy, even on a coin. Whenever I find a coin I see that inscription. It is written on every single United States coin, but we never seem to notice it! God drops a message right in front of me telling me to trust Him? Who am I to pass it by? When I see a coin, I pray, I stop to see if my trust IS in God at that moment. I pick the coin up as a response to God; that I do trust in Him. For a short time, at least, I cherish it as if it were gold. I think it is God's way of starting a conversation with me. Lucky for me, God is patient and pennies are plentiful!

When I was out shopping today, I found a penny on the sidewalk. I stopped and picked it up, and realized that I had been worrying and fretting in my mind about things I cannot change. I read the words, "In God We Trust," and had to laugh. Yes, God, I get the message.

It seems that I have been finding an inordinate number of pennies in the last few months, but then, pennies are plentiful!

And, God is patient...

Have a blessed day!

You always hear the usual stories of pennies on the sidewalk being good luck, gifts from angels, etc. Have you ever heard this twist on the story? Gives you something to think about, doesn't it?

The Fat Lady by Chong Sheau Ching[241]

Hi! How are you?" The woman smiled as she took the seat beside me. She had to lower herself slowly, squeezing her ample bottom into the seat, filling all available space.

Positioning herself comfortably, she plopped her enormous arm on our common armrest. Her immensity saturated the space around us, shrinking me and my seat into insignifiance.

I cringed and reclined towards the window.

She leaned towards me and repeated her greeting in an upbeat, friendly voice. Her face towered above my head, forcing me to turn to look at her. "Hi," I replied with obvious loathing.

I turned away to stare out the cabin window, sulking silently about the long hours of discomfort I was going to experience with this monster beside me.

She nudged me with her meaty arm. "My name is Laura. I'm from Britain. How about you? Japan?"

"Malaysia," I barked.

"I'm so sorry! Will you accept my heartfelt apology? Come shake my hand. If we're going to spend six hours side-by-side on this flight, we'd better be friends, don't you think?" A palm waved in front of my face. I shook the hand reluctantly, still silent.

241

The Fat Lady, by Stephen, Inspirational Stories, June 17, 2011.

Laura started a conversation with me, taking no notice of my unfriendly reactions. She talked excitedly about herself and her trip to Hong Kong to see her friends. She rattled off a list of things she was going to buy for her students in the boarding school where she was teaching.

I gave her one-word answers to her questions about me. Unperturbed by my coldness, she nodded as she made appreciative comments to my answers. Her voice was warm and caring. She was considerate and obliging when we were served drinks and meals, making sure that I had room to maneuver in my seat. "I don't want to clobber you with my elephant size!" she said with utmost sincerity.

To my surprise, her face which repulsed me hours before, now opened into extraordinary smiles, lively and calm at the same time. I couldn't help but let down my guard slowly.

Laura was an interesting conversationalist. She was well read in many subjects from philosophy to science. She turned a seemingly unimportant subject into something to explore and understand. Her comments were humorous and inspirational. When our topic turned to cultures, I was pleasantly surprised by her intelligent comments and well-thought-out analysis.

During our conversation, Laura managed to make every cabin crew who served us walk away laughing at her jokes.

When a flight attendant was clearing our plates, Laura cracked several jokes about her size. The flight attendant roared with laughter as she grabbed Laura's hand, "You really make my day!"

For the next few minutes, Laura listened attentively and gave pointers to the flight attendant's weight problem. The grateful attendant said before she rushed off, "I've got to work. I'll come back later and talk to you about it."

I asked Laura, "'Have you ever thought about losing some weight?"

"No. I've worked hard to get this way. Why would I want to give it up?"

"You aren't worried about cardiovascular diseases that come with being overweight?"

"Not at all. You only get the diseases if you're worried about your weight all the time. You see advertisements from slimming centers that say, 'Liberate yourself from your extra baggage so that you are free to be yourself.' It's rubbish! You're liberated only if you're comfortable about who you are, and what you look like any time of the day and anytime of the year! Why would I want to waste my time on slimming regimes when I have so many other important things to do and so many people to be friends with? I eat healthily and walk regularly; I'm this size because I am born to be big! There is more to life than worrying about weight all day long."

She sipped at her wine. "Besides, God gives me so much happiness that I need a bigger body to hold all of it! Why would I lose weight to lose my happiness?" Taken aback by her reasoning, I chuckled.

Laura continued. "Folks often see me as a fat lady with big bosoms, big thighs and a big bottom that no man would even bother to cast a glance at. They see me as a slob. They think I'm lazy and have no willpower. They're wrong." She held up her glass to a passing flight attendant. "More of this magnificent wine, please." She smiled sweetly at the attendant. "Great service from your crew. May God bless all of you."

She turned to me, "I'm actually a slim person inside. I'm so full of energy that people won't be able to keep up with me. This extra flesh is here to slow me down, otherwise I'll be running everywhere chasing after men!"

"Do men chase after you?" I asked jokingly.

"Of course they do. I'm happily married but men still keep proposing to me.

"Most of them have relationship problems and they need someone to confide in. For some reason, they like to talk to me. I think I should have been a counselor instead of a school teacher!"

Laura paused before she said thoughtfully, "You know, the relationship between men and women is so complicated. Women worship men and call them, 'Honey' until they find out they have been lied to, and then they turn into bitter gourds! Men love women so much that they see them as their soul mates until they look at their credit card bills, and then women become devils with tridents!"

Laura's enthralling conversation had turned the flight into something thoroughly enjoyable. I was also fascinated by the way people were drawn to her. By the end of the flight, almost half the cabin crew was standing near the aisle by us, laughing and joking with Laura. The passengers around us joined in the merry-making too. Laura was the centre of attention, filling the cabin with delightful warmth.

When we waved goodbye to each other at the arrival lounge at Hong Kong's Kai Tak Airport, I watched her walking towards a big group of adoring adults and kids. Cheers sounded as the group hugged and kissed Laura. She turned around and winked at me.

I was stunned, as the realization set in: Laura was the most beautiful woman I had ever met in my life.

Thank You For Hands – Author Unknown[242]

An old man, probably some ninety plus years, sat feebly on the park bench. He didn't move, just sat with his head down staring at his hands. When I sat down beside him he didn't acknowledge my presence and the longer I sat, I wondered if he was ok.

Finally, not really wanting to disturb him but wanting to check on him at the same time, I asked him if he was ok. He raised his head and looked at me and smiled.

"Yes, I'm fine, thank you for asking", he said in a clear strong voice.

"I didn't mean to disturb you, sir, but you were just sitting here staring at your hands and I wanted to make sure you were ok", I explained to him.

"Have you ever looked at your hands", he asked. "I mean really looked at your hands?"

I slowly opened my hands and stared down at them. I turned them over, palms up and then palms down. No, I guess I had never really looked at my hands as I tried to figure out the point he was making.

Then he smiled and related this story:

Stop and think for a moment about the hands you have, how they have served you well throughout your years. These hands, though

---

242

Thank You For Hands, To Touch The Face of God, www.motivateus.com, April 4, 2014.

wrinkled, shriveled and weak have been the tools I have used all my life to reach out and grab and embrace life.

They braced and caught my fall when as a toddler, I crashed upon the floor. They put food in my mouth and clothes on my back.

As a child my mother taught me to fold them in prayer. They tied my shoes and pulled on my boots. They dried the tears of my children and caressed the love of my life. They held my rifle and wiped my tears when I went off to war.

They have been dirty, scraped and raw, swollen and bent.

They were uneasy and clumsy when I tried to hold my newborn son. Decorated with my wedding band, they showed the world that I was married and loved someone special.

They wrote the letters home and trembled and shook when I buried my parents and spouse and walked my daughter down the aisle. Yet, they were strong and sure when I dug my buddy out of a foxhole and lifted a plow off of my best friend's foot.

They have held children, consoled neighbors, and shook in fists of anger when I didn't understand. They have covered my face, combed my hair, and washed and cleansed the rest of my body.

They have been sticky and wet, bent and broken, dried and raw. And to this day, when not much of anything else of me works real well, these hands hold me up, lay me down, and again continue to fold in prayer.

These hands are the mark of where I've been and the ruggedness of my life.

But more importantly it will be these hands that God will reach out and take when he leads me home. And He won't care about where these hands have been or what they have done. What He will care about is to whom these hands belong and how much He loves these hands. And with these hands He will lift me to His side and there I will use these hands to touch the face of Christ.

No doubt I will never look at my hands the same again. I never saw the old man again after I left the park that day but I will never forget him and the words he spoke.

When my hands are hurt or sore or when I stroke the face of my children and wife, I think of the man in the park. I have a feeling he has been stroked and caressed and held by the hands of God.

I, too, want to touch the face of God and feel his hands upon my face. Thank you, Father God, for hands.

All 50 states acknowledge God in their constitutions.

After reviewing acknowledgments of God from all 50 state constitutions, Americans are faced with the prospect that maybe, just maybe, the ACLU and the out-of-control U.S. federal courts are wrong! If you find this to be 'Food for thought,' share this with as many as you think will be enlightened....

Alabama 1901, Preamble -- We, the people of the State of Alabama , invoking the favor and guidance of Almighty God, do ordain and establish the following Constitution...

Alaska 1956, Preamble -- We, the people of Alaska , grateful to God and to those who founded our nation and pioneered this great land...

Arizona 1911, Preamble -- We, the people of the State of Arizona , grateful to Almighty God for our liberties, do ordain this Constitution...

Arkansas 1874, Preamble -- We, the people of the State of Arkansas , grateful to Almighty God for the privilege of choosing our own form of government...

California 1879, Preamble -- We, the People of the State of California , grateful to Almighty God for our freedom...

Colorado 1876, Preamble -- We, the people of Colorado , with profound reverence for the Supreme Ruler of Universe...

Connecticut 1818, Preamble -- The People of Connecticut, acknowledging with gratitude the good Providence of God in permitting them to enjoy...

Delaware 1897, Preamble -- Through Divine Goodness all men have, by nature, the rights of worshipping and serving their Creator according to the dictates of their consciences...

Florida 1885, Preamble -- We, the people of the State of Florida , grateful to Almighty God for our constitutional liberty, establish this Constitution...

Georgia 1777, Preamble -- We, the people of Georgia , relying upon protection and guidance of Almighty God, do ordain and establish this Constitution...

Hawaii 1959, Preamble -- We, the people of Hawaii , Grateful for Divine Guidance ... Establish this Constitution...

Idaho 1889, Preamble -- We, the people of the State of Idaho , grateful to Almighty God for our freedom, to secure its blessings...

Illinois 1870, Preamble -- We, the people of the State of Illinois, grateful to Almighty God for the civil , political and religious liberty which He hath so long permitted us to enjoy and looking to Him for a blessing on our endeavors...

Indiana 1851, Preamble -- We, the People of the State of Indiana , grateful to Almighty God for the free exercise of the right to choose our form of government...

Iowa 1857, Preamble -- We, the People of the State of Iowa , grateful to the Supreme Being for the blessings hitherto enjoyed, and feeling our dependence on Him for a continuation of these blessings, establish this Constitution...

Kansas 1859, Preamble -- We, the people of Kansas , grateful to Almighty God for our civil and religious privileges establish this Constitution...

Kentucky 1891, Preamble -- We, the people of the Commonwealth are grateful to Almighty God for the civil, political and religious liberties...

Louisiana 1921, Preamble -- We, the people of the State of Louisiana , grateful to Almighty God for the civil, political and religious liberties we enjoy...

Maine 1820, Preamble -- We, the People of Maine, acknowledging with grateful hearts the goodness of the Sovereign Ruler of the Universe in affording us an opportunity, And imploring His aid and direction...

Maryland 1776, Preamble -- We, the people of the state of Maryland , grateful to Almighty God for our civil and religious liberty...

Massachusetts 1780, Preamble -- We, the people of Massachusetts , acknowledging with grateful hearts, the goodness of the Great Legislator of the Universe In the course of His Providence, an opportunity and devoutly imploring His direction...

Michigan 1908, Preamble -- We, the people of the State of

Michigan , grateful to Almighty God for the blessings of freedom, establish this Constitution...

Minnesota, 1857, Preamble -- We, the people of the State of Minnesota, grateful to God for our civil and religious liberty, and desiring to perpetuate its blessings:

Mississippi 1890, Preamble -- We, the people of Mississippi in convention assembled, grateful to Almighty God, and invoking His blessing on our work...

Missouri 1845, Preamble -- We, the people of Missouri , with profound reverence for the Supreme Ruler of the Universe, and grateful for His goodness, Establish this Constitution...

Montana 1889, Preamble -- We, the people of Montana , grateful to Almighty God for the blessings of liberty establish this Constitution...

Nebraska 1875, Preamble -- We, the people, grateful to Almighty God for our freedom . Establish this Constitution.

Nevada 1864, Preamble -- We, the people of the State of Nevada , grateful to Almighty God for our freedom, establish this Constitution...

New Hampshire 1792, Part I. Art. I. Sec. V -- Every individual has a natural and unalienable right to worship God according to the dictates of his own conscience...

New Jersey 1844, Preamble -- We, the people of the State of New Jersey, grateful to Almighty God for civil and religious liberty which He hath so long permitted us to enjoy, and looking to Him for a blessing on our endeavors...

New Mexico 1911, Preamble -- We, the People of New Mexico, grateful to Almighty God for the blessings of liberty...

New York 1846, Preamble We, the people of the State of New York , grateful to Almighty God for our freedom, in order to secure its blessings...

North Carolina 1868, Preamble -- We, the people of the State of North Carolina, grateful to Almighty God, the Sovereign Ruler of Nations, for our civil, political, and religious liberties, and acknowledging our dependence upon Him for the continuance of those...

North Dakota 1889, Preamble -- We, the people of North Dakota , grateful to Almighty God for the blessings of civil and religious liberty, do ordain...

Ohio 1852, Preamble -- We, the people of the state of Ohio , grateful to Almighty God for our freedom, to secure its blessings and to promote our common...

Oklahoma 1907, Preamble -- Invoking the guidance of Almighty God, in order to secure and perpetuate the blessings of liberty, establish this....

Oregon 1857, Bill of Rights, Article I Section 2 -- All men shall be secure in the Natural right, to worship Almighty God according to the dictates of their consciences...

Pennsylvania 1776, Preamble -- We, the people of Pennsylvania , grateful to Almighty God for the blessings of civil and religious liberty, and humbly invoking His guidance...

Rhode Island 1842, Preamble -- We, the People of the State of Rhode Island, grateful to Almighty God for the civil and religious liberty which He hath so long permitted us to enjoy, and looking to Him for a blessing....

South Carolina , 1778, Preamble -- We, the people of he State of South Carolina , grateful to God for our liberties, do ordain and establish this Constitution.

South Dakota 1889, Preamble -- We, the people of South Dakota , grateful to Almighty God for our civil and religious liberties .

Tennessee 1796, Art. XI..III. -- That all men have a natural and indefeasible right to worship Almighty God according to the dictates of their conscience...

Texas 1845, Preamble -- We, Utah 1896, Preamble -- Grateful to Almighty God for life and liberty, we establish this Constitution...

Vermont 1777, Preamble -- Whereas all government ought to enable the individuals who compose it to enjoy their natural rights, and other blessings which the Author of Existence has bestowed on man...

Virginia 1776, Bill of Rights, XVI -- Religion, or the Duty which we owe our Creator can be directed only by Reason and that it is the mutual duty of all to practice Christian Forbearance, Love and Charity towards each other...

Washington 1889, Preamble -- We, the People of the State of Washington , grateful to the Supreme Ruler of the Universe for our liberties, do ordain this Constitution...

West Virginia 1872, Preamble -- Since through Divine Providence we enjoy the blessings of civil, political and religious liberty, we, the people of West Virginia reaffirm our faith in and constant reliance upon God...

Wisconsin 1848, Preamble -- We, the people of Wisconsin, grateful to Almighty God for our freedom, domestic tranquility....

Wyoming 1890, Preamble -- We, the people of the State of Wyoming, grateful to God for our civil, political, and religious liberties, establish this Constitution...

While none of the state constitutions require anyone to worship or pray to God, each gratefully acknowledges God's blessings on our country.

Separation of Church and State: Misinformation and Hypocrisy by Dr. Michael Brown.

No sooner had I expressed my differences with the president's announcement supporting same-sex "marriage" than a young man named Collin posted on my Facebook page, "You have to leave your stupid religious dogma behind when talking about state and national issues. You are basing your objection to homosexual marriage on the Bible which would be violating the American principle of separation of church and state."

Not only is this the opposite of what our Founding Fathers intended, but it is also completely hypocritical, since Collin voiced no objection to the president pointing to his religious beliefs in support of same-sex "marriage."

And so, President Obama can invoke "Christ sacrificing himself on our behalf," Speaker of the House Nancy Pelosi can invoke her Catholic faith, Episcopal bishops in North Carolina can invoke the Bible and their religious traditions, even to the point of actively campaigning for gay "marriage," and virtually no one (perhaps with the exception of Barry Lynn) is crying out, "Separation of church and state!"

But let conservative Christians invoke the Bible or quote the words of Jesus or point to their religious traditions in opposition to redefining marriage, and comments like this one come pouring in faster than you can count them: "I live in North Carolina where the separation of Church and State doesn't exist." (This was from "Eric R." after the marriage amendment passed on May 8th.)

I have even been told that I have no right to cast a vote for a candidate or a bill if my viewpoint is based on the Bible. What? This notion is as idiotic as it is outrageous.

Let's set the record straight for those who might be misinformed. First, "the separation of church and state" is not mentioned or alluded to in the Constitution. Second, the concept of "the separation of church and state" is found in the First Amendment, the relevant part of which simply reads, "Congress shall make no law respecting an establishment of religion, or prohibiting the free exercise thereof." In other words, the state needs to stay out of the church's business. It was not until 1947 that the Supreme Court invoked the principle of "separation of church and state" in a legal ruling.

Third, the wording for "separation of church and state" is based on Thomas Jefferson's reply to the Danbury Baptist Association in Connecticut in 1802, but as Yale law professor Stephen Carter pointed out, "The separation of church and state, properly understood, comes from the work not of Thomas Jefferson, as is widely perceived, but from the insights of Roger Williams."

It was Williams who "developed the metaphor of the garden and the wilderness. The garden was the place where the people of faith would gather to struggle to understand God's Word. The wilderness was the rest of the world; the world where the light had not yet been received. Between the garden and the wilderness stood a wall. The wall existed for one purpose only. It was not there to protect the wilderness from the garden; it was there to protect the garden from the wilderness."

What does this mean to us today? Listen again to Prof. Carter: "The wall of separation between church and state is not there to protect the state from the church; rather, it is there to protect the church from the state. It stands as a divide to preserve religious freedom, And one needs to protect the church from the state because the latter will utilize its enormous powers to do what the state has always done – either subvert the religion or destroy it. If we continue our slide toward a state that breaches the wall of separation whenever it is convenient, then I worry about the great risk to religious freedom. In the end, such a breach could destroy our ability to form the communities of resistance that are crucial if we are going to have a chance to transform the nation." (This quote is worth reading again and posting as widely as possible.)

Based, however, on modern misconceptions of the separation of church and state, there could have been no abolition movement to eradicate slavery, since it was led by Christians with the Bible as their principle ideological text, nor could there have been a Civil Rights movement (other than, say, the Malcolm X version), since it too was a church-based movement led by ministers quoting the Bible.

Dr. Martin Luther King, who was one of those ministers, expressed things succinctly when he said, "The church must be reminded that it is not the master or the servant of the state, but rather the conscience of the state. It must be the guide and the critic of the state, and never its tool." But King also gave a sober warning: "If the church does not recapture its prophetic zeal, it will become an irrelevant social club without moral or spiritual authority."

What America really needs, and what many of our country's founders envisioned, is a vibrant, healthy, non-hypocritical church functioning as "the conscience of the state." As John Adams famously wrote in 1798, "Our Constitution was made only for a moral and religious people. It is wholly inadequate to the government of any other."

* This article was reprinted with the permission of Dr. Michael Brown. Dr. Brown holds a Ph.D. in Near Eastern Languages and Literatures from New York University. He is the author of 25 books, including Hyper-Grace: Exposing the Dangers of the Modern Grace Message, and he hosts the nationally syndicated, daily talk radio show, the Line of Fire. Follow him at AskDrBrown on Facebook or @drmichaelbrown on Twitter.

Epilogue

America: Where Great Things Happen was a work of conscience for me. Over the years I have often complained about the dearth of good news we get in our magazines and newspapers. This is even truer in the network television medium.

Television news tends to come to us in sound bites. *Breaking News* flashes across our screens day and night. But, what we get is rarely real news. It's more like stale news. It's the same news we got an hour ago or four hours ago, or sometimes yesterday, repeated ad nauseam so the station can make sure its viewers don't miss anything. Occasionally, it might include a word or two of update, but hardly what anyone would truly consider to be "breaking news."

What comes to mind is the saturation coverage of the missing Malaysian Airlines Flight MH370, with 238 passengers and crew aboard. Three weeks of around the clock hourly "breaking news" coverage of an international 24/7-search effort of the Indian Ocean, that produced no new information, very likely made the viewers weary. The constant updates that included scant information must have also been very hard on the missing passenger's next of kin. With all the media coverage, we know precious little about what happened to that airplane, but we get titillated by "breaking news reports" daily, almost hourly.

Talking heads on television love this kind of story because it keeps viewers on the edge of their seats. It's good for ratings, for a while. At least until the viewers begin to get bored, hearing a constant rehash of what they heard a few hours ago or a few days ago.

The concept of "if it bleeds it leads," is evident in almost all aspects of news reporting. I suspect it's because we are a fairly lazy public that doesn't want to work very hard to find out what's happening around the world, a public that is titillated by death, suffering, gore, profanity, crude behavior, and human failings.

It seems nothing interests us more than watching someone fall from a high place in our society or community. For instance, the public can't get enough news coverage about homosexual pedophile priests, or respected politicians involved in trashy affairs. An otherwise highly respected pastor of a megachurch, who falls from grace by having extramarital affairs or who admits to being addicted to pornography, is good for a weeks worth of daily news coverage.

Workers will meet at water coolers to discuss the latest tragic story they caught on the evening news. But, when was the last time anyone called you to discuss a Brownie Scout who sold 2,000 boxes of cookies, or an organ donor who gave one of his or her kidneys to a complete stranger?

News stories that make the reader or viewer feel good are as rare as an R rated movie without the ubiquitous "F" word, or an Irish celebration on St. Patrick's Day without someone singing *Danny Boy.*

When I began to think about a topic for this book, it occurred to me that the reading public might be interested in a book that has no negative stories. I asked some of my friends this question: Would you be interested in buying a book full of positive community stories about which you rarely ever hear anything? Would you buy a book that has no earth shaking events, yet makes you feel good when you read it?

The answer to both questions was a resounding YES! "Where can we find such a book?" "I haven't written it yet," I replied, "but I'm thinking about writing such a book." Each of them encouraged me to do so.

The next step was to find interesting, feel good stories, with potential national interest, that almost never get more than limited local coverage. It turned out that the Internet was/is full of such stories. It's a tedious but worthwhile and satisfying task to research available outlets to locate interesting people and organizations that do wondrous things few of us ever hear much about.

So I set about pulling together the contents of this book, hoping that readers would find these individuals, corporations, and organizations as interesting and enjoyable to read about as I found them to be in my pursuit of "feel good" stories.

In the purest sense, some of them are not feel good stories, as much as they are stories with a wholesome message that I think is important. All in all, though, I hope when you put this book down you will think you had a great reading experience that made you feel good, and that you will be inclined to tell your friends about it. After all, enjoyable experiences should be shared, right?

If you have any questions or would like to comment on the book, you can reach me at DonaldG000@aol.com. I would love to hear from you!

Donald L. Gilleland

CPSIA information can be obtained at www.ICGtesting.com
Printed in the USA
LVOW04s2011221114

415107LV00003B/3/P